THEOLOGY
AND DIFFERENCE

The Indiana Series in the Philosophy of Religion
Merold Westphal, general editor

THEOLOGY
AND DIFFERENCE

The Wound of Reason

WALTER LOWE

INDIANA UNIVERSITY PRESS

Bloomington and Indianapolis

The poem "Uragami Tenshu Church, Nagasaki" is reprinted by permission of the author and the publisher from *Black Method* by Biff Russ, © 1991 by Biff Russ. Kansas City, Mo.: Helicon Nine Editions.

Chapter 2 incorporates an essay, "Barthes as Critic of Dualism: Re-reading the *Römerbrief*," which appeared in the *Scottish Journal of Theology* 41 (1988). Portions of chapter 3 were published as "Freud, Husserl, Derrida: An Experiment" in *Phenomenology of the Truth Proper to Religion*, ed. Daniel Guerrière (Albany: SUNY Press, 1990). Both appear here by kind permission of the publishers.

The paper used in this publication meets the minimum requirements of American National Standard for Information Sciences—Permanence of Paper for Printed Library Materials, ANSI Z39.48-1984.

Manufactured in the United States of America

Library of Congress Cataloging-in-Publication Data

Lowe, Walter.
    Theology and difference : the wound of reason / Walter Lowe.
       p.   cm. — (The Indiana series in the philosophy of religion)
    Includes bibliographical references and index.
    ISBN 0-253-33611-2 (alk. paper)
    1. Theology—Methodology. 2. Theology—20th century.
    3. Theodicy. 4. Deconstruction. 5. Faith and reason. I. Title.
    II. Series.
    BR118.L69   1993
    209'.04—dc20   92-26531

1 2 3 4 5 97 96 95 94 93

To the memory of my brother,
John William Lowe
1945–1990

Uragami Tenshu Church, Nagasaki

—based on a photograph by Shomei
Tomatsu. The picture shows Christian
statuary thrown on the ground by the
Bomb. Jesuit missionaries once settled in
Nagasaki. The statues are of angels.

—dedicated to my niece

I address this poem
to you Angie
almost nine years old.
You have heard
that I lost my faith years ago.
You want to know if this is true.
Here is my answer:

When you think of me
remember this Japanese photograph.
One day you will learn
how it was made—
of the strangeness of art
and of the spirit.
When you do,
try to imagine Mr. Tomatsu
alone in the quiet of his darkroom.
Half way around our world
he slides his print
into the liquid.
He turns it over with careful tongs
watching the image begin to appear.
It floats like a ghost as he rocks the tray:
the angels emerge
in a flock through the dark,
reluctant like all ghosts to return
but feeling themselves drawn painfully
back, as if they cannot find their way
out of the human mind completely.

—Biff Russ

CONTENTS

PREFACE

> The proud tower built up through the
> great age of European civilization was an
> edifice of grandeur and passion, of riches
> and beauty and dark cellars. Its
> inhabitants lived, as compared to a later
> time, with more self-reliance, more
> confidence, more hope; greater
> magnificence, extravagance and elegance;
> more careless ease, more gaiety, more
> pleasure in each other's company and
> conversation, more injustice and
> hypocrisy, more misery and want, more
> sentiment including false sentiment, less
> sufferance of mediocrity, more dignity in
> work, more delight in nature, more zest.
> The Old World had much that has since
> been lost, whatever may have been
> gained. Looking back on it from 1915,
> Emile Verhaeren, the Belgian Socialist
> poet, dedicated his pages, "With emotion,
> to the man I used to be."[1]

This book is an effort to do two things: acknowledge the chasm which separates us from the nineteenth century *and* think across it. The task is necessary because, among other reasons, the formative theologians of the twentieth century stood in a relationship, however dialectical, with the time that had gone before. Barth and Bonhoeffer had read their Kant and Hegel. Many of *their* later readers have not. Thinking the connection between the centuries would be easier, more natural, if more of those who lived that connection had survived into their later years. The Great War was not only a devastating experience; it was also, because so many died, a devastating loss of experience. Now, in the late years of the twentieth century, we still think across that wound.

The difficulty is reflected in a problem which confronts any teacher in the field, the problem of finding a *conceptual framework* within which to place the various theological options of the twentieth century. Perhaps the most common practice is to treat the options as so many tactics for dealing with the subject-object relationship.[2] Subject and object seem as obvious and neutral a framework as one could ask for. Yet to place the twentieth century options within that framework is to ignore the fact that that very framework was profoundly contested in the nineteenth century, and that many of the early twentieth-century religious thinkers wrote with that history of contestation in mind.

A way of recapitulating something of that controversy is to observe that the usual representation of the subject-object framework—"S" and "O" along a horizontal line—suggests two objects stationed side by side. It is by nature a schema weighted in the direction of scientific empiricism. On grounds both philosophic and theological, one longs for something more. Yet one must be wary of a tendency, too common among apologists for religion, to overvalue the subject. In American culture, various forms of humanistic psychology have become virtual stand-ins for religion; and this, one suspects, is part of a larger tendency which has been widespread since the Enlightenment. Something like Buber's I-Thou is eminently desirable, but any solution has to be such as to bear the scrutiny of Marx and Freud.

Contemporary religionists confronting this issue often appeal to some form of hermeneutics, particularly that practiced by Paul Ricoeur. The linguistic turn promises to bypass the whole metaphysical construct of object and subject; and it is Ricoeur who has taught us to honor and to reckon with the "masters of suspicion."[3] My own study has persuaded me, however, that for Ricoeur the process of hermeneutical "distanciation" is ultimately a detour, a detour which ultimately returns to the experiencing subject. If this is indeed the case, then Ricoeur's twentieth-century proposal must be regarded as a variation on nineteenth-century idealism.[4]

Theodor Adorno contends that the issue of idealism is not confined to one century or to one school of philosophy. "The system is the belly turned mind, and rage is the mark of each and every idealism."[5] Emmanuel Levinas is another who connects idealism and the fetish of system to the violence of our age: "The I is identical in its very alterations. It represents them to itself and thinks them." "Western philosophy has most often been an ontology: a reduction of the other to the same."[6] The significance of Adorno and Levinas for our concerns is to suggest that the subject-object framework is itself an implicit system, and one which leads, unhappily, in the direction of idealism. Adorno, in particular, will be taken as a guide in the present study; but I am aware that it is necessary to mount an argument less delphic than Adorno's own.

In the effort to do so, the study proceeds in two seemingly contradictory directions. On the one hand, it reexamines the thought of Immanuel Kant, the source of much of our modern awareness of subjectivity. Some of the most helpful efforts to get the lay of the land in modern theology have done so by distinguishing the (limited) range of options which are available in light of Kant.[7] On the other hand, the study takes up the work of Jacques Derrida. However idiosyncratic, Derrida does provide an alternative to a broadly Ricoeurian hermeneutic; and his critique of "logocentrism" recalls Adorno's critique of idealism.

Under the combined pressure of this odd pairing—Kant the archetypal rationalist and Derrida the apparent nihilist—an equally odd thing begins to happen. The subject-object framework begins to turn itself inside out. We are accustomed to thinking of critical awareness in philosophy as a matter of being appropriately aware of the role which the subject plays in the knowing process, and then of balancing this with an appropriate awareness of the role of the object. And we think of Kant as the one who introduced this awareness of subjectivity, though we also tend to reckon that he underrated the role of the object. This way of thinking has the effect of placing the notion of critical thought within the subject-object framework, and thus delimiting it. But is reason really that limited? Might it be possible to *reverse* the relationship? Might it be possible, that is to say, to suspend the subject-object framework *within* the medium of critical thought? That is the reversal which one begins to sense, juxtaposing Kant and Derrida. One must ask whether just such a reversal, in its very difficulty, might not be the elusive issue which underlies much of modern theology.

The possibility is tantalizing. But it is unsettlingly close to a notion one often encounters in the philosophy of religion, that of "transcending the subject/object split." That notion, it seems to me, flows directly into idealism. Paddling against the current, one again finds Adorno helpful. For Adorno sensed that the attraction of idealism derived from a larger problem—namely the all-too-human tendency to deny and disguise the reality of suffering. Adorno is in this regard a proponent of what John Caputo has recently termed "radical hermeneutics"—rigorous reflection which would face up "to the limits of our situation, to the illusions of which we are capable, to the original difficulty of our lives."[8] Perhaps, then, the way to find an alternative to idealism is to cleave close to that difficulty, allowing the difficulty itself to repel the illusion. And perhaps, just perhaps, that is what Kant and Derrida are doing. On such a reading, Derrida would be something more than the playful nihilist. Deconstruction would testify, directly or indirectly, to the reality of human brokenness. As for Kant, at least one commentator has pointed to the role of theodicy in his early thought.[9] Subsequently, it is clear, he disavowed the notion of a metaphysical solution. But one can abandon the search for a speculative solution, yet still be haunted by evil as a problem. What if Kant's critical thought were approached as being, in some sublimated way, an extended struggle with the *question* of theodicy? On such a reading, one might even find encouragement in the one thing Kant and Derrida do indisputably have in common, namely the notorious inaccessibility of their respective writing styles. Even those obstacles might relate, in some illuminating fashion, to the struggle to overcome human resistance—to the irreducible harshness of life.[10]

Another way of accounting for the present book is to say that it explores the possibility of an alternative to the theological method of correlation. That purpose was not in the forefront of my mind when I started out, and even now I am far from claiming to have the formula for an alternative method. Nevertheless, I am prepared, with the sagacity of hindsight, to make an argument along the following lines.

Any critique of correlation will quickly be confronted with the question, "Well, what do you offer as an alternative?" For those who wish to affirm both the role of reason and experience, on the one hand, and the authority of revelation, on the other, some form of correlation would seem to be, almost by definition, the method of preference. In fact, for those who have chosen to work that particular terrain—or that particular boundary, as Tillich would say—the question becomes whether there *is* any method other than (one or another form of) the method of correlation.

That is the question I wish to pursue. It is one thing to affirm that within a given domain one particular approach commends itself as the method of common sense. It is something else to say that, within that domain, this is the only viable method; that there is no plausible alternative. Such a prospect, with its absence of conceptual tension, might give the most ardent correlationist second thoughts. Yet that does seem to be the situation with which we are faced. Barth is, of course, the figure over against whom correlation defines itself; but he would not seem to represent an alternative *within* the designated domain. The criticism repeatedly lodged against him is precisely that, by refusing to seriously entertain the claims of experience and reason, he has denied—obtusely—the reality or the legitimacy of that domain. When it comes to faith *and* reason, he has refused to get into the ring. And conversely, the same thing is said from the other side regarding the philosophic sources. Certainly the correlationists are attentive to contemporary movements within philosophy: the surest way of sorting out the various correlationist proposals is by noting the particular philosophical (sociological and psychological) sources they draw upon. But of themselves, the philosophic sources must treat religion "within the limits of reason alone," and the correlationist is after other game.

This seems, in broad outline, the situation. Given that one wishes to grant a certain integrity to the claims of experience and reason and to the claims of revelation, some form of correlation would seem the only option. Criticism of the method is left with only the slightest toehold, in the form of a misgiving—can this really be the *only* viable method? Can it be that correlation, which is so committed to pluralism and dialogue, does not itself have an "other"? It is from this uncertain perch that the present study of Kant and Barth begins. Barth and Kant are, after all, the key representatives of the two alternative methods which were judged, because of their alleged partiality, to be noncontenders within the assigned domain. It might be worth looking more closely, to see whether the gesture of exclusion is, itself, so definitive, so secure. Perhaps these pioneering thinkers have more in common than the correlationist's placing of them to the one periphery or the other would suggest. If a linkage between them could be found, a "coincidence of opposites" effected, something interesting might result.

A note on language: Much of the argument of this book is directed against an ideological monism which would suppress difference. The pervasiveness of that monism is reflected in the fact that even those I wish to claim as allies—Adorno, Kant, Barth, Metz, Derrida—have used gender-biased language. I have occasionally drawn attention to this symptomatic phenomenon; after some hesitation, however, I declined the more intrusive option of thoroughly reediting the passages in question.

Any writer who invokes the Frankfurt School has a special obligation to be mindful of the material conditions which make it possible to pursue a long project of writing. As a gesture in this direction, I gratefully acknowledge the support provided over a number of years by Candler School of Theology, Emory University, and by the Association of Theological Schools in the United States and Canada. I am also pleased to acknowledge that the research was assisted by a fellowship from the American Council of Learned Societies under a program funded by the National Endowment for the Humanities.

Similarly, deconstruction makes a writer acutely aware that one's words are the words of others; one's ideas are so many debts. I wish to express my particular gratitude to Henrik Boers, Rebecca Chopp, Cassie Fahey, Ed Farley, Wayne Floyd, Tom Flynn, Cliff Green, Ronald Green, Jim Gustafson, Cliff Guthrie, Ted Hackett, Julian Hartt, Brooks Holifield, George Hunsinger, Rod Hunter, Kit Kleinhans, Mark Knauff, John Leavey, Rudi Makkreel, Bill Mallard, John Moore, Steve Olson, Don Saliers, Robert Scharlemann, Steven Smith, Mark C. Taylor, Meg Watzek, Merold Westphal—and the members of the Duodecim theological discussion group. I wish to express my special gratitude to Jacques Derrida for the generosity with which he gave of his time during my sabbatical stay in Paris in the spring of 1983.

In its early stages the project gained much from the support and guidance of Hans Frei. I, along with many others, mourn the loss of this beloved mentor and friend.

The greatest debt, however, is that which I owe to my wife, Barbara DeConcini. She has been companion and conversation partner during years of effort and celebration. For her love and her friendship, I am profoundly grateful.

THEOLOGY
AND DIFFERENCE

I

INTRODUCTION
VIOLENCE AND REASON

Theology in our century was born amid the darkness of war. It has been struggling ever since to emerge from the shadow of mass violence cast by "the Great War" and the events which followed in its wake. In the nineteenth century experience had become the touchstone for doing theology. With the twentieth century, experience became unbearable. The sea of violence had, in Theodor Adorno's words, "breached the barrier against stimuli beneath which experience, the lag between healing oblivion and healing recollection, forms."[1] For experience to crystallize as experience, there is required a certain psychic space. In the century of total war that space collapsed.[2]

The struggle to emerge from darkness is in part the effort to reopen such a space. In contemporary appeals to experience one senses a note of urgency, even desperation, which reflects the inherent bind. Experience has become overwhelming; therefore we seek the stability of some confirming experience, some sign of grace. But because experience has become so overwhelming, the very possibility of confirming experience, the psychic space within which it might take place, can no longer be assumed. An experience can be sufficiently destructive that it no longer counts as simply one experience among others, e.g., as an "experience of being overwhelmed." That is the testimony of the walking wounded from Verdun to Vietnam. What is at stake is not this or that experience, but the possibility of experience itself. Speaking of French combatants in World War I, Modris Eksteins writes,

> Life came to be looked on as a reprieve. Nothing else. Men stopped asking questions, deliberately. They ceased to interpret. "Just as he tried to delouse himself as regularly as possible," said Jacques Rivière, "so the combatant took care to kill in himself, one by one, as soon as they appeared, before he was bitten, every one of his feelings. Now he clearly saw that feelings were vermin, and that there was nothing to do but to treat them as such."[3]

Simone Weil writes: "At the very best, he who is branded by affliction will keep only half his soul."[4]

This may explain the sense one has in the present culture of there being simultaneously too much experience and too little. Too much experience because, in a time of psychic numbing, culture seeks to assure itself through the quantity and intensity of its experience that it is still somehow alive. Too little because in such a time assurances are ephemeral at best, and never quite persuasive.[5] Psychic hunger and urgency conspire, making us acutely susceptible to promises of "ready-made enlightenment." This is the delusion Adorno identifies in contemporary culture, which is modern in the sense that it wishes to think itself enlightened, but wants its enlightenment ready-made. Seeking enlightenment on the cheap, one winds up with myth, the very thing to which enlightenment is supposed to be opposed. "False clarity is only another name for myth; and myth has always been obscure and enlightening at one and the same time: always using the devices of familiarity and straightforward dismissal to avoid the labor of conceptualization."[6] The delusion derives, by a peculiar justice, from a refusal of suffering. It derives from the culture's refusal to recognize that insight cannot be mass produced, that the power of insight is equal, in Adorno's words, to "the energy and suffering that it cost" to gain it.[7]

The present book seeks to reclaim, in a theoretical mode, the possibility of the needed psychic space. The effort is a wager that in a time of mass violence—and perhaps especially in such a time—there are indeed insights "whose power equals the energy and suffering that it cost to gain them." The project may thus be summarized as an effort to think through three meanings of enlightenment. Enlightenment as the struggle to emerge from the darkness of mass violence. "The Enlightenment" as the historical movement which elevated reason in a manner which led to the debacle. And ready-made enlightenment, which promises to save us effort and pain through the experience of some simple and self-justifying "presence."

Pitfalls of Enlightenment

The struggle for a psychic space within which experience might crystallize is part and parcel of the religious quest of our times. A constant stream of books on meditation and esotericism, self-help and spirituality attests to the need. But the struggle, if it is to be effective, must be aware of how readily it can be coopted, short-circuited and merchandised.[8] Already in his own time Hegel found it necessary to position himself not only against a shallow empiricism (that target was obvious enough) but against the formless enthusiasm for an "indeterminate" romanticism as well. "Just as there is an empty breadth," he cautioned, "so too there is an empty depth."[9]

Contemporary exercises in empty depth tend to exhibit a common pattern. With remarkable consistency they begin where our own reflections began a moment ago, with the sense that something has gone wrong in the modern world. They then observe how much of what is wrong can be laid at the doorstep of that which distinguishes the modern world, namely its reliance on science, technology, and thus a certain sort of reason. In some cases the argument is mild in its criticism of reason, simply saying that something is missing; in other cases it is strident. Either way, the sermon of empty depth concludes (and this is its identifying mark) by depicting some alternative realm: a realm transcending the limitations of reason, which we are to enter by some special path, by following some recommended procedure.

The problem with ready-made enlightenment lies, I think, with the very thing which gives it its appeal, namely the simplification effected by its either/or. The problem is precisely that it proposes an *alternative*. For in so doing, it sets reason to one side and the realm of emancipation to the other. To the one side the realm of (technical) reason, to the other side the realm of transcendence, imagination, meditation or whatever. The irony of such efforts, however well intentioned, is that in their determination to escape the confinements of modern society, they mimic the very division of labor which dominates modern society. Labor division is central to what Max Weber labeled (with no implicit approval of the phenomenon) the "rationalization" of society; it is society as dominated and defined by "instrumental reason."[10] Ready-made enlightenment adds to "rationalized" society one more compartment, a sort of vacation spot for the spirit. It claims the addition will transform one's entire life; but the truth is reflected in how little the addition disturbs the workings of the larger society, how readily the spiritual getaway becomes a department within that larger system.[11]

On reflection, the outcome is not so surprising. If ready-made enlightenment fails to disturb the status quo, it is because, being ready-made, it requires that one accept certain things as they are. Its prefabricated language and thought forms bear the imprint of the very situation it professes to resolve. "Inner" versus "outer," "consciousness" versus "matter," "higher" versus "lower"—these terms and distinctions, these reified differences, are not the timeless truths they profess to be but products of history which need to be examined as such. Failing to recognize this, the flight from reason obediently follows, as if by an invisible tether, the promptings of social "rationalization."

Nor does it help much to protest that one does not wish to find a realm opposed to reason, but wishes instead to find a larger realm which *includes* that of narrow, technological reason while simultaneously transcending it.

For that ploy of "subsuming" technological reason is the very proposal which was formulated by Hegel in the early nineteenth century, during what was in many ways the high point of the modern period. Hegel is remembered as the arch-rationalist, the philosopher of system. But what drives his thinking and eventuates in the system is a determination to transcend the limitations of a narrow, abstract mode of thought which he called *Verstand*—mere "understanding." In the chapters which follow I will argue that Hegel remains the unacknowledged inspiration of many of those who aim, by whatever means, to transcend reason. (Whether or not they are true to Hegel, especially the best of Hegel, is another question. I shall not attempt to resolve that matter here. As reminder that the linkage to Hegel remains a complex question, I shall often refer not to Hegel specifically, but to "idealism."[12]) In any event, one link to at least certain aspects of Hegel is that in the contemporary proposals, as in classical idealism, there is posited a certain underlying conception of the self. In the following pages, I will specify that conception in terms of what I shall call "the idealist diamond." For the moment it is enough to observe that Hegel sought to transcend the limits of reason—and that it was precisely because of that that he concluded by making *un*limited claims for reason. That already presages a kinship with those who proclaim a transcendence of reason, yet wind up reinforcing a limitlessly "rationalized" status quo.

The element of truth in even the crudest effort at enlightenment is the conviction that there are limits to what can be rationalized and controlled. Each effort is at some level a way of surrendering (rational) control. But in the final analysis—are we *really* prepared to surrender control? Are our gestures of letting go anything more than a tactical maneuver, like that of the executive who allots a certain time to meditation in order to gain a competitive edge, returning to work with additional energy? Is this not the reason why our preferred forms of enlightenment disturb so little? Do we not seek in them a larger, more all-embracing control: control of mind, yes, but control of spirit and soul as well? In this possibility we catch sight of the religious temptation of our time, an instrumentalization of the soul. The critique of idealism may be of greatest use to us, in the end, as a way of exposing the logic of our own doublemindedness.

Of contemporary theologians, none has reflected more vigorously on the pitfalls of enlightenment than Johann Baptist Metz. In *Faith in History and Society: Toward a Practical Fundamental Theology*, Metz warns of the temptation to surrender to the march of events, as if whatever happens could be its own justification. A certain notion of "evolution," often left intentionally vague by its own proponents, "functions as a quasi-religious symbol of scientific knowledge." At bottom it amounts to "a basic acceptance of technical rationality." The attendant sense of helpless resignation is partly cause and partly reflection of a pervasive situation:

> Man's consciousness of his own identity has become weaker and more dam-
> aged in the course of human progress. Man . . . feels that he is caught up
> in the waves of an anonymous process of evolution sweeping pitilessly over
> everyone. A new culture of apathy and lack of feeling is being prepared
> for him in view of his experience of fragile identity.[13]

The human subject, both male and female, is imperiled. The danger em-
anates from "a technical reason which at once reduces everything to the
level of an object" (44). The lesson for theology, it might seem, is that
theology must spring to the defense of the beleaguered subject. Quite un-
derstandably that is what much of modern theology has proceeded to do.
But *who is* this subject we are summoned to defend? Metz's work is especially valuable in alerting us to the complexities of this question. For the
rise of technical reason did not happen of itself. It is the work of a particular subject: for Metz it is the middle class or bourgeois subject, who came
on the scene at the time of the Enlightenment. One mark of the bourgeois
individual is precisely the pride taken in his or her status as a subject.
Subjecthood itself is regarded as a sort of property (28–29).

Shortly, in an introductory section on deconstruction, I will stress the
importance of thinking which is non-oppositional. There is real risk that
by zeroing in on the bourgeois subject, I myself may slip into an ideological, polarizing approach. If nevertheless I suggest such a critique, it is in
order to avoid a contrary pitfall, that of an evenhandedness bought at the
price of becoming ahistorical—a pitfall to which deconstruction itself is
peculiarly prone. Lacking the space for a fuller analysis, let me simply say
that I take the bourgeois subject to be no more than an instance, but a
peculiarly apt, peculiarly modern instance, of a broader historical phenomenon.[14]

One reason to keep an eye on the specifics of history is that what has
been true throughout history remains true in the modern period. The
victors define, at least in their own minds, the meaning of their particular
period. They marginalize others and justify the exclusion by taking themselves as norm of what it means to be a subject, a fully realized person.
Modern advertising is one clear example of this triumphant self-affirma-
tion, an unremitting celebration of the self-image of the bourgeois subject,
fulfilled, content, and in control. Theology may wish to indict an ob-
jectivizing reason for much of the violence of modern times; but, as alternative, it is not enough to champion a deeper subjectivity. Theology must
ask who this subject is, lest its very effort at resistance wind up affirming
the prevalent ideology.

In such a context, it avails little to protest, as religious apologists often
do, that what is meant by deeper subjectivity is not the subject of modern
self-aggrandizement, but a profounder, more inward conception of the

self. For, despite repeated assertions that one must first change people before one changes the world, this characteristically religious turn toward a privileged, inward space exacts too high a price. Indeed the word "privileged" here is telling. By its very nature the move inward deflects attention from the outward, objective conditions, the history of violence, upon which the privileging of inwardness depends. For want of attention to history, "theology, which believes that it is bound to defend the contemporary human subject uncritically as a religious subject," becomes "simply a late reflection of . . . middle-class religion (*'bürgerliche Religion'*)."[15]

Religion in this context "no longer belongs to the social constitution of the identity of the subject, but is rather added to it" (33). Simply adding a tasteful touch of transcendence to the existing order, Christianity becomes a form of ready-made enlightenment. Reacting against this cooptation, the religious impulse, sensing its own deformation, struggles to fight free. It gropes for a sanctuary in which to find shelter and a basis from which to critique. But where is sanctuary to be found when psychic space has collapsed; what criterion is to be found when religion has become a business, and meditation a commodity?

The Dissolving of Difference

"Business," "commodity": with these terms a neglected dimension of the problem comes into view. This is the specifically economic dimension. In Western religious circles it is not sufficiently remarked that the historical Enlightenment and the rise of bourgeois individualism are profoundly linked to the rise of capitalism; and that it is in the nature of capitalism to reduce everything without exception to a single, monetary framework. The advent of capitalism undoubtedly introduces a certain kind of freedom; but it entails this darker side as well, in that nothing is valued for its own sake, nothing has significance in its own right. All values are reduced to exchange value and in this sense every object becomes, at least potentially, a commodity. "The objects could be regarded as an unqualified mass in philosophy because economic reality had leveled them, rendering all things equivalent to money as the common denominator. . . . The less human beings think of reality in qualitative terms, the more susceptible reality becomes to manipulation."[16] Martin Heidegger noted that postulating a certain "mathesis," a sort of mathematical grid upon which all of reality was to be laid out, provided the necessary condition—the necessary framework—for modernity.[17] Heidegger observed the grid at work in the Newtonian conception of space and time and in modern geography.

Modern capitalism is, in effect, the economic form of this same reductive gesture. In a historical sketch which bears quoting at length, Metz touches upon the two sides of this complex phenomenon, at once liberating and reductionistic:

> The way of life of the middle-class citizen is ultimately contained within the concept of "private." The middle class is no longer sustained by any all-embracing traditions, let alone religious traditions. It owes its existence and survival largely to an economic and political struggle against social systems and economic structures, such as feudalism and absolutism, that were sanctioned by religion. It is supported by a new principle which regulates and underpins all social relationships—the principle of exchange. Production, trade and consumption are all determined by this middle-class principle of exchange. All other values, which may have had a decisive effect on society in the past, but which no longer directly contribute to the functioning of the modern middle-class society of exchange, have receded into the sphere of private, individual freedom. (35)

This is to say that the emergence of capitalism represents a significant, albeit partial, liberation.[18] At the same time, it is, for all its complex structures, a gesture of economic simplification. What I wish to stress in the present context is the extent to which this simplification is responsible for the modern alchemy whereby "all that is solid melts into air."[19] This needs stressing because capitalism is fond of presenting itself as the defender of "traditional values." Such claims serve to reinforce established patterns of privilege, even as the system generates the acids of modernity.

It is in order to counter this economic simplification, this confinement to economics, that Metz calls for a *political* theology.[20] The point of contrast becomes clear when Metz suggests that the bourgeois economic self represents a failure of nerve, a stunted form of the revolution struggling toward birth in the Enlightenment. Drawing on Kant's essay "What Is Enlightenment?" Metz postulates a specifically political dimension of enlightenment springing from the "decision and courage to make use of oneself without the guidance of another" (39). It is just such courage and decisiveness which, historically, the middle class individual has lacked; "the propertied citizen . . . lacks the moral strength to make use of his own intellect and to become politically what he has already been both socially and economically for a long time" (43). Savoring the benefits of an economic revolution and fearing that to couple the economic with an authentic political revolution might put those benefits at risk, the bourgeois individual was content to stop halfway. But that meant that, for all their real and apparent power, the bourgeoisie themselves never thought and decided "without the guidance of another." They thought and decided, instead, within the predefined parameters of the system of exchange. Allowing this system to define (political) value, the middle class embraced an "enlightenment" which came to them ready-made.

Such failure of nerve has historical repercussions. It seems fair to say that the middle class's failure to take political responsibility for its professed values, and its allowing of all to be dissolved within the medium of exchange, harbored an unavowed nihilism. With the mass violence of the twentieth century, that nihilism became exposed. In the Great War it was all too evident that soldiers had become cannon fodder: human beings had become commodities. "Mankind is giving way to human matériel according to the expression the war has already made familiar. . . . The German factory is absorbing the world."[21] As Adorno observes, "the mechanism for reproducing life, for dominating and for destroying it, is exactly the same . . . [W]ar was a business."[22] He continues (in a passage in which gender-exclusive language is particularly conspicuous):

> If all psychology since that of Protagoras has elevated man by conceiving him as the measure of all things, it has thereby also treated him from the first as an object, as material for analysis, and transferred to him, once he was included among them, the nullity of things. The denial of objective truth by recourse to the subject implies the negation of the latter: no measure remains for the measure of all things.[23]

Western society was entranced by the notion that two things could go together: an orientation toward control *and* the assumption that man is the measure of all things. After all (so the reasoning went), it is man the measure who will be in control.

The bargain was a Faustian one. For *control requires a system*—on this count Hegel remains instructive. And the human subject, having been lured into the convenient and self-serving assumption that taking oneself as measure is the same as thinking independently, became enclosed *within* the subject's own system. Who begins as Faust must end as the sorcerer's apprentice. Economic man believed his thinking remained enlightened and undeluded simply because it was a relentless calculation in terms of his own "self-interest." This was cynicism posing as insight, enlightenment on the cheap. Blind to the fact that the self of economic self-interest was no simple or natural reality, it accepted selfhood as defined by the system of exchange: the selfhood of which it could rightly be said, "every person has his price." Through what one might provisionally call a dissolving of differences, and for want of political resistance to that dissolution, the proud middle class, which had begun in protest against various established systems of authority, ended by submitting itself to a system of its own devising—a system in which the human subject must share in "the nullity of things." Thus "the principle of human domination, in becoming abso lute . . . turned its point against man as the absolute object."[24]

The Memory of Suffering

Ready-made enlightenment would not be complete did it not provide, among its trappings, a form of theodicy. Implicitly or explicitly it appeals to an ongoing process—part nature, part history—which will justify the suffering it entails. One triumph or another, the triumph of science or the triumph of the state, will make good the sacrifices made in its name. At the same time one can discern behind these bland assurances a harsher voice which says that like it or not, the triumph is inevitable. Best stop resisting and be resigned. It is this summons to spiritual surrender which Metz has in mind when he exhorts us against a certain notion of "evolution." "The logic of evolution is the rule of death over history—in the end, everything makes as little difference to it as death." Precisely: in the end, everything makes as little difference to it as death. The dissolving of difference is extended to a cosmic scale. Each concrete, particular being is subjected to an all-embracing "continuity" which renders each "indifferent and without grace."[25]

How, then, to think in a way which resists such annihilation of difference, in a way which refuses to surrender hope? How can we gain leverage on a system which recognizes no difference and thus permits no critique? Metz, for his part, looks to a few stubborn realities which remain outside the system of exchange, realities which have been ignored precisely because they have no value as commodities. It is upon this premise that he turns to memory and narrative, and especially to the memory of suffering. In the eyes of modern society, suffering is almost by definition that which is to be rejected and cast out. Painful, undesired, it cannot be enclosed within the system of exchange. And what is true of suffering generally is true *a fortiori* of *past* suffering, that "about which nothing can be done." For the secure and "healthy minded," past suffering is that suffering which is most easily put out of mind.

For those not among the privileged and the secure, however, such memories retain a peculiar power, precisely because they do exceed the system of quantification and exchange which privilege assumes to be universal. Memory refuses the false theodicy. It insists that "the happiness of the descendants cannot compensate for the sufferings of the ancestors and social progress cannot make up for the injustice done to the dead."[26] The memory of suffering gives voice to the suppressed question to which the system cannot reply. It exceeds the system's supposed universality by an "irrational" yet profoundly human gesture. This gesture is the demand that the justification of suffering be nothing less than the *redemption* of suffering; and that redemption, if it be redemption, must embrace the living *and the dead*. Mere improvement is no redemption, for "no improvement of the condition of freedom in the world is able to do justice to the dead or effect a transformation of the injustice and the non-sense of past suffering."[27]

So understood, the memory of suffering performs at least three crucial functions in Metz's argument. (1) As we have just seen, it establishes a *critical standard*. It insists that "truth is what is relevant to *all* subjects, including the dead and thus who have been overcome or conquered."[28] (2) Closely related to this first function, it establishes a *universal human solidarity*, providing the inspiration for "a new form of . . . responsibility towards those most distant from us, inasmuch as the history of suffering unites all men like a 'second nature' " (105). Finally, (3) it establishes a *religious context*. We have seen how the memory of suffering transforms the demand for justification into a cry for redemption. Within the Christian community, it elicits, as well, the memory of the cross, the memory of redemption effected by the suffering of Christ. As Metz observes, this Christian affirmation "remains controversial and controvertible: the power to scandalize is part of its communicable content" (111). With all its scandal, with all its "apocalyptic sting," witness to the cross is the most essential Christian gesture. It is the confession of "the God of Jesus' passion as the subject of the universal history of suffering" (73; cf. 111, 117).

I have followed Metz in some detail because of the affinity I feel between his project and my own: an affinity deriving in part from our common debt to Adorno.[29] I would be pleased if the present book, for all its theoretical character, could contribute to a political theology along Metz's lines. Indeed I might almost say that I have, regarding his work, only one reservation—but a reservation which it will take this entire book to articulate.[30] That "reservation" has to do with Metz's understanding of *reason*, what it can and cannot do. Granted, political theology does indeed require "decision and courage," and thus an orientation toward *praxis*. And granted, Metz has good cause to be wary of the surrender to bourgeois preconceptions which occurs when Karl Rahner predicates theology upon an abstract, so-called transcendental notion of the human subject.[31] In my judgment, however, these legitimate concerns lead Metz to affirm "the primacy of praxis" in a way which risks (to state the issue dramatically) a dismemberment of reason.[32]

Again let me say with a minimum of irony that my criticism of Metz is in a sense a minor one. He intends no dichotomy. He is emphatic that *praxis* or practical reason does not dispense with concepts; "conversion, metanoia and even exodus are not simply moral or educative categories— they are also and above all noetic categories" (51). But he leaves unexplored the extent to which theoretical reason (and most particularly the transcendental reason he so distrusts) can move in the direction of *praxis*—and even in the direction of that crucial, broken but perceptive thinking represented by the memory of suffering. Reuniting the disjointed parts to make that long connection between transcendental reason and the memory of suffering, and showing that it is not so very long after all: such is the task of the present book.

The subtitle "the wound of reason" attempts to intimate the connection.[33] Clearly enough, the phrase evokes the wound which reason *inflicts*, the alienation and disequilibrium which reason visits upon humankind. Specifically it denotes the devastation wreaked by Western culture under the aegis of instrumental reason. But what is crucial to the use I propose to make of the phrase is its capacity to intimate the existence of something more—a something more which cannot be subsumed within the all-embracing healthy-mindedness which ready-made enlightenment too cheerfully recommends. The notion of a wounded reason is a humbler alternative, but one more in keeping with our time. It suggests a wound which reason—at least a certain sort of reason—might *bear* within itself. A reason aware of its own brokenness might prove, in the end, a better guide than one committed a priori to healthy-mindedness. Thus Adorno's painful maxim, "the splinter in your eye is the best magnifying glass."[34] Insights got in this manner might be proportionate to "the energy and suffering that it cost to gain them."

As for Metz, he images the two revolutions, the all-too-successful economic one and the aborted political one, as a battle between two giants.

> One of them is weaker and is on the brink of defeat yet manages to keep going and finally free himself from the other's grasp. He is able to do this because a tiny hunchback sits in his ear, urging him on and continually whispering new defensive ploys. This might serve as a parable for the struggle between technology and politics, between purely economic-technological planning and a political draft for the future. (105)

For Metz, "the dwarf stands for the memory of . . . suffering." But that tiny, contorted figure whispering its canny advice—is it not also a good place to start if one wishes to imagine a wounded reason?[35]

In the present book the imagining proceeds under the tutelage of the arch-rationalist Immanuel Kant and the contemporary deconstructionist Jacques Derrida. Linking two such disparate figures should provide, if nothing else, a stimulus to imagination. Since I have committed myself to arguing that theoretical reason can share some of the burden which Metz assigns to the memory of suffering, it might be useful for me to offer an initial sketch of how a consideration of Kant and Derrida might point the way toward such a reappraisal of reason.

(1) For Metz the memory establishes *a critical standard*; it provides a crit-

ical leverage. But "critical" is precisely the term which classically describes the Kantian philosophy; and it is no stretch at all to say that in some significant sense of the term Derridean deconstruction is also determined to be critical. As a sort of down payment on my assurance that pursuing this line of thought can prove fruitful for theology, chapter 2 will use Derrida to reinterpret and reappreciate that most critical (but seemingly unphilosophical) of theologians, Karl Barth. Barth, so reinterpreted, is paradigmatic of the theology I am working toward. Thus we treat him in a preliminary way in chapter 2 and return to him in the concluding chapter, chapter 6.

(2) The memory of suffering establishes a *universal human solidarity*. Reason is often taxed with being analytic, dichotomizing, and divisive. In defending our two philosophers (and using them to explore an alternative understanding of reason) I shall be fighting on two fronts. (a) For those who first encounter the movement, the association between "deconstruction" and "destruction" is too close for comfort.[36] And many of those who have attached themselves to the movement have shown little concern to dispel the impression that deconstruction is inherently nihilistic. Chapter 3, which offers a basic orientation to deconstruction, takes the question of truth as its theme. I argue that while deconstruction is highly critical of most formulations of this question, it is not indifferent to the question as such. Quite the contrary, deconstruction implicitly depicts the human condition as a condition of radical brokenness and insecurity—and it (implicitly) offers this depiction as true. As a depiction of the human condition, this provides a basis, albeit a rather tragic basis, for human solidarity. As a depiction of brokenness, it obviously has everything to do with the memory of suffering. (b) On the Kantian front, I will deal with the sort of charge implied by Metz when he denounces "a technical reason which at once reduces everything to the level of an object" (44). In chapter 3 I will develop a distinction between technical or instrumental reason, which does tend to *objectify*, and a mode of theoretical reason which is in quest of authentic *objectivity*.[37] In chapters 4 and 5 I will argue, with particular reference to Kant, that transcendental reflection represents, in both the theoretical and practical spheres, an effort toward objectivity in the sense of impartiality, and thus toward that to which all reasonable persons might freely assent.[38] That must be one key element of what Metz has in mind when he calls for universal solidarity.

(3) Finally, the memory of suffering establishes a *religious context*. Chapters 4 and 5 place Kant in the foreground, with Derrida in the near background. Issues of difference, and of the relation of finite and infinite, are very much in view. I argue that Kant's thought is informed early and late by a distinctive way of handling these issues. I further contend that what commends this approach and makes it distinctive is the way Kant manages to maintain at one and the same time an acute sense of human finitude

and a deep respect for the powers of reason. So often finitude and reason are pitted against one another. Kant shows that this doesn't have to happen, that each can incite the other to a greater radicality. Pascal's vision of the human being as thinking reed has never had an abler advocate. Finally, I also argue that the nature of this radicality is, in a broad sense of the term, religious. This I try to indicate by speaking of such thought as proceeding *coram Deo*. By the time we get to practical reason in chapter 5, I think it will be apparent that here too there are deep convergences with a wounded reason and the memory of suffering.

Making Sense of Derrida

If there is a single theme running through much of recent theology, it may well be the issue of difference or otherness. On various fronts, Western culture, including Western theology, stands charged with having neglected other peoples, other modes of experience, the otherness of the natural world. In a similar vein, I have argued that an authentic theology must stand against the dissolving of difference; it must resist the manifold pressures toward a "one-dimensional" world. There is a good *prima facie* case, therefore, for theology's attending to the work of Jacques Derrida, who has reflected so insistently on the distinctive character of the notion of difference—on what makes "difference" different.[39]

It might be said that Derrida's thought amounts to a series of strategies for undercutting or "deconstructing" the twofold lure of metaphysical monism (which collapses difference into one) and metaphysical dualism (which dichotomizes difference, creating opposition). Derrida deals with the threat of monism by speaking of a pervasive desire for "*presence*." The term "presence" in this context refers to any reality which is taken to be autonomous and self-sufficient, and which is regarded as being at some point accessible in a direct, unmediated fashion.[40] Philosophical examples are as various as the empiricist's notion of "sense data" and the idealist's conception of the Self. As for the second lure, that of dualism: Derrida speaks of a widespread penchant for *oppositional* structures of language and thought, and, related to this, a penchant for oppositional or adversarial ways of relating to the world at large.

The point of using these general terms, "presence" and the "oppositional," is to stress that they point to tendencies which are by no means confined to philosophy, tendencies far more pervasive than our initial references to "metaphysical monism" and "metaphysical dualism" might suggest. We have to do here with penchants and predilections which so permeate our language, character, and thought that they are never definitively overcome. No one can step cleanly beyond these involvements and dependencies; and it is evidence of Derrida's rigor that he does not claim for himself a prophetic exemption from the quandaries and dilemmas he describes. In such a situation, one's method is never definitive, never more than a series of *ad hoc* devices for resisting the monist/dualist undertow. And that is what is meant by "deconstruction."

Having introduced the issues of presence and oppositionalism, we now need to attend to how the two play into one another. Let us take as point of departure the observation which has become a commonplace in structuralist linguistics and anthropology, that human language and thought commonly proceed by way of various binary distinctions, such as left/right, stranger/friend, the cooked and the raw. Such distinctions may seem innocent enough. But time and again they become invidious. We know that to "discriminate" may mean simply to distinguish, but it may also mean a great deal more. Distinction transmutes into hierarchy—"one of the two terms governs the other (axiologically, logically, etc.), or has the upper hand"—and hierarchy brings with it the temptation to attempt to banish the disdained reality altogether.[41] The implicit goal, in such a case, is to establish a pure linguistic domain predicated solely upon the acceptable terms, whether defined socially as acceptable speech, or philosophically as well-founded categories. And it is Derrida's contention that in each such case the various terms will circulate around a central term or set of terms which itself is regarded as stable, self-evident. The center is regarded, that is to say, as a "presence."

Thus we see how, despite the apparent contradiction, a certain dualism issues in attempted monism. Accordingly, deconstruction of oppositional thinking must go hand in hand with critique of presence. Similarly, an analogous point may be made by beginning at the other end, with critique of presence. For when one encounters a term which has acquired such power as to define a linguistic domain, the effect is, for those within that domain, as if the term were self-explanatory, immediately comprehensible. But closer inspection may reveal that the defining term is in fact dependent, dependent in its very meaning, upon a whole network of associations, and particularly upon certain contrast-terms. Indeed—and this is perhaps the distinctively Derridean turn—one is apt to find that the original term draws upon the other terms not just negatively, by way of contrast, but *positively*, i.e., to supplement its meaning and its authority. Derrida never tires of tracing these subtle processes of supplementation as a way of demonstrating that the various presence terms actually lack the serene self-sufficiency which has been attributed to them. The threads of unacknowledged dependence then become the point of entry for a linguistic and conceptual deconstruction, in the sense of a careful, textual relativization of the avowed opposition or dichotomy.[42]

An example treated at length in *Of Grammatology* is the primacy accorded by Western thought to the immediacy of spoken language over the written. The author shows how those who have sought to affirm the primacy of the spoken word have had frequent recourse to metaphors which actually draw upon the peculiar character of *written* language.[43] Another instance of supplementation, encountered in contemporary theological debates, may be suggested by means of a somewhat stylized example. One is often advised that the classical Christian tradition is hopelessly wedded to a "static" conception of God, and that what is required in the contemporary world is a thoroughly "dynamic" conception of deity. Clearly this is a proposal to center a linguistic domain upon one set of terms, while resolutely excluding another. But suppose one were to ask, half seriously, "Tell me more about this dynamic character of God. Is it something that comes upon God occasionally, like a fever?" The response, somewhat offended perhaps, would be to this effect: "You have not begun to understand the dynamic character of God if you can imagine it to be episodic. No, God is *permanently* dynamic." The banished vocabulary of unchangeability is thus reintroduced as clarification or supplement at the very center of the purportedly purified domain.

Derrida was not the first to discover the issue of difference. Much as deconstruction echoes Heidegger's call for the "destruction" of Western metaphysics, so the Derridean *différance* recalls Heidegger's "ontological difference." Less explicitly but in some ways more penetratingly, Adorno foreshadowed the notion of difference in his *Negative Dialectics*. For Adorno the task of dialectics is to unfold "the difference between the particular and the universal." The quasi-utopian vision which informs this effort, Adorno terms "reconcilement": "Reconcilement would release the nonidentical, would rid it of coercion, including spiritualized coercion; it would open the road to the multiplicity of different things. . . . Reconcilement would be the thought of the many as no longer inimical."[44] Moreover, Adorno is more explicit than Derrida about the historical and political dimensions of his discussion. "Derrida . . . shares a penchant for dialectics with Adorno, is sensitive to the unexpected ways in which philosophical opposites slide into one another, but is unable to link this concern with an account of the natural-historical genesis of the self."[45] A theology informed by Derrida will need something like Adorno's conceptualities in order to rejoin liberationist concerns. But Adorno, even more than Derrida, requires of his readers a grounding in the history of philosophy. (Deconstruction, in fact, may be *too* readily detached from its classic philosophic background; but that is another problem, which we seek to rectify in chapter 3.) To keep matters from becoming more complex than they already are, therefore, we will allow Derrida and deconstruction to occupy center stage. But Adorno will not disappear. I consider his perspective to be ultimately more comprehensive and more concrete than Derrida's. Thus Adorno will continue to guide us—whispering, as it were, from the prompter's box.[46]

To shift metaphor, we will sail under the colors of deconstruction, but the flag will not be nailed to the mast. We will seek to avoid the notion, prevalent in some quarters, that deconstruction itself might become the basis for a newly purified linguistic domain. No doubt Derrida would be unsettled by some of the things I will say regarding a certain notion of radical transcendence. I will remain as sensitive as I can to the concerns of deconstruction; at times I will argue that those concerns are well served by the theological moves I wish to make. But eventually theology must honor the difference between its own task and Derrida's. Having learned what it can, it must proceed on its own, trusting its own best lights. As Derrida himself affirms in a remarkable interview:

> in general, to summarize very succinctly, the point would seem to be to liberate theology from what has been grafted on to it, to free it from its metaphysico-philosophical super ego, so as to uncover an authenticity of the "gospel," of the evangelical message. And thus, from the perspective of faith, deconstruction can at least be a very useful technique. . . . And [the point would also seem to be] a real possibility for faith both at the margins and very close to Scripture, a faith lived in a venturous, dangerous, free way.[47]

Tradition in Question

What then *are* the implications of deconstruction for theology, and particularly for theology rooted in traditional Western culture? Clearly the culture is ridden with hierarchies, dichotomies, and privileged terms. One thinks, for example, of the distinctions of "inner" versus "outer," and "consciousness" versus "matter" noted earlier in speaking of ready-made enlightenment. Derrida shows how such conceptions are inextricably linked in Western thought to the notion of an inward presence—a presence of oneself to oneself. Belief in self-presence underlies the Western preference for a "logos" often characterized as the "living presence" of the spoken word in contrast to the "dead letter" of the written. John Henry Newman, to pick one vulnerable example from many, urges that the word *logos* "stands both for *reason* and for *speech*, and it is difficult to say which it means more properly. It means both at once: why? because really they cannot be divided,—because they are in a true sense one."[48] These familiar assumptions regarding what is dead in language and what is living, Derrida terms "logocentrism."[49]

One should not underestimate the rhetorical power of logocentrism. Who would choose to miss out on what is "living" in order to speak on behalf of what is "dead"? On this fundamental point, Derrida's proposal is as odd as that of Metz. Derrida's critique of logocentrism is, in fact, very useful as a way of understanding why enlightenment is not always what it seems. He helps us see, for example, how the common critique of the technological mindset—as being rigid, codified, and "dead"—actually plays into the most fundamental, and indeed the most rigid, of Western preconceptions. A set of assumptions as old as Plato laments the impoverishment which allegedly occurs when language is externalized, written down, detached from the living presence of the spoken word. As venerable as Plato, such conceptions are also as contemporary as Martin Buber's "I-it" and "I-Thou." Buber is quite explicit about the significance he ascribes to presence.[50] If Derrida is right, the best Buberian intentions cannot prevent "presence" from gravitating toward "self-presence," thus diminishing all that is other.

But how, then, are we to proceed? Traditional theology is scarcely conceivable apart from *some* use of contrast terms along the line of "lower" and "higher," "world" and "spirit," "darkness" and "light." (Indeed my own talk about the search for authentic enlightenment has been playing upon the last of these.) On first approach, the answer seems obvious: any theology which takes deconstruction seriously must clean house. It must identify and expel from its vocabulary that entire lexicon of terms which serve the metaphysics of presence. Such is the conclusion to which many have come on first considering the relation of deconstruction and theology. But there is a profound irony here. The terminological housecleaning which deconstruction would seem to commend bears more than a passing resemblance to the effort which we virtually defined deconstruction as *rejecting*, namely the effort to banish certain terms and conceptualities, and to establish thereby a purified linguistic domain.

So we find ourselves in a puzzling situation. What *is* the significance of deconstruction for theology? Are certain terms to be censured? Or is censorship itself to be censured? The answer, I believe, is that both of the options are true, both are to be affirmed—and that the result, viz. the puzzling situation in which we find ourselves when both options *are* affirmed, is precisely where deconstruction intends to place us. Indeed the process of situating us at this difficult intersection, and keeping us there, is a good deal of what deconstruction is about. Deconstruction makes us suspicious of a whole network of terms *and* it makes us aware that the network is, in effect, without end, so that *all* of our language is affected. To borrow an image from Derrida, deconstruction requires that we write continually with two hands, using terms *and* correcting them.[51] Which means that, so far from conveying an esoteric knowledge which would enable us to float free above the Western tradition, what deconstruction actually does is to place us in a more complex—one might well say, more dialectical—relationship to it.[52]

In its engagement with the philosophic tradition, deconstruction has a Heideggerian precedent. Heidegger initiated the "destruction" of Western metaphysics which has been been taken up in various ways by a host of poststructuralist prophets. What is the practice behind the slogan? How does Heidegger deal with the tradition, in actual practice? Let us pause long enough to consider an example. Of all the figures in Western philosophy, there is perhaps none more antithetical to Heidegger's way of thinking than René Descartes. Descartes initiated the turn toward the subject, opening up the subject-object dichotomy which Heidegger is so determined to overcome. Such, in any case, is the common picture of Descartes, the picture of one "who came and doubted and so became a subjectivist," thus launching the sterile debates of modern epistemology. Heidegger does set forth such a portrait of Descartes—but only in order to deride and reject it, calling it "at best . . . only a bad novel."[53] So far from dismissing Descartes, Heidegger dismisses the caricature.

And he does so in order to enter into what Nietzsche has called a "loving combat": Descartes has been called a subjectivist, has he? Very well, let us see what lies behind this disputed term "subject." Heidegger pushes back—in Descartes's text—beyond the notion of "subject" as thinking being to "the subjectum," which is "that about which [a proposition] says something." Without entering into the details of his argument, it can be said that Heidegger carries out a sort of conceptual excavation which exhibits within the Cartesian notion of subject something more fundamental than the solitary human "I." More fundamental is that which "underlies—*hypokeimenon, subjectum*—the *subjectum* of the positing as such." Admittedly, Descartes associated this underlying reality with the "I," and "hence it came about that ever since then the 'I' has especially been called the *subjectum*, 'subject.' "[54] But that is also to say, then, that even on Descartes's terms, the "I" deserves the name "subject" only insofar as it is so associated with that which underlies. Thus in and through its very name as subject, the "I" is relieved of its supposed absoluteness, its supposed centrality. Its very claim as subject depends upon something other.

Thus does Heidegger, the scourge of ontotheology, deal with the tradition. He proceeds internally, arguing from within Descartes's language and premises, showing how they say far more than Descartes is commonly understood to say. Heidegger assumes, and in plying his immanent critique confirms, that the Cartesian moment is not simply a blind alley to be forgotten. It becomes "a story in which the movement of Being becomes visible." This statement expresses Heidegger's enabling conviction that there is a fundamental situation in which Descartes found himself, which Descartes tried to think; and that Descartes cannot be rejected out of hand, because his situation is related to the fundamental situation which we ourselves are impelled to think.

Now we can return to our question "what are the implications of deconstruction for theology?" by way of the question "what are the implications of Heidegger's thought for theology?" Some of the best theological minds of a generation applied themselves to the latter question; yet I think it is fair to say that the effort never fulfilled its promise.[55] One indication of the usefulness of Derrida for theology is that he helps us understand this disappointment. Derrida cites Heidegger as pioneer of the critique of presence. In a sense, all Derrida did was to take with full seriousness the assertion in *Being and Time* that classical metaphysics failed because in such metaphysics, "entities are grasped in their Being as 'presence'; this means that they are understood with regard to a definite mode of time—the *Present*."[56] Derrida argues that Heidegger's philosophy falls short of Heidegger's own best insights. Much of the time, Heidegger's notion of getting beyond presence seems to mean meditating upon what makes presence possible—viz. presencing. Thus Heidegger's heavy investment in terms such as "neighboring, shelter, house . . . voice, and listening" which derive their aura from the fact that they suggest a (deeper) presence.[57] It was to just these terms that theology was drawn, unwavering in its conviction that the aura had somehow to do with the numinous, the Holy.[58]

If this is the way that Derrida comes into the conversation—and historically I think it is: historically he was deeply formed by Husserl and Heidegger—it becomes impossible to view Derrida as a flat, undialectical break with the tradition. A more complex relation is suggested by Derrida's own comments about his relationship to tradition: "I like repetition: it is as if the future trusted in us, as if it waited for us, encoded in an ancient word—which hasn't yet been given voice. All of this makes for a strange mixture, I realize, of responsibility and disrespect."[59] After all, deconstruction does not come out of nowhere; it is born of an effort to out-Heidegger Heidegger. In fact Derrida's term "deconstruction" is more fitting than Heidegger's term "destruction" as a formulation of what it means to have a Heideggerian relationship to the tradition. Lifting a term from Derrida's treatment of Hegel, we may say that in Heidegger the critique of presence remains "restricted."[60] Accordingly the question of deconstruction's bearing upon the Western theological tradition depends upon the question, what is the meaning of *un*restricted critique? Would it be a flat rejection—the example of Heidegger on Descartes notwithstanding? Or would it be something richer and more complex?

That is the question we will pursue in chapter 3. Ultimately it will lead us to Kant.

Contextualization

I would now like to make a positive proposal about our relation to the Western tradition, and thus about the implications of deconstruction for theology. The proposal is conveyed by a somewhat distinctive use which I wish to make of a term which has already gained some currency, the term *contextualization*.

Perhaps the best way into the proposal will be to note a number of distinct though related uses of the term "contextualization." (1) "Contextualization" may designate the procedure, familiar since the emergence of historical scholarship in the nineteenth century, whereby particular ideas or texts are related to their historical setting. In its extreme form, as "historicism," the procedure reduces the various expressions to the status of being nothing more than a function of the setting. Thus, in a familiar example, the confrontational style of Barth's *Commentary on Romans* is often "explained" as a reaction to the extreme circumstances of the War. The implication is that our own circumstances are not so extreme and that, as a result, Barth's early theology is only partially relevant, at best, to the needs of contemporary thought. Further, (2) "contextualization" may designate the procedure just described, the relating to historical setting, with the important addition of one or another form of the "hermeneutic of suspicion." The effect of that hermeneutic is to suggest that the generally accepted version of history is actually an ideology devised to protect certain interests, and that history looks quite different when one penetrates beneath the ideology to a more basic level. The Marxist reading of history is, of course, the paradigm of this approach; more recently, the genealogical analyses of Michel Foucault have lent the tactic new vigor. Viewed from the underside of concrete economic situations, the phrase "free market" describes something quite other than an equal and unconstrained social interaction. Similarly, it is disingenuous to claim that the term "man" includes women as well, when it is used in a social setting distorted by a long history of male dominance. As a way of signaling the importance of such social-historical awareness, theologians, particularly theologians of liberation, have introduced their particular usage of the term "contextualization."[61]

A good deal of theological ink has been spilt over challenges posed by the first sense of contextualization. Could biblical claims to revelation hold up under scrutiny by the historians? What can we know of the historical Jesus? Adopting a distinction made by Juan Luis Segundo, we may say that such questions have their roots in the rationalist, "first Enlightenment." They set the terms for generations of historical and theological debate.[62] Similarly, the more recent shift from the first to the second sense of contextualization parallels a widespread shift to the concerns of "the second Enlightenment," which finds its paradigm in a Marxian hermeneutic of suspicion.[63] Not validation by historical science, but empowerment of the disenfranchised, became the goal of theology. Attention shifted from theoretical to practical reason, or "praxis."

Accordingly my concern at this juncture, as in the conversation with

Metz, is to affirm the claims of practical reason without surrendering the distinctive and necessary offices of "theoretical" reason. Since the claims of the practical are often buttressed by disparagement of the theoretical, this becomes an important point. As an initial corrective, I shall propose two further senses of "contextualization." (3) The first of these further senses has to do with the question discussed in the previous section, viz. the status of the Western tradition and particularly Western metaphysics. Current critics of "foundationalism" are only the most recent to have charged that metaphysics is in large part a means of control, an effort to gain for oneself a secure, invulnerable position. Adorno cautioned earlier that "the attempt to deduce the world in words from a principle is the behavior of someone who would like to usurp power."[64] My proposal is to suggest that, as valid and important as this caution is, it may not be all there is to say about the metaphysical impulse. After all, to call metaphysics a defensive reaction is already to suggest that it is born of a quite accurate awareness—an awareness that in point of fact we are *not* in control of our existence. And if this is so, might it not be that, at some level and in some part, the metaphysical effort is informed by this awareness in a manner which is positive and orientational, and not simply negative and reactive? Might it even be that metaphysics—let us say, "metaphysics at its best"—actually *seeks* to remind us that we are *not* in control? In that case the disorienting prefix "meta-" would not simply be a mark of hubris. It would be an effort to gesture beyond what we can know with precision, toward a larger context—with the understanding that it is a context *which we can by no means comprehend, but of which (and in which) we can nevertheless make some sense.*[65] Adorno, for all his denunciation of metaphysics, affirms that "to happiness the same applies as to truth: one does not have it, but is in it. Indeed, happiness is nothing other than being encompassed, an after-image of the original shelter within the mother."[66] The maternal image of "being encompassed," evoking that which is psychologically our earliest context, intimates that metaphysics may be suited for something more than domination; that there may be some sense in which metaphysics *contextualizes us.* It suggests that metaphysics at its best may have a positive penchant toward acknowledging ourselves—and itself—as *being contextualized.*[67]

Antifoundationalism stands in a long lineage which has consistently assumed that the enlightened can distinguish relatively easily between bad thinking, which is "metaphysical," and good thinking, which is in some sense "critical." Once again we observe the inveterate impulse toward a purified linguistic domain. My proposal is a corollary of the failure of such edicts of linguistic hygiene. If it has been impossible to segregate "critical" from "metaphysical," it may be because the critical requires the metaphysical, as a supplement. I would propose specifically that the metaphysical may help one become more *self*-critical. In principle those who practice contextualization in the first and second senses of the term ought, in all consistency, to apply the procedures equally to themselves. But there is a human, all-too-human tendency to grant special exemption to one's own point of view. The critical contribution of metaphysics is to enforce the "ought" with an "is": the two cases ought to be thought of in the same manner because the situation of the two cases, ourselves and others, *is* fundamentally (not to say foundationally) the same.

Specifically, metaphysics at its best may be said to aid the critical effort on three counts. First, it affirms that there is a context which is in some sense common, inclusive. Further, it affirms (cf. the best use of "meta-") that the context exceeds that which we can comprehend. And yet, finally, it affirms that there is no stark barrier; it is always possible to make a certain sense of (and in) the context. Thus the question of truth persists, it refuses to be declared inoperative.

To summarize regarding the third sense of "contentualization": self-critical thinking goes against our grain; it requires that we swim against the current. To meet the challenge we need all the help we can get. If metaphysics can contribute, by all means let us use it, though here as elsewhere critical thinking must receive assistance guardedly. But having said this, it is possible to take one further step. For just as we cannot simply cut ourselves off synchronically from contemporary metaphysical discourse, so too we cannot simply sever our diachronic dependence upon past forms of discourse. We cannot by fiat float free of the tradition. Thus we are led to a final sense of contextualization: (4) the sense in which we are contextualized *by the tradition.*[68] To acknowledge such contextualization does not by any means spell capitulation to the tradition. The tradition must be engaged with all the critical energy which is evoked by Heidegger's "destruction" and Derrida's "deconstruction." But our engagement must proceed in full awareness that our questioning—even our rebellion—is indebted and dependent in ways we can only partially surmise.

This point needs to be emphasized. We who attempt theology in the twentieth century are susceptible to the appeal of those shortcuts and devices which promise to rid us of "static thinking," "ontotheology," and "logocentrism"—while simultaneously sparing us the considerable labor of having to reckon with a tradition. The reckoning comes ready-made under such dismissive labels as "ontotheology." A bit of self-critical reflection should alert us to the way in which such attitudes toward past and tradition work hand in glove with the dissolving of difference and the modern frenzy for the "new-and-improved." Adorno's explanation is that the law of exchange which rules bourgeois society "is in its essence something timeless"—which "means nothing less than that remembrance, time, and memory, as a sort of irrational remainder, become liquidated."[69] Following Adorno, Russell Jacoby observes that "an obsolete social system . . . staves off its replacement by manufacturing the illusion that it is perpetually new." In such a context, genuinely critical reflection must pit itself against an amnesia of spirit, the "planned obsolescence of thought."[70]

The Idealist Diamond

Every revealing is simultaneously a concealing. In the language of Heidegger, "the illuminative clearing happens only as concealing."[71] Bonhoeffer speaks of more than his own people when he writes, "I think we Germans have never properly understood the meaning of 'concealment.' "[72] "Enlightenment" is a pitfall by its very nature, for the word itself gives promise of an untroubled revealing in which concealment plays no part. To lay hold of an unambiguous showing, an immediacy or presence—that would be enlightenment. In his critique of this chimerical notion Derrida surpasses even Heidegger. In case after case he shows how notions which appear foundational and unequivocal actually mask various unacknowledged dependencies.

To these reflections, our section on contextualization added a corollary suggested by Heidegger's respectful handling of Descartes and often forgotten by relativist expositors of Derrida: namely the thesis that every *concealing* is simultaneously, in some sense, a *revealing*. As I hope to show, it is possible to use this formula without its becoming a cover for smuggling all of the tradition back in. It is possible to use it in such a way that the revealing is not construed as a presence. So used, the corollary affords a viable way of reengaging the tradition. Just how such engagement might proceed is a subject for the chapters which follow. In the present section I offer a few anticipatory hypotheses which are set down in brief, even telegraphic fashion.

The "first Enlightenment," which had as its paradigm Newtonian physics, forced a recognition of *nature* as an autonomous order, to be explored by disciplined investigation. By contrast a second, more praxis-oriented, political Enlightenment had its paradigmatic moment in the early phases of the French revolution. That event may be said to represent a discovery of *history*: i.e., a discovery that existent social structures are not mandated by heaven, but can be refashioned by the collective will of humankind.

These two instances are moments of enlightenment in the sense that each broke the spell of a specific form of mystification which the earlier tradition, to its lasting shame, strove to perpetuate. As a way of specifying the forms of mystification, let us recall the classic distinction between moral evil and natural evil. *Moral* evil is suffering which occurs as the result of a deliberate act which willed, more or less intentionally, that some such suffering should occur. In theological language, one speaks of sin.

The child abuse which tormented Ivan in *The Brothers Karamazov* is an example; someone was responsible. In contrast the Lisbon earthquake which posed such questions for Voltaire is an instance of *natural* evil. The event proved problematic precisely because it could not be explained as resulting from (e.g., being the punishment for) any specific human act.

Mystification number one, then, lay in the tradition's tendency to treat *all* of human suffering as ultimately a function of moral evil. Augustine wrote that all the evil we know in this life is "either sin or punishment for sin."[73] Is it possible on such a premise even to conceive of a distinctively natural evil? For that, there is required the notion of a natural order with its own autonomous operations, interactions, and collisions. Only then can one speak of certain cases of suffering as occurring not by direct divine fiat, the punishment for sins, but simply as the result of natural causes. But once one does know the cause, a remedy becomes imaginable. The optimism of the first Enlightenment seems less naive when seen as the liberating discovery that sufferings which had been passively endured as being a function of moral evil were found to be instances of natural evil which might possibly be put right.

Mystification number two was the converse of number one: here moral evil was disguised as natural evil. Ills springing from an unjust social order were treated as if they were beyond the range of human responsibility. Kings were meant to reign, they were noble by birth; women required protection and discipline, one saw in their bodies the evidence of their frailty. Such notions are instances of what the Frankfurt School calls "second nature": certain characteristics—they may be real or imagined, but they are in any case secondary, socially derived—are treated as if their existence were independent of the social order. So conceived, they are offered as justifying questionable practices, e.g., instances of violence, occurring within that order.[74] From the theories of Marx to the practices of contemporary base communities, the critique of ideology requires a gesture of demystification whereby the guise of nature is dispelled and social responsibility exposed.

There was, however, a darker side to the two Enlightenments. Once the distinctive character of natural evil has been exposed, it is difficult to resist the implication that certain forms of suffering are more or less ingredient in the simple fact of being finite. Granted, it is hard to specify just what these hardships are. There is always the tantalizing possibility that everything, even mortality itself, might in time be remedied. Thus Kierkegaard lampooned the modern assurance that some all-redeeming System might yet be perfected—perhaps even by next Sunday. This suggests that where Enlightenment optimism did become excessive, the reason may not have been simple naivete. Perhaps an all-too-real awareness of vulnerability was being covered over by the veils of aspiration.

The work of the second Enlightenment was in part to expose the ideologies of the first. To this purpose the "discovery of history" was admirably suited. The new thought forms which the first Enlightenment justified by appeal to an eternal Reason were subjected to a process of contextualization in the second of our several senses of the word. By the time of Marx the thought forms of the first Enlightenment seemed themselves a function of certain social historical forces, which they simultaneously fostered and obscured. Thus the second Enlightenment, like the first, had its darker side. From the time of Plato, Western thought had been unsure what to do with temporality. Now history bids fair to become the universal solvent, eroding the stable ground which even the critic seemed to require in order to have a fulcrum for critique. The only apparent fulcrum was a moving one, the process itself. The process must be trusted. The process becomes the new Reality. This is how critique becomes coopted by what Metz calls evolution. The net result is a diachronic form of ready-made enlightenment, the desperate trust that the System will somehow perfect itself.

In effect, what was most unsettling about the Enlightenment at large was precisely the fact that its discoveries were *twofold*, the discovery of a certain autonomous nature *and* the discovery of history.[75] To put the matter in terms of the point just discussed, what was unsettling was the dawning awareness that history did *not* have the stability, the inherent order, which was being ascribed to nature. And so it was that tacitly, inchoately, the modern mind began to grope its way toward a *reunification* of nature and history. At one level this might be put simply as an aspiration, a hoped-for *telos*, that one day human doings might become harmonious and our alienation from nature be overcome. But in order to make that hope something more than wistful, to give it some grounding in reality, it is altogether natural, and perhaps logically necessary, to posit a confirmation, an actual unity, at some place in the present or some time in the past. From this it is a small step to a fullblown narrative which proceeds in three parts: the *archē* of a primal unity, an original innocence; the division or fall into disunity and alienation; and the *telos*, whether assured or merely hoped for, of restoration and reunification. Unity, separation, reunion: a three-part story—or, figuratively, a diamond.

If the Enlightenment was unsettling in what it suggested of human suffering, the three-part story was correspondingly powerful in that it provided an implicit theodicy. To bring this out, one need only make a slight addition to what has already been said. One need only add that the restoration is not simply a restoration; but that the final state of things is all the richer and more real for having passed through the second stage, the stage of estrangement and conflict. To the modern mind especially, original innocence seems insipid and uneventful; release from an eternity of tedium becomes something positive. Regarded as liberation into a larger world, it becomes a "fortunate fall." We will always carry with us a nostalgia for the lost innocence of childhood, but growth into maturity requires the chaos and conflict of adolescence; and as with the individual, so too with the human race. In retrospect the pain is positive, by virtue of what it contributes to individuation and growth.

"Who strives always to the utmost, him can we save." This line from *Faust* suggests something of the insight and aspiration which makes the modern theodicy so compelling. The insight is allied with the Enlightenment clarification of the reality of natural evil: conflict, pain, and struggle are not alien to life, they are part and parcel of it. "Man errs, while his struggle lasts"; for one who would truly live, pain and error are not to be shunned, but acknowledged and embraced.[76] Only thus can one hope that somehow, in and through the struggle, alienation may be overcome and salvation achieved.

So far, so good. But in order to serve as theodicy, the three-part story must do more than articulate a disturbing insight and an uncertain aspiration. It must provide a quasi-metaphysical justification for the sufferings undergone. And in the effort to justify, it generates a narrative quite different from the memory of suffering. As Metz observes, oppressed peoples commonly maintain their sense of themselves by telling their own stories, which are often stories of suffering. Characteristically these stories do not place the suffering within some larger, quasi-explanatory framework. In contrast, the oppressor's view of history is just such a quasi-explanatory framework, a tale of Manifest Destiny. It celebrates the victories, investing them with an aura of righteous inevitability. Against such triumphalism, those who have suffered have nothing to set but the simple, brute fact of their suffering. Yet that fact in its starkness and simplicity becomes a powerful form of protest. Together, teller and tale resist assimilation; they disturb the victor's totalizing claim. In Metz's phrase, they give voice to "dangerous memories."

One might say, then, that we have here two views of history. But surely we must also say that one view, that of the oppressed, cleaves closer to the reality of history—history with all its gratuitous, unreconciled suffering—whereas the other is less a view of history than an alternative to it, a flight from history's open-ended reality. To put the matter another way, if history as distinguished from nature is the realm of a certain degree of freedom, then the oppressed people's tale, in the very pain of it, is closer to what history is. For, in the very act of their being told, stories from the underside of history testify that they are not, as the victors would have it, the stories of lesser beings who are inherently deserving of oppression. They are stories of human beings endowed with freedom and dignity. It is just this that imbues the stories with such sadness. In contrast, the actors celebrated in the victor's tales are presented as "a force of history." Their self-congratulatory tale casts upon the outcome a mantle of inevitability precisely contrary to the open-ended it-could-have-been-otherwise character of history.[77] For those who have suffered it is wrenching to think "it could have been otherwise." But there is, perhaps, a poetic justice in the fact that, with this reflection, their memories become the guardians of (the reality of) history. Conversely, it is fitting that the victor, in resisting the "it could have been otherwise," implicitly exiles himself from the very realm of his purported triumph, the realm of history.[78]

So we must ask whether the three-part life story of innocence, conflict, and reconciliation does not have, however unintentionally, the same effect as the victor's story. Doesn't it also tranquilize one's sense that "it could have been otherwise" by accommodating suffering within a quasi-explanatory framework? And might it not also tend to assimilate a certain language of nature, with terms such as "force" and "inevitability," to the proper language of history? But here as elsewhere, history will not become whatever one wants it to be. History does not consent to its designated role within the projected super-history. This is why I call the diamond "idealist." It is idealist in that, despite its intention, it is ahistorical. The diamond intends to capture history, but history withdraws from it like the tide. One is no longer talking about the reality of history. The framework is left stranded on the shoals of ideology.

The Kantian Opening

The idealist diamond does not begin with the avowed intention of being idealist. Neither does it set out to be metaphysical in any negative sense of that term. Rather, as we have seen, it aims to *overcome* the dichotomized, "metaphysical" mode of thinking which the term "idealist" seems to suggest. The diamond aims to accomplish the sort of contextualization which I have said is characteristic of metaphysical thinking at its best. And in this effort the diamond, while speculative, has common sense on its side. For surely to choose *either* "mind" or "nature" is to settle for a half truth; surely the basic error is to pit the one against the other, to pose a dichotomy in the first place. Such dichtomization was the fatal error of the historic Enlightenment. Subsequent thought must reunite what that movement put asunder, and it must do so by a deeper recognition, an enlightenment of the Enlightenment.

C. G. Jung captures something of the dynamic of this recognition when he speaks of encountering one's "shadow." As the language suggests, Jung's retrieval of the shadow side was a thrust against the historical Enlightenment, for which darkness was not to be affirmed but overcome. Jung observed that on encountering that which is other than myself, I spontaneously regard it as strange, even threatening. I resist it, I define myself over against it. Yet with time I may come to discover unsuspected connections. I may begin to surrender my defensiveness, allowing myself to be contextualized by a larger reality in which I and the other both participate. Thus is alienation overcome. As Emerson proclaimed in "The American Scholar," "The world—this shadow of the soul, or *other me*—lies wide around. Its attractions are the keys which unlock my thoughts and make me acquainted with myself."[79] And if Emerson seems too distant or metaphysical, something very similar may be rendered in the contemporary, hermeneutical language of Paul Ricoeur, who writes that "reflection is the effort to recapture the Ego of the Ego Cogito in the mirror of its objects, its works, its acts."[80]

Recognition of the shadow is meant to break open the closed, too-brightly-lit Enlightenment world. It is meant to be an act of contextualization. Whether it succeeds as such is, however, another question. For in the nature of things, or at least in the nature of Jung's argument, the crucial recognition has to be the recognition of a certain shared reality, a certain unity. And that is all that is required in order to generate something like the diamond. The recognition is a *re*-cognition of an original unity; by its nature as an overcoming of the appearance of irresolvable division, it is a movement toward reunification. But reunification of what? And where does the self stand with respect to that unity? Must we not say that ultimately the self *is* the unity? This is the line of questioning which causes one to doubt whether an act of contextualization (viz. a contextualization of the self) and a consequent overcoming of metaphysics have really been achieved. Has the self really been relativized vis-à-vis a larger context—or is it rather the *other* which has been relativized, made a means toward a larger end, namely the self's triumphant self-recognition and consequent expansion? Emerson, for his part, is quite clear. After the passage cited, he writes:

> so shall the dumb abyss be vocal with speech. I pierce its order; I dissipate its fear; I dispose of it within the circuit of my expanding life. So much only of life as I know by experience, so much of the wilderness have I vanquished and planted, or so far have I extended my being, my dominion.[81]

It is a statement which reflects all too well the period in American history in which it was written.

Recalling the two pitfalls Derrida seeks to avoid, we may say that the diamond is symptomatic of modern thought in that it is much concerned to avoid oppositional thinking, while showing no commensurate sensitivity to the issue of presence. Conversely, Derrida's particular contribution is to have countered this tendency by clearly articulating presence as a distinctive issue.[82] Once alerted to the issue, we begin to see how the modern period has fallen into oppositionalism in its treatment of the received tradition. It tends to think in terms of Dark Ages versus Enlightenment, static thought versus dynamic, closed world versus infinite universe. And it tends to identify itself with one member of the distinction, which became thereby a presence term, self-evidently good. Further, one can see how the modern period, when it does thematize the issue of oppositionalism and seeks to overcome it, implicitly does so in the name of an underlying presence which is generally associated with the subject or self. Thus, notwithstanding its aim of going beyond idealism, thought which reflects the diamond pattern deserves the title "idealist."

To put the matter another way (and this point is central to Derrida's usefulness) it will not do to accuse the diamond of being "idealist" or "subjectivist" or whatever *directly*. That will only prompt another round of the debate in which proponents of the diamond will aver that, quite to the contrary, they are seeking to overcome the idealism/realism dichotomy, they are seeking to overcome the subject/object dichotomy, et cetera, et cetera. Those who criticize the diamond in this way only wind up repeating it, so that "misconstrued, treated lightly, Hegelianism only extends its historical domination."[83] Rather, one must criticize *indirectly*, by way of a concrete, textual critique of presence. One must begin by showing that at one point or another (and given the figure of a diamond, the term "point" is particularly apposite here) a certain presence has been posited; and one must show concretely that *as a result* there has been a skewing in the direction of idealism, in the direction of the subject, or whatever.[84] Without this indirect, inductive criticism, one is left with the empty gesture of saying the nineteenth century was rationalist, we have gone beyond that; the nineteenth century was optimistic, we have gone beyond that—shopworn formulas which are the familiar stock of ready-made enlightenment.

So far I have been using the notion of the idealist diamond quite broadly, as a type. Questions of where the type applies must be determined case by case. In chapter 3 I shall argue that Paul Ricoeur, a formidable thinker who certainly aims to eschew idealism, turns out to be an instance of the type. Like Jung, Mircea Eliade is a clear example; and Paul Tillich, with his structuring narrative of dreaming innocence, alienation, and reconciliation, must be reckoned another.[85] That these names should constitute a virtual honor roll of those who have shaped theology and the study of religion in America during this century, shows how pervasive is this mode of thought. Yet there is a fundamental incompatibility between this pervasive pattern and the crucial memory of suffering. I have spelled out the nature of this incompatibility elsewhere.[86] Here suffice it to observe that one reason these various thinkers have been influential is because they do in fact respond to a profoundly human aspiration; but that the *way* in which they respond diminishes the poignancy and pain of history, and along with that our sense of human reality.[87]

Of the Enlightenment, too, it is true that every revealing is simultaneously a concealing. The great temptation of the Enlightenment may be associated with its very name, that is with the implication that there can be an enlightening or a revealing which is *not* simultaneously a concealing. Where then is the concealing? What is the difficult reality which is obscured by the open, accessible truth of the Enlightenment? The answer, I would suggest, lies in the *twofold* character of the Enlightenment, the *difference* internal to the Enlightenment. This is a difference concealed by each reference to "the" Enlightenment. Earlier we saw that there were at least two Enlightenments; and that they point in rather different directions, the one toward (a certain understanding of) nature, the other toward (a certain understanding of) history. We also saw that while each held out a certain promise, in that it contributed to a better understanding of a particular form of evil, each also exposed—rendering more poignant—a particular form of suffering which it might or might not be able to overcome. It is this last, the reality of suffering exposed—natural evils which simply happen and are not directly the result of divine decision; moral evils which are the result not of some eternal order, but of particular systems of injustice—which we find difficult to contemplate, and which we cover over in our anxiety for a solution. And it happens that the surest cover is to collapse the two Enlightenments into one; to think, for example, that there could be such a thing as a "scientific socialism"; and thus to generate the self-justifying monster, half nature, half history, which Metz labels "evolution."

What is required in order to stave this off is a distinctive mode of thinking which would grant primacy to neither of the two Enlightenments, but would think the two dialectically. This even Metz does not provide. To begin to resource such a mode of thought in theology is the purpose of the present book. As a way of adumbrating what I am after, I can do no better than to quote a long, mentally nourishing passage in which Susan Buck-Morss summarizes Adorno's negative dialectic. According to Buck-Morss, Adorno *had*

> no concept of history in the sense of an ontological, positive definition of history's philosophical meaning. Instead, both history and nature as its dialectical opposite were for Adorno *cognitive* concepts, not unlike Kant's 'regulative ideas,' which were applied in his writings as critical tools for the demythification of reality. At the same time, each provided a critique of the other. Nature provided the key for exposing the nonidentity between the concept of history (as a regulative idea) and historical reality, just as history provided the key for demythifying nature. Adorno argued, on the one hand, that actual past history was not identical to the concept of history (as rational progress), because of the material *nature* to which it did violence. At the same time, the "natural" phenomena of the present were not identical to the concept of nature (as essential reality or truth), because . . . they had been historically produced.

Let me continue Buck-Morss's description, interspersing comments of my own. Thus "by insisting on their dialectical interrelationship, their nonidentity and yet mutual determinacy, Adorno refused to grant either nature or history the status of an ontological first principle." In other words, he refused to regard either as a presence. "His purpose was to destroy the mythical power which both concepts wielded over the present, a power which was the source of a fatalistic and passive acceptance of the status quo." Cf. Metz's "evolution." "This demythifying process relentlessly intensified the critical tension between thought and reality instead of bringing them into harmony." In effect, it stuck with the reality of suffering. "In the space, which he later called the 'force-field' generated by this process, Adorno placed his hope for the future realization of freedom, which Hegel had prematurely attributed to the history of the past."[88]

Such a "force-field" offers us our best shot at responding to the problem with which we began, the need to reopen a space for experience. Thus the aim of this book is not to perfect a method, but to help open a certain space. Now if Hegel is the thinker in whom, paradigmatically, the two Enlightenments seemed for a moment to unite, then Kant, I wish to suggest, has peculiar resources for keeping them distinct. Undoubtedly Kant is often pilloried for having "dichotomized" subject and object, nature and history, pure and practical reason. The very repetitiveness of the accusation is evidence, one begins to suspect, of the hold which idealism continues to have upon us. It may be that Kant does not miss Hegel's issues, but rather approaches them in another way. Yirmiyahu Yovel concludes in *Kant and the Philosophy of History* that "the closer Kant anticipates Hegel, the *more* antinomic his own position becomes."[89] So far from being evidence of obtuseness, Kant's characteristic tension of thought may be just the thing that is needed in order to keep sight of human finitude.[90] Antinomic thinking, properly pursued, might be a virtual prescription for avoiding presence. And there may be realism in Kant's keen awareness that unity is indeed an aspiration of the human heart—but only an aspiration. A certain unity is a requirement of reason, a genuine requirement, but it is not necessarily a requirement of reality. What seems to be needless division on Kant's part may prove to be, on closer inspection, a respect for difference.

In philosophy too the histories tend to reflect the viewpoint of the victor. At one time histories of thought portrayed Kant's mature philosophy as a pinnacle of lucidity, from which most of subsequent idealism was to decline. Eventually Kantian historians were displaced by the followers of Hegel, and accounts appeared in which Kant's work appeared as a mere base camp, a transitional phase in the ascent to the Hegelian heights.[91] According to the latter account, Hegel's ascent transcended metaphysics. Kant, while he pointed beyond metaphysics, remained captive to certain metaphysical presuppositions, such as that of the "thing-in-itself" and an irresolvable distinction between subject and object. But the effect of Derrida's concept of presence is to give us a more inclusive critical concept. It allows us to imagine what one might call a "metaphysics-1" before Kant—and a "metaphysics-2" coming after.

The moment you think in these terms, your sense of the tradition gets reconfigured. It becomes possible to think of Kant as working at the margin—at the fold, transition or "force-field"—*between* two forms of metaphysic. No doubt even on such an account there would be much in Kant which would need correction, even rejection; no doubt what is revealing in his thought will be simultaneously a concealing.[92] Nevertheless it becomes imaginable that from this space which is no space but a fold, transition, or turning, we may derive strategies of use in our own time, at the turning of the century.

Bonhoeffer writes that "Kant in his Anthropology makes the very sound remark that anyone who fails to grasp the significance of the false appearances in the world . . . is a traitor to humanity."[93] It is in this sense of a vigorous, critical resistance that we may speak of a Kantian opening. Provided only that we remember, an opening can also be a wound.

II

QUALITATIVE DIFFERENCE
BARTH'S EPISTLE TO THE ROMANS

This chapter amounts to an experiment, a test case for my thesis that deconstruction may shed light on the theological tradition. Applied to the work of Karl Barth, the effect of Derrida's categories would seem clear: deconstruction would seem to corroborate the common reading of Barth, and specifically the common reasons for rejecting him. As regards the Derridean notion of presence, Barth has long stood accused of a "positivism of revelation." And as regards oppositionalist thinking, his work—especially his commentary on Romans—continues to be regarded as the very paradigm of theological dualism. Barth, who railed against the mixing of philosophy with theology, would seem to stand convicted of being metaphysical in the most negative sense of that term.

Let us focus on the Romans commentary and, while remaining sensitive to the issue of presence, let us take as our guiding thread the issue of dualism.[1] The grounds for criticism are not far to seek. Barth announces in the preface to the second edition, "If I have a system, it is limited to a recognition of what Kierkegaard called the 'infinite qualitative difference between time and eternity' . . . ."[2] That distinction is succeeded by a series of others—revelation versus reason, the Gospel of God versus the ways of humankind, faith versus religion, etc.—which rule out of court every conceivable form of human initiative. Little wonder then that from the time of its publication, readers of the *Römerbrief* have been left to wonder whether Barth's God serves any other function than that of a cipher for the repudiation of all that is finite, earthly or mortal.

Yet those who persevere may discover passages which resist such interpretation. Barth's hostility toward religion, for example, is well known. It is commonly cited as a prime instance of his dualism, in which he sets at naught what is perhaps the highest of human capacities. But what is one then to make of the fact that what Barth singles out for critique is nothing other than religion's tendency to be, precisely, dualistic?

> More than any other human possibility religion is scarred with the dualism of "There" and "Here," presupposition and fact, truth and reality; the re-

ligious man above all others is not what he intended to be. A dualism con-
trols the world of religion, and, consequently, there sin—"abounds" (v. 20).
(231, cf. 268)

In these lines we find Barth the presumed dualist denouncing in the
harshest terms, terms associated with the condemnation of sin, the effects
of religious dualism. Faced with such an anomaly, one must conclude either that Barth is hopelessly inconsistent or that the common reading of
him has been inadequate.

A clue to the nature of that inadequacy may be found in the self-des-
ignation adopted by the theological movement which Barth helped
launch. That movement was determined to break with the liberalism of
the previous century; yet in calling itself "dialectical theology" it adopted
a term which was profoundly rooted within that very period. By this act
the new movement may have signaled that its relationship to what went
before was not to be understood as flatly negative, but rather as being,
itself, dialectical. If this be so, how are we in our own time to pursue the
clue? One approach would be straightforwardly historical, a reexamina-
tion of the labyrinthine debate running from Kant through Hegel and
Kierkegaard. But there is another possibility as well: we might begin with
a recent thinker who stands significantly within the tradition of Kant and
Hegel, and we might then "question back" from the current embodiment
of that tradition to Barth. Such a procedure has its risks, of course, but it
is possible that with the passage of time certain issues may have gained in
clarity. It is worth exploring the premise that certain contemporary debates might illumine retrospectively lines of thought which were already
operative, but not fully explicit, within Barth's own reflection.

Qualitative Difference

Such is the rationale for pairing Barth with Derrida. Now the most pressing challenge for the venture is indeed Barth's invocation of "the 'infinite
qualitative distinction'" [den "unendlichen qualitativen Untershied"] between
time and eternity. That phrase, which appears in the preface to the second
edition, is a direct quotation from Kierkegaard (10 [xiii]).[3] In the course
of his own exposition, however, Barth does not hesitate to alter the
Kierkegaardian language. One finds him speaking simply of "the qualitative distinction" [des qualitativen Untershieds] between God and the world
(39 [14]) and of "the qualitative distinction [jene qualifizierte Distanz] between men and the final Omega" (50 [26]). He chooses, in other words,
to drop the term "infinite." The result is perplexingly mild, not at all what
one would expect in a prophetic tract. We should be reluctant, I think, to
dismiss as accidental a change in so crucial a phrase, and a change which

takes so unexpected a turn. Is there some other way of making sense of it?

Prompted by Derrida, I propose the following. First, Barth may intend to free the notions of difference and distinction from any connotation of necessary *opposition*. Much of Derridean deconstruction is, in effect, an extended reminder that that which is different from us does not necessarily stand in opposition to us. This might be a truism, were it not for a further thesis which I wish to ascribe to Barth (and to Derrida). For both seem to imply that it is actually quite difficult to maintain an open-ended sense of "difference" and to avoid casting matters in terms of a clearcut and (therefore) conceptually controllable "opposition."[4] And this leads directly to the third thesis, which is that the term "infinite," so far from heightening one's sense of authentic difference, may actually undercut that sense. Such a reversal occurs when, to quote a crucial passage in Barth, "We assign [God] the highest place in our world; and in so doing we place [God] fundamentally on one line with ourselves and with things" (44).[5]

Barth contends that we move by imperceptible degrees from postulating an opposition (finite versus infinite), to regarding the opposition as constituting the poles of a spectrum (from finite to infinite), to considering the spectrum itself as reflective of an underlying presence or sameness. The net effect is to obscure the reality of the very difference which we would affirm. We place God "on one line with ourselves" the moment we entertain the fantasy of "some prolongation into infinity" (44). As antidote to such confusion, a straightforward notion of "difference" might prove more radical than the misleading "infinite." The seemingly mild affirmation of "qualitative difference" may offer the sharper critique.

Memory of God

The test of any line of interpretation is the light it casts on the text at large. Regarding the opening chapter of Barth's commentary, one may offer five observations.

(1) Barth frequently describes God's impact upon our world as a calling into question. The Gospel proceeds by "setting a question-mark against the whole course of this world" (40, cf. 43). What is revealed thereby is "the universal questionableness of human life" (40, cf. 42, 46). Such language is well suited to steering between pitfalls which Derrida characterizes as opposition and presence. For to question is not to contradict, but neither is it to submit to the way things are. To question is to insinuate alongside the accepted reality another possibility or another point of view which is simply different.

In a similar vein, one may consider these lines at the head of the section entitled "The Theme of the Epistle":

> In announcing the limitation of the known world by another that is un-
> known, the Gospel does not enter into competition with the many attempts
> to disclose within the known world some more or less unknown and higher
> form of existence. . . . The Gospel is not a truth among other truths.
> Rather, it sets a question-mark against all truths. (35)

Here again Barth's distinctive point is elusive but crucial. The Gospel stands apart; but it does so in the manner of a question. It does *not* do so in such a way as, in Barth's phrase, to "enter into competition."

(2) While it does not set itself in opposition, the questioning does have an effect. In the paragraph following that just quoted, Barth says of God's power that "being completely different, it is the KRISIS of all power" (36). Simply by virtue of being (completely) different, it precipitates a *krisis*. Now the word *krisis* comes to our ears so laden with associations drawn from existentialism and the world wars that it is hard to conceive a *krisis* which is not a function of opposition. Assistance may be sought in Derrida, who speaks of how certain possibilities foreign to a linguistic system have the effect neither of negating that system nor of leaving it undisturbed, but of eliciting within that system "a certain trembling, a certain decentering."[6] Barth may be seeking to describe (or to effect) something similar when he says, still within the sentence just quoted, that the power of this world "is pronounced to be something and—nothing, nothing and—something" (36).

The pattern of "something and—nothing, nothing and—something" reappears in the assertion that "by the Gospel the whole concrete world is dissolved and established" (35). In this passage the German word translated as "dissolved" is *Aufhebung* (xiv). Whatever one is to make of the migration of this cardinal term from Hegel to Barth, it is safe to assume that it does *not* denote a flat, oppositional negation. Barth says as much by coupling *Aufhebung* with *Begrundung*. The resultant phrase, translated as "dissolved and established," recurs so frequently as to constitute a fundamental trope of the Barthian argument (30, 36, 38, 46, 51). In another connection Barth writes, "In so far as 'piety' is a sign of the occurrence of faith, it is so as the dissolution of all other concrete things and supremely as the dissolution of itself" (40, cf. 49, 50). The language of dissolution provides a way of speaking of *krisis* without becoming entangled in opposition. It is as if the presumptive structures of this world collapsed under the weight of their own pretensions once they were immersed in the medium of the Gospel.

(3) It should be stressed that the structures which are so dissolved are

indeed *presumptive* structures. They are not the structures of creation as such, but the structures which humankind has *projected upon* the world. And what are these projected structures, specifically? It seems in keeping with the sense of Barth's own text to suggest that they are, in effect, the structures of presence and opposition. Regarding the projecting of patterns of opposition, I will have more to say when I treat "the wrath of God." For the moment, let us attend to the issue of presence. In the opening pages of his text, Barth lays down a cardinal rule for interpretation: "Paul's position can be justified only as resting in God," and it is only in this way that his words can "be regarded as at all credible, for they are as *incapable of direct apprehension* as is God Himself."[7] The denial of immediacy, whether in the form of "direct observation" (29), "direct communication" (41), "romantic direct communion" (50), or "direct experience of God" (52), is an insistent theme throughout the text. In support of this refusal Barth quotes Kierkegaard's dictum that "to be known directly is the characteristic mark of the idol" (38). In a similar vein Kierkegaard affirms, "All paganism consists in this, that God is related to man directly, as the obviously extraordinary to the astonished observer."[8] What is disallowed is the notion that God could become for humankind a "presence."

Commentators have been more or less cognizant of Barth's insistence upon a necessarily indirect character of divine communication. Nevertheless, Barth continues to be accused of espousing, in Bonhoeffer's fatal phrase, a "positivism of revelation." If knowledgeable observers persist in pressing this charge, it must be that they do not see how Barth's disclaimers, however emphatic, can possibly comport with the rest of what he is about. In light of our present interpretation, however, the repudiation of direct communication not only comports with other themes in Barth—it is positively required by them. The denial that revelation constitutes a presence susceptible of direct communication can now be appreciated as being of a piece with Barth's avoidance of oppositional constructions, which we have already observed. An alleged presence is thought to be self-explanatory and self-sufficient. But we noted in our initial discussion of the linkage between presence and opposition that, in the very act of opposition whereby a purported presence is set apart as "self-sufficient," the term is in fact confirmed in its dependence upon a whole network of reference and exchange. Thus the Gospel—which is, as one might say with due trepidation, the one true presence—can be present to our awareness only insofar as it is simultaneously absent. This would seem to be the logic of Barth's affirmation: "The Gospel does not expound or recommend itself. It does not negotiate or plead, threaten, or make promises. It withdraws itself when it is not listened to for its own sake" (38–39). For this is to say that it is precisely *because* it "does not negotiate or . . . threaten"—because it does not enter into the human system of exchange and opposition—that the Gospel must be "listened to for its own sake." And that when the Gospel is not so received, its response is simultaneously one of non-presence and non-opposition: it simply "withdraws."

(4) At the same time that he insists upon the indirect character of all knowledge of God, even in Jesus Christ, Barth follows Paul in asserting that "that which may be known of God is manifest" to all of humankind (45). It was discerned, for example, by "Plato in his wisdom" (46). In the preface to the second edition Barth affirms that the " 'infinite qualitative distinction' " between God and the human "is for me the theme of the Bible *and the essence of philosophy*"(!)[9] Here again we have something that goes against the common picture of Barth, for it is apparent that he is affirming *some* sort of general revelation. But what is it that is so revealed? The twofold answer may be couched in terms of the foregoing discussion: what is revealed is the differentness of God and the questionableness of this world. (a) The first of these Barth treats under the heading "that which can be known of God," where he speaks of "the recognition of the absolute heteronomy under which we stand" (46). The word "heteronomy" does sound oppositional (one thinks of Tillich's use of the term), but the root meaning of "hetero-," we should remember, is simply "other." And that which is other, *even that which is "Wholly Other,"* does not necessarily stand in a relationship of opposition. Indeed in the next, extraordinary sentence Barth makes this very point, even at the risk of collapsing the sense of distance: "When we rebel, we are in rebellion not against what is foreign to us but against that which is most intimately ours" (46).

Barth clarifies this remarkable convergence of the thematics of intimacy and otherness through a notion of *memory*: "Our memory of God accompanies us always as problem and as warning. He is the hidden abyss; but He is also the hidden home at the beginning and end of all our journeyings. Disloyalty to Him is disloyalty to ourselves" (46). Readers of Barth's commentary have often objected that Barth does not identify any human capacity to which revelation can relate. The "memory of eternity" (48) introduces just such a capacity. In our own concluding chapter, we will return to this puzzling notion of a "memory of God," a "memory of eternity," which is so anomalous within his theology, yet so crucial to his argument. For the present, it is enough to note how tenaciously he holds to the idea. On the penultimate page of his first chapter, and thus *after* the discussion of "the Night," Barth affirms that "there still, however, remains a relic of clarity of sight, a last, warning recollection of the secret of God" (53). Only at the last, extreme point in Barth's exposition does he mention the disappearance of the capacity ("but even this can cease" [53]). Only then does the memory of God fall victim to "the final vacuity and disintegration" (*Zersetzung*—no longer *Aufhebung*). And only then does Barth declare, "His judgement now becomes judgement *and nothing more*."[10]

(b) Barth addresses the second aspect of the revelation, namely the questionableness of this world, under the heading of "the invisible things of God" which "are clearly seen" (46). In keeping with what he has said about memory, Barth affirms that these things can be seen "by calm, veritable, unprejudiced religious contemplation" (46). Regarding the character of these "invisible things of God," he contends:

> The insecurity of our whole existence, the vanity and utter questionableness of all that is and of what we are, lie as in a text-book open before us. What are all those enigmatic creatures of God—a zoological garden, for example—but so many problems to which we have no answer? (46)

Earlier in Barth's exposition an act of questioning generated a certain tension without becoming oppositional. Now the notion of the "questionableness" of the world serves to give to Barth's general revelation a content which is not a simple presence; nor is it, for that matter, a simple absence. Rather it is the fact that what *is*—seemingly—present, namely the reality of this world, is in point of fact quite thoroughly questionable. This then is the crucial, predictable reservation which attaches to Barth's unexpected affirmation of a general revelation. There is a human capacity—but that capacity does not provide a presence. In pointing beyond a one-dimensional "world without paradox" (48), in testifying to the differentness of God and the correlative questionableness of the world, the capacity is thus far from providing any foundation for human security, any ground for religious "boasting."

Question and memory converge in Barth's treatment of the problem of evil. If there exists a single key to the *Römerbrief*, it may well lie in this radical inquiry, which puts at issue "the consistency of God with Himself." So radical a question cannot be answered (or even addressed) by the "No-God" who is "the complete affirmation of the course of the world and of men *as it is*."[11] Thus Barth asserts, in words that anticipate Jürgen Moltmann's (qualified) defense of "protest atheism," that "the cry of revolt against such a god is nearer the truth than is the sophistry with which men attempt to justify him."[12] Barth's treatment of the problem of evil takes on the contours of Metz's "dangerous memory."[13] Barth writes that "there still abides . . . that profound agreement between the will of God and that which men, longing to be freed from themselves, also secretly desire" (41). So indispensable is this way of protest and resistance that Barth can say, "There is no other relation to God save that which appears upon the road along which Job travelled" (48).

(5) While the realities to which memory and protest attest do not step forth in the mode of presence, Barth is emphatic in saying of them that "these things ARE . . . " (43). They do exist, that is to say, independently of the attitude we choose to adopt regarding them. In this specific sense, one may find in Barth's commentary a form of ontology. And in the dis-

tinction between reality and our attitude toward it we have a way of clarifying a topic which is too often obscured in discussions of Barth, namely the subject of "the wrath of God," which Barth treats under the heading of "The Night."

The section on "The Night" constitutes an important test for the reading of Barth which I have been setting forth, for in these pages the language unquestionably does become oppositional. The problem with the common reading, however, is the tendency to assume that the entire commentary is about "the Night"—a night in which all creatures would indeed be black. The inadequacy of such a reading is indicated by a glance at the table of contents. The heading "The Night" is situated in the middle of chapter one, dividing it in two in a manner which is not repeated in any of the other chapters. *Before* that heading, one finds the section entitled "The Theme of the Epistle." Thus the very structure of Barth's exposition gives one to understand that the "theme of the epistle" is something other than "the Night." So it is, if our exposition of "the theme" in terms the differentness of God and the questionableness of the world has been correct.

And so it is in the text, provided that the reader bear constantly in mind that the realities are one thing and our attitude toward them quite another. This distinction is absolutely central to Barth's treatment of "the Night"; for when Barth does speak of "the wrath of God," he speaks of it as "the questionableness of life *in so far as we do not apprehend it*" (42). Similarly, one might say that the wrath of God is (the reality of) the otherness of God *insofar as we do not accept it*. Earlier, in denying "direct immediacy," Barth held that "the power of God . . . can . . . be received and understood by us, only as contradiction" (38). But that contradiction is not an opposition. Or insofar as it *is* in opposition, it is in opposition to *our customary ways of understanding*.[14] The contradiction is not opposed to our true reality. Thus it becomes possible, in a formula which serves as a virtual definition of faith, "to accept a contradiction and rest in it" (39).

The section on "the Night" is about the human resistance to this contradiction. It is about the fact that we do not "see the great question-mark that is set against us" (43) and do not rest in it. When this happens, when we do not trust, *then* "the barrier remains a barrier and does not become a place of exit. . . . *Then is the contradiction not hope, but a sorrowful opposition. . . . And Negation is then—what is normally meant by the word.*"[15] Barth could hardly be more explicit in signaling that what he has meant by contradiction up to this point has *not* been opposition; and that it is only now, now that one considers the absence of faith, that it becomes "a sorrowful opposition." Similarly it would be difficult for him to indicate more straightforwardly that all that he has said heretofore that seemed to imply simple negation—all that he has said about the otherness of God and the *krisis* of creation—has *not* been negation (or opposition) in the sense of "what is normally meant by the word."

The Christ Event

The foregoing observations provide a means of access to the contested topic of Barth's early Christology. In this matter it is especially vital that one keep close to the text. Pages 29–31 contain the oft-cited images drawn from geometry: the intersecting planes, the line tangential to the circle. But it is striking how little use there is in these pages of the spatial distinctions (or oppositions) such as "above" and "below" which are often assumed to encapsulate his thought.[16] Rather, the recurrent contrast is between the "known" and the "unknown." It seems fair to conclude, therefore, that Barth means this "unknown" to be taken with full seriousness: i.e., as calling all other (known) distinctions into question, *including* such distinctions as "below" and "above." Barth is signaling that we scarcely know how else, with what other term than "unknown," to point to the divine occurrence.

Even as regards the contrast of the known and unknown, moreover, the emphasis falls not upon the unknown (or the known) as such, but upon the intersection of the two. And what happens at this intersection is not mere bafflement, but an occurrence which Barth seeks to depict in carefully balanced terms. On the one hand, "the relation between us and God, between this world and His world, presses for recognition"; on the other hand, this reality, this pressing, "is not self-evident" (29). It is, in short, a situation analogous to that described earlier with regard to general revelation, where a question (or a general questionableness) pressed for recognition while yet not constituting a presence.

Barth proceeds to specify what happens in this instance:

> The years A.D. 1–30 are the era of revelation and disclosure; the era which, as is shown by the reference to David, sets forth the new and strange and divine definition of all time. The particularity of the years A.D. 1–30 is dissolved [*aufhebt*] by this divine definition, because it makes every epoch a potential field of revelation and disclosure. (29)

The passage offers a key to Barth's use of the concept of *Aufhebung*. In and through the particularity of these years there comes to light a situation which transcends the time. It is on this basis that Barth can say in the preface to the first edition, "If we rightly understand ourselves, our problems are the problem of Paul" (1). Not only is our world, like Paul's world, questionable, as can be known "by calm, veritable, unprejudiced religious contemplation"; it is, like Paul's world, actively questioned. Yet this is a reality which cannot be known apart from these years; the reality of being questioned cannot become a "standpoint" which one might assume without reference to the specificity of the years (cf. 19). It is in this sense that Barth intends that the specificity of the years be at once transcended and established. "The Resurrection from the dead is . . . the transformation: the establishing or *declaration* of that point from above, and the corresponding discerning of it from below" (30).

Images of tangents and intersecting planes seem apt for suggesting a frontier or threshold at which there occurs an otherness without opposition.[17] The matter is a good deal less clear as regards the imagery of explosion. If one emphasizes the explosion as such, the image stands as counterevidence to the reading I have been proposing; for whatever else it may be, an explosion has got to count as an extreme form of direct communication, a relationship of "the obviously extraordinary to the astonished observer." We would then have to think in terms of two contradictory thematics, one of direct communication and the other of indirect, both at work within the *Römerbrief*. Before resorting to that explanation, however, one should note that the text itself seems to direct attention not toward the explosion as such, but toward "the effulgence, or, rather, the crater made at the percussion point" of the exploding shell (29). If explosion is an archetype of presence, emphasis upon the crater entails a note of absence; and indeed Barth's immediate gloss speaks precisely of "the void by which the point . . . makes itself known" (29).

It is thus possible to regard the crater in the manner in which Derrida speaks of the "mark." This Derridean concept can be explained by means of an image. The physical act of writing, particularly in its early forms, often required the pressing of a pointed instrument into some receptive substance, such as wax. The resultant impression is quite literally nothing, a negative space; yet at the same time it represents a great deal, a whole network of significations. The mark epitomizes a peculiar modality which is neither simple absence nor presence.[18] Once attuned to this distinctive character of the imprint or mark, the reader finds similar notions scattered throughout the *Römerbrief*. The most striking instance is undoubtedly Barth's affirmation that "the whole world is the footprint of God" (43). More generally, it becomes possible in this manner to understand how Barth's frequent use of the notion of "void" may indeed be negative, yet not simply negative. "The importance of an apostle," for example, "is negative rather than positive. In him a void becomes visible" (33). But in becoming visible, the void becomes, precisely, a sign; and in becoming a sign, a nexus of signification, the apostle becomes "something to others."[19]

A further way in which the imagery of the christological section extends into the chapter at large is via the thematics of dimensionality. "The wisdom of the Night" issues in folly "because it holds firmly to a two-dimensional plane, a plane persistently contradicted by actual occurrence" (54). Wedded to this stance, one is unable "to see the new dimensional plane which is the boundary of our world and the meaning of our salvation" (45). Instead one is left with "the picture of a world without paradox" (48). The result is the loss not only of the otherness of that other plane, but of the relative otherness which exists *within* this world as well. "If this 'breaking in' does not occur, our thought remains merely empty, formal, critical and unproductive, incapable of mastering the rich world of appearance and of apprehending each particular thing in the context of the whole."[20] On these grounds it is possible to suggest a positive, analogical relationship between the "qualitative difference" between God and the world, on the one hand, and, on the other hand, the lesser but nonetheless real differences which obtain within this finite world.

An Analogy of Difference?

Barth does hold that all of humankind stand under the wrath of God. If that be grounds for calling him a dualist, then dualist he is, along with much or most of the Christian tradition. But that is a matter of what we may call *moral* dualism—righteous God versus sinful humanity—which is quite distinct from dualism of a *metaphysical* or ontological bent. Presumably critics who tax Barth with being dualistic, and thereby distorting the Christian faith, have the latter, metaphysical dualism in mind.

More precisely, the complaint against Barth would seem to be that he is indifferent to the distinction just made. That is to say, he has projected the moral conflict upon the metaphysical realm, thereby promulgating an unnecessarily oppositional understanding of the relationship between God and creation. "Eternity" and "time," after all, should not be ranged over against one another in the same way as "divine righteousness" and "human sin." Such would seem to be the grievance against Barth. But on the evidence of the text it would seem that, far from having ignored the distinction between the metaphysical and the moral, between reality and our attitude toward reality, Barth has assumed that very distinction as the grounding for his distinctive dialectic. Moreover, in delineating the real situation—the "metaphysical" reality toward which we adopt our moral stance—Barth is at some pains to fashion a vocabulary of simple difference, eschewing the rhetoric of opposition.

In addition, Barth emphatically holds that insofar as there *is* in our world a penchant toward metaphysical dualism, that tendency is a function of our own moral wrongheadedness, which is epitomized in religion. "In religion, dualism makes its appearance. . . . Religion breaks men into two halves" (268). One need not contend that Barth is perfectly consistent in this regard. A comprehensive account of his early writings might well find itself speaking of two contending viewpoints or languages, one resistant to metaphysical dualism, the other not. But if our study of the opening chapter of the *Römerbrief* has merit at all, those dismissals of the text which label it as unreflectively dualistic will have to be rethought.

Barth, for his part, would of course be skeptical of anything that proceeded under the heading of metaphysics or ontology. Yet regarding the matters we have discussed—the questionableness of the world, the differentness of God—he readily affirms that "these things ARE . . . " A further implication of our study would seem to be that even within creation one finds intimations of a (created) reality which transcends our oppositional distortions, what one might call a realm of "innocent difference." One thinks in this connection of the Edenic resonances implicit in Barth's choice of example when he speaks of the zoological garden.[21] Certainly, in any event, the effect of his remarks on "the things of God" which "are clearly seen" is to profoundly interrelate the acceptance of innocent difference within this world, the recognition of the questionableness of the world at large, and the acknowledgment of the differentness of God.

Any attempt to specify further the nature of this interrelationship would take us beyond the bounds of the present essay. But we may already have sufficient grounds for suggesting that beyond Barth's rejection of the *analogia entis*, and entirely in keeping with that rejection, when that rejection is properly understood, there exists a further possibility: a distinctive strategy which one might call, with a final nod toward Derrida, an analogy of difference.

Theology and Difference: The Argument in Brief

The usual criticism of Barth is twofold: (a) he has a dualistic view of the relationship between God and creation; and as a result (b) he is not able to make the necessary distinctions *within* the created order. He gives us pure presence or pure absence, a night in which all cows are black. In parallel fashion, a defense of Barth's position, as we have interpreted it, would hold that (a) what appears to be dualistic is simply a clear recognition of the most fundamental difference, which is carefully kept from becoming oppositional; and that precisely because Barth has gotten that first difference right—or because St. Paul has gotten it right—(b) it then becomes possible to honor, in appropriate ways, the lesser distinctions within the created order. Moreover, we have seen that Barth's commentary includes a counterattack against his critics. Barth implies that (a) the alternative position which his critics represent is of a piece with religion's recurrent effort to soften or blur the fundamental difference, placing God and creation on a single line. Barth also implies that (b) the corollary of this religious impetus is the emphasizing of some distinction within the

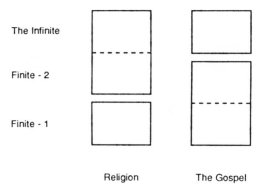

Schema 1. Barth's view of the theological options: initial typology

created order—elevating some finite reality as idol, as presence, as point of contact with the divine—which inevitably generates within the created order an opposition.

Barth's counterattack makes clear that he has his own distinctive view of matters; and that on this view what looks like dualism may rather be a strategy for defending difference. The value of bringing Derrida to Barth has been in adumbrating this distinctive perspective. To bring it more fully to light, I now wish to set forth a typology. Let us call it a *polemical* typology, for its purpose is not that of a neutral instrument, but that of a device for understanding how things look from within the position which Barth is advocating, and what it is that Barth is driving at. A first step is to sketch the two alternatives as Barth envisages them (Schema 1). The figure to the right corresponds to the defense of Barth's position, as given above, and the figure to the left corresponds to Barth's counterattack. Set aside for the moment the question of whether one shares Barth's viewpoint. These figures are useful in pointing up the fact that we are dealing with *two kinds* of differences or distinctions (call them strong distinctions and soft distinctions); that much depends on how these two kinds of differences are related; and that there are two junctures at which the differences arise or the distinctions are made—namely, the finite/infinite and the finite/finite.

Running these factors through the possible permutations, we arrive at Schema 2. The position to the far left would presumably be a form of pantheism. Perhaps it is ungracious of me to label it type 0, but I think it is fair to say that it does not figure as a major option within the present discussion. For our purposes the more interesting new arrival is type 2, a position exemplified, though not exhausted, by classical existentialism. This position thrives upon certain tensions or conflicts within the realm

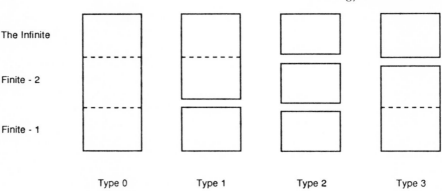

Schema 2. Barth's view of the theological options: full typology

of the finite (e.g., the for-itself and the in-itself; the spirit and the flesh).
Propelled by the sheer force of that tension, the religious existentialist
"leaps" toward the infinite.[22]

Using the typology, we may begin to get inside the early Barth's assessment of his theological options; we may begin to understand his particular
polemic. The first option, type 1, would represent the failure of the liberal
theology (including, perhaps, its complicity in the class divisions of the
finite, social order). Where to find an alternative? As is well known, the
theology of Kierkegaard—cf. type 2—influenced Barth enormously. But
gradually he worked his way to a new position distinct from at least the
common reading of Kierkegaard; and that is type 3.

Now it is intriguing, in view of our larger purpose, that a formally identical typology might also be applied to Kant—which is to say, to Kant's
own view of the philosophical options. Certainly, the upper portion of
type 1 reflects what Kant so distrusted in metaphysics, viz. the speculative
flight into the infinite. "The light dove, cleaving the air in her free flight,
and feeling its resistance, might imagine that its flight would be still easier
in empty space."[23] Type 2 represents the textbook interpretation of Kant,
particularly when one takes into consideration both the first and second
Critiques. Human reason, faced with certain irresolvable antinomies—human action is free, human action is not free—postulates a transcendent
reality by which the antinomies might be resolved. And type 3? That is
the question which I will press in chapters 4 and 5. There I will draw
Kant into our discussion of theology and difference by showing that he
makes use, sometimes explicitly and more often implicitly, of a position
remarkably like type 3.

Thus the typology points to a possible convergence between Barth and
Kant, by way of Derrida. And it does so not simply by looking at a few of

their ideas and placing them within one pigeonhole; that would be an external comparison. Rather, it does so by suggesting something of the dynamic of their thought—how the options looked to them, what they were reaching toward and what they sought to avoid. In this sense a polemical typology is all to the good; it helps us to see the particular figures from inside, not as "holding a position" but as actively seeking and avoiding, as engaged in a way of thinking. The remainder of this book aims to clarify this distinctive mode of thought. I will argue that type 3 does need to be regarded as a distinctive mode of thought, with a logic and integrity of its own; that we understand it better once we, like Barth and many others of his generation, have wrestled with Kant; and that, once recognized, this mode of thought opens a space or "force-field" within which theology can be done today.

Undoubtedly the objection will be raised that the entire project goes against the spirit of Derrida. Surely, it will be argued, the making of "strong distinctions" is tantamount to oppositionalist thinking. The objection needs to be considered because, if sustained, it would pose a stark either/or. We would virtually have to choose between doing deconstruction and doing theology. But is the alternative position so obvious and desirable—viz. the position which tacitly assumes that all differences should ultimately be of the same order, of the same sort? Derrida himself makes a strong distinction between *différance* and any other category of thought; he has even been accused (unjustly, I think) of making that notion into an absolute.[24] Any discourse is going to have its strong, orienting concepts: its god terms, so to speak. And while I believe it a mistake to draw any quick theological conclusions from this fact (by means of a notion of "ultimate concern," for example), I also believe there is little point in trying to expel such terms from the field of discourse altogether. The question is not the existence of such terms, but *how* they function; whether they function in such a way as to suggest that they are not simply distinctive and important, but self-evident and unquestionable. The question in short is not whether they are present, but whether they function *as presences*. And that is a relational question, to be resolved not by considering the strong distinction in isolation, rejecting a text when it seems to contain such a term; but by looking to the *relation or dialectic between* that difference and the larger field of differences. The matter has to be decided on a case-by-case basis. We must bear in mind that deconstruction, too, may be served up as a ready-made enlightenment. Metaphysics is not so easy to spot as some would have us think.[25]

III

TRUTH AND
CONTEXTUALIZATION
FREUD, HUSSERL, DERRIDA

So far we have made do with the brief account of deconstruction provided by the section, "Making Sense of Derrida." With the previous chapter as evidence that deconstruction is worth pursuing, it is time to examine the topic at closer range. I propose to focus on the issue of truth; for as surely as it will seem strange to some to ally Barth the dogmatician with Derrida the deconstructionist, it will seem odd to others to yoke Derrida the apparent nihilist with Kant the rationalist. As a way of drawing out Derrida's stance toward the truth question, I shall examine his formative relationship with the arch-rationalist of twentieth-century Continental thought, Edmund Husserl. In one provocative remark among many, Derrida classifies Husserlian phenomenology as an instance of Western "metaphysics." But, he goes on to specify, "metaphysics in its most modern, critical, and vigilant form."[1] With this qualification the charge becomes interesting. It holds out the possibility that in and through their debate the contrasting thinkers might exhibit a certain continuity. And a continuity which would not be a function of happenstance or concession, but an index, suggestive for rapprochement with Kant as well, of what it means to be "critical and vigilant."

At the same time, we need to honor the otherness of Derrida, to preserve something of the strangeness of deconstruction. To this end I propose to introduce another figure who is more familiar, but who also has a way of sticking in the craw of common sense. The difficulties in Freudian psychoanalysis, I shall argue, are such that even Paul Ricoeur has not done justice to them. These difficulties provide a second, less rationalist line of approach to Derrida. And conversely it may be that Derrida's acute sensitivity to method will give us some better understanding of what Freud, and the "hermeneutic of suspicion" which he represents, is all about.

We shall thus proceed by a process of triangulation, getting our bearings on Derrida by taking sightings from two other distinct points of view. Our argument will carry us from a preliminary consideration of Freud, through a comparison and then contrast of Husserl and Derrida, and will conclude with a number of reflections regarding the issue of nihilism and the question of truth.

Freud and the Logic of Suspicion

Half the problem with psychoanalysis has always been getting clear on the exact extent of the truth claims made in its name. In brief, schematic fashion, there are four possibilities. It may be said that (1) psychoanalysis claims to say everything about everything; (2) more modestly, it claims to say everything about something; (3) more modestly still, it claims to say something about something; and (4) finally and most intriguingly, it claims to say something about everything.

"Everything about everything" is the classic formulation of reductionism. Freud says that everything is sex, everything is phallic symbol or vaginal symbol—*tertium non datur*—and if you voice reservations, that is sure sign of your own resistance. Freudianism thus appears as a closed, self-referencing system, a sort of metaphysic. Either one buys the whole program, at the price of intellectual capitulation, or one stands by common sense and dismisses it altogether.

In contrast, the "everything about something" reading sees psychoanalysis as more circumspect. Every science has its proper object; Freud's achievement was to have brought to light a hitherto unrecognized object, namely the unconscious. Obviously the unconscious is not everything, but it *is* something, and we in the twentieth century would be foolish to deny it altogether. Often this second approach is cast in the language of hierarchy: what Freud says holds true for certain lower aspects of human experience, but there are other, higher aspects as well, which cannot be explained away.

The third approach, "something about something," is an extension of the second. Once again the unconscious is acknowledged as legitimate object or area of study, but now questions are raised as to the founder's adequacy even there. Freud is regarded as a sort of Columbus, for having set foot upon a new world, but also for having misnamed and misconstrued it. He was led astray, it is often said, by the Helmholtzian physics of his day. The antidote is an alternative hermeneutic, such as the existentialist or the Jungian.

What is striking in our account of the three approaches is how closely linked are the ways of defining Freud and the ways of responding to him. The moment you cast psychoanalysis in any one of these ways, the rest of the discussion seems foreordained. In the first case, it is simply a matter of dismissing the entire enterprise, perhaps by humor and irony, perhaps by turning it upon itself. In the second and third cases, it is a matter of exploiting the fact that psychoanalysis has been defined, in the root sense of the word: limits have been set to its validity. Attention quickly shifts to other matters.

The very predictability of these critiques of Freud might be enough to pique one's interest in something new. Certainly the fourth alternative, "something about everything," is remarkable in the extent to which it avoids a number of the moves observable in the other three. It does not portray psychoanalysis as seeking total control of the conceptual terrain; yet neither does it delimit a priori the conceptual space within which or about which psychoanalysis is allowed to speak. And this very fact, were the fourth alternative to prove valid, would help explain the peculiar reception which has been accorded psychoanalysis. It would explain how, without its making the sort of truth claim characteristic of an absolute reductionism, psychoanalysis might nevertheless seem reductionistic. After all, for the person on the receiving end, a psychoanalysis which proposed to say "something about everything" might very well *feel as if* it were claiming to say "everything about everything." For there would still be that peculiar insistence: it would always be there, it would presume to speak about even the most trivial matter. There would be no way of de-fining, no way of setting limits to it—no way of securing for oneself a safe and privileged space.

This, I want to suggest, is what it is like to be on the receiving end not simply of psychoanalysis, but of *any* form of the hermeneutic of suspicion. The interpretation is only an interpretation, it claims only to say *something* about everything. It is not a metaphysic, it only voices a suspicion. But the suspicion is insidious, it continually insinuates itself, it leaves no place to hide. Here, in the received impact of psychoanalysis, we have an important clue to the distinctive character of what Freud was about, a clue to what distinguishes the hermeneutic of suspicion from the apparent predecessors, such as mechanistic metaphysics, with which it is too freely confused.[2]

Having fashioned a minimal terminology with which to talk about Freud, we now need to do something similar with Husserl. Undoubtedly this effort, which will occupy the next two sections, will entail considerable simplification; for the reader versed in phenomenology, it will mean going over familiar ground. But the very generality of the account may serve a purpose, in that it will provide a common language which can then be applied, as well, to Derrida.

Kant and the Issue of Objectivity

It is a truism that the thought of Immanuel Kant represents a watershed for the modern discussion of religious belief and truth. As to the exact nature of the Kantian influence, however, there is less agreement. Responses range from celebration to lament, with lamentation to the fore. It is commonly asserted that the new development which one finds in Kant is a turn to the subject, a heightened awareness of the role the subject plays in constituting human knowledge. The gain in such a turn is heightened self-awareness. But that gain has brought with it a grievous loss or misdirection, which is portrayed as one or more of the following: (1) an obsession with questions of epistemology, (2) an entrapment within the subject, and (3) a disabling skepticism about the knowability of the object.

Like the criticism of Freud, the castigation of Kant breathes a reassuring air of common sense. Certainly we know that there are things which actually exist and that, in the end, we should not let ourselves be bamboozled by hyperreflective introspection. But that common sense is utterly reliant upon what Husserl calls "the natural standpoint"; which is to say, it is shot through with unexamined assumptions. To set the framework for our argument, it is useful to state these assumptions as clearly as possible. Reviewing in reverse order the points of a moment ago, the common assessment of Kant aims (3) to reaffirm the reality and knowability of the object. Here it is important to state explicitly what would seem to require no comment: namely that the critique of Kant focuses upon the fate of a particular entity, the object. Indeed, its reaction against Kant's alleged overemphasis upon the subject leads it to focus upon that entity which is *most clearly* an entity. The character of the subject, after all, is somewhat more ambiguous. But once this focus and apparent clarity are assumed, the subject too is apt to be regarded as an entity—simply an entity of a peculiar sort. This is an altogether crucial conceptual move, yet it readily escapes notice because it is underwritten by a seemingly self-evident framework which is unquestioningly assumed in the critique of Kant. For when Kant is taxed with having skewed the subject-object balance, the very notion of such a balance implies some common structure, some conceptual framework, embracing both subject and object. The moment any such framework has been assumed, only the greatest vigilance can prevent the subject from sharing the status of the object, as entity.

Concern for the reality of entities and a predilection for construing reality itself as a set of relationships among entities is characteristic of metaphysics, in the somewhat negative sense of the term which I am assuming here. However, (2) should this be pointed out and should one seek to approach the subject in some alternative manner, the proposal will inevitably appear to the eyes of common sense *cum* metaphysics as yet another exaltation of the subject. This helps one understand why the critics of Kant are so intense in their (often implicit) adherence to the notion of a common structure. For the notion is not just a conceptual convenience. It is tacitly regarded as a way, indeed the only way, of keeping subject and object on the same footing. Thus it is appropriate to say that in the critique of Kant (1) metaphysics is being allowed to preempt—indeed it is being actively employed precisely in order to preempt—a discussion which is properly epistemological. And once again the move seems from the natural standpoint so obvious as hardly to require mention, much less defense. Epistemology, after all, is a labyrinth; retaining a thread of common sense (and certainly the bare juxtaposition of subject and object would appear the sheerest minimum) seems just the thing to keep from losing one's way. Nevertheless, the modest proposal has a grossly disruptive effect. For it dictates a priori that epistemological questions shall not be posed and pursued *in their own right*. Indeed, and this is the measure of the distortion, it is difficult in this context even to conceive what it would *mean* to pursue the epistemological, or as I would prefer to say, the epistemic, in its own right.[3]

This recognition opens the way to a serious engagement with phenomenology. The effect of that engagement may be summarized in formulaic terms as a shift of focus from object to *objectivity*. For the natural standpoint a certain notion of the object is focal, in the sense that it defines the terms of objectivity. The natural standpoint begins with the notion of an object existing independently "out there," and proceeds to define objectivity as just such a condition of out-there-ness. Objectivity, understood as independence of the subject, becomes defined in terms of a presupposed metaphysical framework, as existence "outside" of the subject. The Husserlian response, faced with these assumptions, is not one of denying the reality of the object, nor even of denying the reality of the object conceived as existing independently "out there." Such a denial would still be metaphysics, albeit in a negative mode. Rather the response is simply to hold the entire question of existence in abeyance.

In one sense a very modest act, this Husserlian bracketing. It does not prejudge; it is in fact the very essence of *not* prejudging. It simply holds the metaphysical judgments in abeyance. And yet in its very modesty it is a resistance and a refusal—a refusal which elicits a shudder within the natural standpoint. For viewed from within that standpoint, the Husserlian abstention is an incursion of strangeness and a removal of security. It must seem, from within that standpoint, that Husserl, in displacing the existence of the object from its defining position, has surrendered the one sure guarantor of objectivity. He seems to have allowed objectivity to float free. And one's apprehension is heightened when Husserl proceeds to relocate the now-freed notion of objectivity in the closest correlation with the activity of the subject. It must seem then that he is tumbling irretrievably in the direction of idealist self-enclosure.

I dwell upon this strangeness and shuddering, this apprehension before a position which might prove arbitrary and enclosed, because it suggests the extent to which the impact of Husserl—the rationalist, the champion of the scientific spirit—can be like that of Derrida. It suggests the possibility of engaging the two thinkers not at the point of their obvious dissimilarities, but at the point of their received impact, which is the point where each is most "critical and vigilant." Husserl proposes a methodological wager with no guarantee. It is possible that the quite understandable misgivings will be realized. But who could be unmoved by the thought that objectivity might have a breadth, and the epistemic a distinctive integrity, which have yet to be explored? It is this the possibility, this promise, which guides and justifies the labor of phenomenology.[4]

Husserl and the Western Discovery of Objectivity

How, then, does Husserl propose to bring forward an alternative understanding of objectivity? His solution is to observe, in effect, that when one sets aside the notion of defining objectivity in quasi-spatial terms, as existence "out there," it is still quite possible to understand objectivity by reference to time—namely, as invariance across time; and more specifically, as invariance across a series of "imaginative variations." A classic example is the geometric figure of the circle. In and through various imperfect and transitory representations one grasps a single concept, which is that of the circle. Something analogous may be said of the word: we write "circle" and we speak it; we find it in a variety of accents and scripts, and may imagine a greater variety still. Yet in and through those particularities, we understand a single meaning. The compelling character of this sense (here the geometric example is especially apt) cannot be reduced to mere convention. In Husserl's formula, "A meaning can be treated *as* self-identical only because it *is* self-identical."[5]

This invariance of sense, this transcendence of contingent fact, constitutes Husserl's first and fundamental understanding of objectivity. As such, it informs and determines his other, derivative understandings. It informs, for example, his concept of the noematic pole of experience, which has a certain objectivity by virtue of its invariance in and through the variety of (noetic) stances which I adopt toward it: I see the chair, I walk around the chair, I admire the chair, I doubt the chair . . . Indeed the invariant sense accounts for the crucial and ineluctable correlation of noesis and noema: the sense which I intend *is* the sense which the noema has. Similarly, the meaning which is emptily intended is identical to the meaning which is subsequently fulfilled.

The importance of this theme of invariant sense cannot be overstressed. Certainly in proposing such a notion Husserl went against common sense, exposing himself to the charge of Platonism. But it was Husserl's firm conviction that without such invariance, common sense, and the European sciences along with it, made no sense; both stood powerless in the face of cultural crisis. Only through a robust reappropriation of the original Greek vision, for which Platonism is by rights a proud title, could European culture rebound from its failure of nerve. Thus it is that in Husserl invariance of sense provides a foundational level of objectivity, which allows one to then speak of the objectivity of the noema. And based upon the objectivity of the noema, one proceeds to certain specific cases, cases in which "what is experienced has the sense '*transcendent*' *being*."[6] It is this latter sense which prompts one to speak of the object as existing "out there."

This, then, is the process by which the object "out there" is dethroned, relieved of the prerogative of dictating the meaning of objectivity. Instead, the object "out there" appears as a secondary, derivative subset within a larger, more inclusive sense of objectivity. The result is at least a partial vindication of Husserl's methodological wager; for whereas within the naturalistic the relationship between subject and object was always somewhat enigmatic, the correlation of noesis and noema within the phenomenological standpoint may be observed with remarkable clarity. Skeptics will object, however, that the Husserlian solution is only a conjurer's trick, and that far from resolving the issue, it has actually made matters worse. For the noetic-noematic correlation, it will be charged, is no more than a correlation "within" consciousness; the endless examination of the contents of consciousness and the continual postponement of the lifting of the phenomenological brackets amount to solipsism of a more subtle and seductive form.

The response to this objection must be twofold. The first point is to acknowledge, indeed to affirm, that it was never a part of Husserl's purpose to demonstrate the existence of an "outside world." Rather, assuming such an objectivity, he asked, "How are we to understand the fact that the intrinsic being of objectivity becomes 'presented,' 'apprehended' in knowledge, and so ends up by becoming subjective?"[7] In short, "the point is not to secure objectivity but to understand it."[8] But beyond this, the response must call into question the terms of the objection. For we misconstrue the Husserlian project (or at least fail to take it on its own terms) the moment we say "within consciousness" in such a way as to suggest that consciousness itself is a thing lying alongside other things. And we only elaborate the misconstruction when we speak of consciousness itself as containing a series of entities, called "mental objects," which stand in uncertain relationship to other things outside. This is not so much an objection as an unreflective return to the hegemony of metaphysics over the epistemic. Yet it is a distortion which can readily take hold within phenomenology itself. To forestall it, one must energetically affirm that the act of phenomenological bracketing does not give us a new set of objects as such; rather it enables us to inquire into objects' "subjective manners of givenness, i.e., into *how* an object . . . exhibits itself."[9] We attend to *the way in which* the whole range of already-familiar objects appear or are presented. Similarly it must be stressed that the *whole* range of familiar (and unfamiliar) objects is so inspected; there is not some other range, a range of actually existing objects, set apart somewhere beyond.

These points are quite obviously crucial if phenomenology is to be accorded the courtesy of being understood, at least initially, on its own terms. What is remarkable is how similar they are to the points we made earlier, when we sought to understand psychoanalysis on *its* own terms. To recast the recent discussion in the earlier terminology: phenomenology does not purport to say everything about everything, i.e., to reduce all of reality to (a function of) consciousness. But neither does phenomenology confine itself to saying something (or everything) about a restricted region, i.e., about those things which are within consciousness as opposed to other things without. Rather it undertakes precisely to say something, having to do with the mode of presentation, about everything (that is presented). We thus have an intriguing formal similarity between two modes of investigation which are in many ways antithetical: between phenomenology, which seeks to save the phenomena, and psychoanalysis, which receives all phenomena with suspicion and seeks to look behind. I shall argue that this similarity is by no means accidental, but that it signals the possibility of a more meaningful encounter between the two perspectives. For assistance toward that goal we now turn to Derrida, from whom we may anticipate a critique of Husserl, as well as clarification of the logic of suspicion.

Derrida and the Deconstruction of Objectivity

We have seen how invariance of sense constitutes the foundational level of Husserl's understanding of objectivity. Husserl is of course aware that, in point of fact, this invariant sense is commonly conveyed by a material mark or sound. But for Husserl the principal implication of this fact is that the sense must be clearly distinguished from the variable and per se inchoate matter which is its vehicle. "When we normally express something, we do not, *qua* expressing it, live in the acts constituting the expression as a physical object . . . but we live in the acts which give it sense."[10]

These Husserlian premises already provide the necessary foothold for an abbreviated form of Derridean deconstruction. For the position invites two conceptual moves, both of which have become hallmarks of deconstructive criticism. The first is a distrust of emphatic distinctions or oppositions, which the deconstructionist suspects are born of a desire to protect the purity of one member of the distinction from being compromised by the other. Such a distinction so maintained is well on the way to becoming a hierarchy, and the second deconstructive move is indeed a distrust of hierarchy: a determination to show in a case-by-case manner how the "higher" element in various purported hierarchies not only depends upon, but in the proponent's textual practice actually becomes confused with, the "lower" element from which it pretends to insulate itself.[11] A good deal of deconstruction can indeed be accounted for in these terms. The method is a sort of return of the repressed whereby the material aspect of the sign, long regarded as peripheral, moves to center stage. Hence Derrida's fascination with puns, and his penchant for treating proper nouns as common nouns and ringing the changes on an author's name. And perhaps one might argue that Derrida is already introducing his own distinctive sense of "objectivity" in the tenacity with which he treats the sign's materiality in its own right. But left in these terms, deconstruction must seem, like the materiality it champions, peripheral. And so it has seemed to many: an intellectual prank, momentarily amusing perhaps, but hardly of moment for persons committed to serious reflection.

For this reason it is important that we undertake a longer approach to the deconstructionist goal, one which sides *with* the significance of sense, rather than proceeding, at least seemingly, against it. In point of fact, Derrida's point of entry into phenomenology is not unlike that of his teacher, Paul Ricoeur. Ricoeur observes: "Consciousness is doubly intentional, in the first instance by virtue of being a signification and in the second instance by virtue of being an intuitive fulfilling."[12] Ricoeur trades here upon the Husserlian distinction between an ("empty") *intention* (what Ricoeur calls a "signification") and a ("fulfilled") *intuition*. An example would be my referring to the city of Paris, in the abstract, on the one hand, and, on the other hand, my actually being there, experiencing the city—or my imagining it or remembering it with something of its texture and Gallic density. One starts to retrieve the scent of Gauloises cigarettes, the sound of water running down the street in the early morning, the banter in a corner café, et cetera, et cetera.

So the empty intention, which Derrida labels the "formalist" moment, is abstract and formal indeed. It is the sort of knowing which is often derogated as merely intellectual, devoid of the abundance Ricoeur celebrates in phenomena such as imagination, parable, and religious experience. As a result, we may be surprised at the way in which Derrida, the supposed irrationalist, actually proceeds once he has distinguished the "formalist" and "intuitionist" moments. For, instead of lamenting the formal and siding with intuition, Derrida proves intensely concerned with *holding to the distinctiveness of the formal* and keeping it from being lost in the all-too-ready embrace of intuition. He recognizes that the act of meaning anticipates and is directed toward a relation with an object (whether perceived, remembered or imagined). But he argues that in principle that object, that *telos, can be dispensed with*. That is the extraordinary possibility which Derrida takes to be the distinctive significance of the formal moment. In Husserl this is a marginal possibility, barely acknowledged but clearly implied. What Derrida does is to take hold of that possibility and draw out its full implication—namely the implication that "the fulfillment of the aim by an intuition is not indispensable"; that it belongs to the original structure of expression to be able to dispense with the full presence "of a perceived, remembered or imagined object." From this it follows that "in order for speech to take place, it is enough that" an intention—even a totally empty intention—"should animate the body of a signifier."[13]

Derrida's proposal here is paradoxical, but it is a paradox which can be rendered in simple terms. What the formalist aspect of Husserlian phenomenology implies is that "one can speak without knowing."[14] One can speak—*and make sense*—without knowing! To understand how this is possible, one does not have to go beyond Husserl. One just has to take very seriously the Husserlian distinction between *Widersinnigkeit* and *Sinnlosigkeit*—i.e., the distinction between that which has a certain contrariness of sense and that which is without sense.

> If it obeys certain rules, an expression may be *widersinnig* (contradictory, false, absurd according to a certain kind of absurdity) without ceasing to have an intelligible sense that permits normal speech to occur, without becoming nonsense (*Unsinn*). It may have no possible object for empirical reasons (a golden mountain) or for *a priori* reasons (a square circle) without ceasing to have an intelligible sense, without being *sinnlos*.

"The absence of an object (*Gegenstandlosigkeit*)"—i.e., the absence of an object given to intuition—"is hence not the absence of meaning (*Bedeutungslosigkeit*)."[15] Derrida believes that to have brought this forth is Husserl's distinctive accomplishment—and yet the entire effect of Husserl's theory of truth is to cover over this very point. For, despite his implicit insight, Husserl's understanding of truth remained steadfastly oriented toward a *telos* of intuition, fulfillment. Thus, for example, Husserl writes:

> If "possibility" or "truth" is lacking, an assertion's intention can only be carried out symbolically: it cannot derive any "fulness" from intuition or from the categorial functions performed on the latter, in which "fulness" its value for knowledge consists. It then lacks, as one says, a "true," a "genuine" meaning (*Bedeutung*).[16]

In short, the ground gained by Husserl's "purification of the formal" is surrendered forthwith to "a concept of *sense* which is itself determined on the basis of *a relation with an object*."[17]

Earlier we experienced some of the shudder Husserl evoked within the natural standpoint. Now we may sense something similar within the Husserlian phenomenology, a tremor occasioned in part by strangeness and in part by recognition of one's own distinctive yet only half-acknowledged commitments.[18] Henry Staten observes that like Husserl's bracketing of the existence of the object, Derrida's crucial methodological move of thinking representation *as such*, apart from the fulfillment by the object, constitutes a sort of wager. Its fruitfulness and legitimacy can be judged only in the trying. The proposal:

> to think representation *as such*, the essence of standing-for short of what is stood-for, performs a conceptual operation that is, considered in isolation, a new way of looking at things, comparable in a way to the new operation by which Husserl attained the phenomenological standpoint, and the question "is it valid?" must be suspended while we consider the full scope of the possibilities it opens.[19]

It is, moreover, a considered wager, arising from a close reading of the Husserlian texts and seeking to secure the gain, the *extension* of the realm of sense, effected by the text.

Specifically, Derrida's proposal may be regarded as cogent clarification of Husserl's seminal liberation of meaning from dependence upon, and confusion with, the presence of the *object*. This is the gist of the Derridean critique of "presence," where presence is anything—sense datum, spirit, or whatever—which asks to be considered as self-explanatory, a final recourse, having meaning in and of itself. The role of final recourse is commonly assigned to the "simply given," the object. Can it then be argued that Derrida's move away from the object, so far from being arbitrary, is an effort toward a deeper truth, indeed a deeper objectivity?

Ricoeur and Theological Hermeneutics

It is now possible to consider the pertinence of these considerations to theology. As point of departure, we may note that the inspiration for much of the most creative theology in the first half of this century was existentialism. Tillich was not alone in regarding existentialism as God's providential gift to theology. In the second half of the century, in contrast, the primary frame of reference has been provided by various forms of hermeneutics. This shift in the conceptual landscape is familiar enough, yet how much can we really say about the rationale for our having made it? It is not enough to speak of the discovery of the importance of language. What makes this discovery more important than some other? Nor will it do to invoke a turn from the existential individual to the social. Are we so confident that in the present setting, when the individual is besieged before and behind, it is the social which requires reinforcing?

A more considered rationale is offered by an essay in which Paul Ricoeur, who is as responsible as anyone for the shift to hermeneutics, examines the thought of the paradigmatic existentialist theologian, Rudolf Bultmann. In his "Preface to Bultmann" Ricoeur begins with a characterization of "hermeneutics in general" as being "in Dilthey's phrase, the interpretation of expressions of life fixed in written texts."[20] He then distinguishes three strata, all comprised in Bultmann's project of demythologizing: the demythologization effected by modern consicousness, that effected by existential philosophy, and finally that effected by the kerygma itself. The theme common to the three strata is, in effect, that demythologization stands in opposition to every form of false objectification.

But what does it mean to be so opposed? We may formulate the matter thus: If one places the emphasis upon false *objectification*, the antidote is (authentic) subjectivity. But if one, equally legitimately, places the stress upon *false* objectification, the antidote is rather authentic objectivity. Ricoeur's reading of Bultmann is, I take it, that in principle Bultmann wants both of these, but that he lacks the conceptual resources to adequately secure a notion of authentic objectivity. He lacks the resources to distinguish objectiv*ism* from an appropriate objectivity; and thus, *volens nolens*, his thought continually lists to the side of subjectivity. What Bultmann has failed to recognize is that the kerygma is not sheer event, but "event and meaning together."[21] Ricoeur now proceeds to shift his argument somewhat so that it becomes even more clearly an *internal* critique of Bultmann. Ricoeur suggests that on this important point Bultmann's exegetical practice proves wiser than his theory. For in the course of exegesis, indeed in undertaking exegesis at all, he implicitly recognizes a moment "of 'meaning' which, as Frege and Husserl have said, is an objective and even an 'ideal' moment."[22] By "ideal" in this context Ricoeur wishes to indicate a meaning which "has no place in reality, not even in psychic reality. We thus return to the Husserlian theme of invariance of sense, and meaning whose grounding is not psychological; meaning which, despite its being, so to speak "unreal," is no less significant. Ricoeur presses Bultmann to affirm fully this moment of ideal meaning which he, Bultmann, has implied; to clearly distinguish it from the moment of appropriation, or existential signification; and to acknowledge that interpretation must do justice to the former before proceeding to the latter. For:

> A theory of interpretation which at the outset runs straight to the moment of decision moves too fast. It leaps over the moment of meaning, which is the objective stage, in the nonworldly sense of "objective." There is no exegesis without a "bearer [*teneur*] of meaning," which belongs to the text and not to the author of the text.[23]

Contra Bultmann, Ricoeur is even able to affirm, "The act of God has its first transcendence in the objectivity of meaning which it announces for us."[24]

Nevertheless, Ricoeur's remains a *relative* criticism: Bultmann simply "moves too fast." Ricoeur continues to share with Bultmann a common framework, a common understanding of the *archē* and the *telos* of interpretation. About the *telos* he is explicit: interpretation does indeed move toward existential signification. As regards the *archē*, Ricoeur does not question, and his other writings seem to confirm, the conviction enunciated by Dilthey and carried forward by Bultmann that hermeneutics has its source in certain "expressions of life" which have become "fixed in written texts." It is *within* this shared context that Ricoeur seeks to make his point that Bultmann has insufficiently appreciated the inherent, positive importance of the middle (generally written) stage, the stage of objectification.

The force of Ricoeur's argument springs from his having identified a contradiction internal to Bultmann's thought. Bultmann the exegete trades upon a reality unsanctioned by Bultmann the hermeneutician. How could this have come about? The answer is not far to seek; it lies with the conception gained from Dilthey (and "an overly anthropological reading of Heidegger"[25]) whereby all objectifications are understood as "expressions of life." Given that governing assumption, any talk about ideal meaning—"ideal in that meaning has no place in reality, not even in psychic reality," objective "in the nonworldly sense of 'objective' "—must seem to Bultmann the existentialist the most wrongheaded form of objectivism. But the moment we have said this much, a further question cannot be suppressed. Can Ricoeur himself avoid the same contradiction? For, whatever his reservations, he continues to operate within Dilthey's framework.

The question might seem captious. After all, it is Ricoeur who pressed upon Bultmann the entire issue of objectivity. More generally, it is Ricoeur who has made current the notion of "distanciation"; and it is about distanciation that we are talking here. What is in question, however, is not commitment or intent, but the systemic balance, the conceptual pressures and counterpressures, which constitute the force field of Ricoeurian thought. Are the structures in place which can guarantee that the second moment, the moment of objectivity, will have significance *in its own right*? One cannot assume that they are—because the Diltheyan framework has its own origins and debts. It borrows from German romanticism and idealism the vision of the self or of life as proceeding out from itself, encountering resistance and objectivity, and then returning strengthened and enriched to a fuller, more self-aware identity with itself. In his classic study of romanticism, M. H. Abrams describes this "circuitous journey." He notes that a number of late eighteenth and early nineteenth century German thinkers adapted the Christian fable of a lost and future paradise into a theory which neatly fused the alternative views of history as either decline or progress. This they accomplished by representing man's fall from happy unity into the evil of increasing division and suffering as an indispensable stage on his route back toward the lost unity and happiness of his origin, but along an ascending plane that will leave him immeasurably better off at the end than he was in the distant beginning.

In this form, the framework served very specific purposes—purposes of theodicy, even theophany. Such an implicit agenda may be welcomed by those who, like Bultmann, are anxious to make connections between hermeneutics and theology. But it is bound to give to the framework a powerful telic thrust, thus virtually foreordaining that, also as with Bultmann, the second, medial moment will be excluded from having significance in its own right. Moreover, the presence of *any* metaphysical agenda within the Ricoeurian hermeneutic is legitimate cause for concern. For it is commonly assumed, though seldom formulated so, that "the linguistic turn" has accomplished something analogous to what Husserl sought in the act of bracketing. That is to say: just as Husserl bracketed the natural assumption of the existence of the object, similarly much of current linguistic and hermeneutical theory has set aside the natural assumption of a direct correspondence between linguistic sign and object. In both cases the counterintuitive move was made in order to assure that a new realm of reflection (that of phenomenological description, that of linguistic study) might be considered without prejudice or preconception, in its own right. The linguistic turn was meant to free reflection from bondage to metaphysics: to open up a space apart from one's natural, telic drive toward (one might almost say, one's appetite for) the object. Yet now there is reason to suspect that, at least in the case of Ricoeur, what is excluded is simply metaphysics of one particular sort, while metaphysics of another no less powerful variety is reinforced.[26]

The same question can be raised in a slightly different way, in terms of what is distinctive to hermeneutics. Ricoeur's own assessment of Bultmann seemed to imply that the birthright of hermeneutics, what set it apart from the ambient existentialism, was the discovery or reaffirmation of a certain objectivity. But now that discovery is at risk of being swallowed once again, swallowed by what is undoubtedly the Ur-source of much of existentialism, namely a certain combination of romanticism and idealism. Thus the question is not extrinsic; it is a concern about whether (Ricoeurian) hermeneutics can adequately preserve and pursue its own distinctive achievement.[27]

Now this talk of preserving a text's distinctive achievement, contra the leveling tendencies within the text itself, recalls the account of deconstruction at the end of the previous section. Similarly, our recent worry that the leveling effect may arise specifically from an *archē* and a *telos* which bear promise of theophany recalls the deconstructionist critique of "presence." What I have sought to accomplish in this treatment first of Bultmann via Ricoeur, then of Ricoeur himself, and finally of hermeneutics as such has been to raise deconstructionist issues without appeal to alien terms or conceptualities. In the end, this is the only possible approach to a method which, its pervasive jargon notwithstanding, intends nothing more than to deal with a text on that text's own—implicit—terms.

Hermeneutics and the Idealist Diamond

Having attended to the lines of continuity between Husserl and Derrida, we may now have a context in which to understand the very real differences between them. As a means of entry into the polemical dimension of their encounter, there is no better method than to ask after the ethical concerns which inform the two philosophies. For there is about the effort toward objectivity an inherent paradox. Consistency requires that objectivity be pursued in a manner which is itself objective, dispassionate. Yet precisely because it is so demanding, so rigorous, the enterprise would scarcely be contemplated by one who was not stirred by some deep and passionate commitment. And indeed that commitment must be kept in view, lest the notion of objectivity become utterly trivialized. Both Husserl and Derrida are, in this respect, thinkers of intense commitment. To understand this is to take a further step toward understanding what binds them and what sets them at odds. It is also a further step away from the portrayal of Husserl as arid rationalist and Derrida as gleeful nihilist.

In Husserl the concerns are often unthematized, but with *The Crisis* and the Vienna lecture they become both evident and urgent. Already in "Philosophy as Rigorous Science" he had delineated the cultural impasse represented by the mutual confrontation of naturalism and historicism. The two opponents, the "scientist" and the "humanist," seem to exhaust the alternatives; "and yet both are at work . . . to misinterpret ideas as facts and to transform all reality, all life, into an incomprehensible, idealess confusion of 'facts.' The superstition of the fact is common to them all."[28] What must be dispelled, then, is precisely this "superstition of the fact," this tendency to treat objects (naturalistically conceived) in abstraction— this objectivism. But an overcoming of abstraction is possible only through a re-cognition in the root sense of the word, a reawakened awareness that the objects of modern science are not ultimate realities, simply given, but rather *achievements*: the result of an original turn of thought which continues to constitute the peculiar genius of Western culture. What has happened, as Husserl's later work makes clear, is that the Western mind has lost touch with the foundational insights which accord it its distinctive "entelechy," and thus has lost its way.[29] One handles the currency of language without knowledge of how it is funded, in ignorance of its proper use. Little wonder, then, that there should exist such widespread alienation. What is required is a retrieval of the original *archē*, which would return the free-floating objectivism to its proper grounding, and restore to the culture at large a sense of human meaning and connectedness.

Yet this *archē* which Husserl is determined to reclaim is functionally identical with the *archē* which Derrida believes has already undercut the second, intermediate moment. This issue of the status of second, intermediary moment, however that moment be understood, is the real matter at stake between Husserl and Derrida in the struggle over the status of speech and writing, over the question of "logocentrism." From Husserl's side, the salient fact is that in writing an original insight is externalized. It follows that the outward form can exist, command attention, and have certain effects quite regardless of whether it has been properly understood. Thus while objectification guarantees that what once was thought will not be totally forgotten, it entails the risk that the outward form may come to seem self-sufficient, thereby obstructing the original insight. About writing there is, in short, a certain duplicity, in his wariness of which Husserl is indeed representative of a grand succession of Western thinkers. At one end of the tradition, Plato gives reasons for mistrust in his mythological treatment of the origins of writing; at the other end, the sober linguist Ferdinand de Saussure sheds scientific dispassion when he speaks of writing as a "trap," a "tyranny" which is potentially "pathological."[30] Here are ethical concerns indeed. And yet the writing so denounced is the same writing which, from Derrida's viewpoint, but on grounds which are arguably Husserlian, embodies the distinctive achievement and insight of the Husserlian phenomenology. We begin to understand how Derrida can find so much in Husserl to emulate and yet regard him as exemplifying the blindness of metaphysics.

All this is made concrete when one contrasts two readings of Freud, the one by Ricoeur, under the guidance of Husserl, the other by Derrida. Ricoeur's monumental *Freud and Philosophy* begins with an excellent formulation of the problem confronting any Freud interpretation. "Freud's writings present themselves as a mixed or even ambiguous discourse, which at times states conflicts of force subject to an energetics, at times relations of meaning subject to a hermeneutics." He then enunciates the purpose which will set his study apart from all the philosophic studies of Freud which have gone before: "I hope to show that there are good grounds for this apparent ambiguity, that this mixed discourse"—so far from being a muddle on Freud's part, so far from being a category confusion—"is the *raison d'être* of psychoanalysis."[31] The clear implication is that of Freud's two languages—the language of force exemplified by such terms as "drive," "repression," "explanation" and the language of sense exemplified by "symbol," "denial," "interpretation"—*both* are equally essential.[32] Yet those who have time and patience to work through Ricoeur's actual exposition will find the thrust almost entirely in *one* direction: toward showing that Freud's language of force is never without some relationship to the language of sense, and that Freud's way of thinking, therefore, is never narrowly reductionistic. Almost totally lacking is any equally emphatic account of how Freud's language of sense is dependent upon the language of force, and of why it is appropriate that it should be.[33]

A second chance arises in Book III, when Ricoeur introduces the concepts of "archeology" and "teleology," by which he proposes to draw together the threads of his exposition. Once again Ricoeur is determined to give Freud his due: Freud is paradigmatic of a distinctive mode of thought, an "archeology" to which Ricoeur means to accord an indissoluble place vis-à-vis the more familiar "teleology." Taken together the two will make up the "Dialectic" announced by the title to Book III. Yet once again in practice something very different occurs. For the sake of brevity, the conceptual slippage may be indicated by citing two passages from an able observer. First, here is Don Ihde on Ricoeur's method: "the excess of psychoanalysis must be balanced by an equal excess from within reflection—and the figure to provide this excess is Hegel." Now Ihde on the result:

> Hegel inverts Freud, and Ricoeur ultimately sides with Hegel. . . . In the last analysis the self is constituted primarily in terms of progression: "the positing or emergence of the self is inseparable from its production through a progressive synthesis." Thus at the end of this set of dialectical exercises the weighted focus of phenomenology—now in Hegelian guise—is restored.[34]

An unannounced move from Hegel the "excessive" counterpoint to Hegel the adequate and all-embracing whole cannot be dismissed as oversight. And Ihde is correct in tracing the move to Ricoeur's phenomenology.

The connection becomes explicit in a more recent work in which Ricoeur takes up Karl Marx, that further voice of suspicion. In *Lectures on Ideology and Utopia* Ricoeur defines his method as that of a "genetic phenomenology in the sense proposed by Husserl in his *Cartesian Meditations*."[35] George Taylor, the book's editor, summarizes what that phenomenology means for Ricoeur.

> We begin with an experience of belonging or participation in the culture, class, time, and so on that give us birth, but we are not completely bound by these factors. Instead, we are involved in a dialectic of understanding and explanation. Understanding—indicator of the relation of belonging—

"precedes, accompanies, closes, and thus envelops explanation." In *The Rule of Metaphor* Ricoeur identifies the tension at work here as "the most primordial, most hidden dialectic—the dialectic that reigns between the experience of belonging as a whole and the power of distanciation that opens up the space of speculative thought.[36]

It is the familiar Diltheyan theme of hermeneutics as having its source in "expressions of life." For Ricoeur this life and its correlates constitute *both* the true *archē and* the true *telos*. From this it follows that *archemac* and *telos* cannot be fundamentally different, and thus that the *archē* cannot in fact be used to ground a truly distinctive "archeology." So, despite the verbal affinity between *"archē"* and "archeology," there remains for the Marxian suspicion, as for the Freudian, only one possible location: namely the intermediary moment. There it will find itself doubly circumscribed (or to use Ricoeur's own term, enveloped): first, because enclosed between *archē* and *telos*; and second, because even within the intermediary moment, it is only a subset of a larger category, which is that of "distanciation."[37] In Ihde's apt characterization, the Ricoeurian focus is "weighted" indeed. Only thus can one explain the astonishing spectacle of Ricoeur, student of the radical thinkers Marx and Freud, blandly offering an unqualified assurance that "the distorting function covers only a small surface of the social imagination, in just the same way that hallucinations or illusions constitute only a small part of our imaginative activity in general."[38] A statement so lacking in critical acumen forces one to conclude that Ricoeur has forfeited his sense of the very thing which made the hermeneutic of suspicion worth studying in the first place—namely its discomforting insistence upon saying "something about everything."

This is not to deny the considerable power of Ricoeur's hermeneutical argument, which derives from its capacity to function on two levels. Most simply he says in his fashion what Dilthey, Husserl, Saussure, and others said in theirs, namely that a certain distanciation, a certain surrender of immediacy, is a legitimate and necessary activity; but that the products, records, marks, expressions, or inscriptions of that distanciation must never be regarded in spurious isolation, apart from the life context which "precedes, accompanies, encloses and thus envelopes" them. At a second level Ricoeur contends that this same message—viz. the necessity of regaining the original rooting in life-process—is the message which the (Marxist) critique of ideology wishes to deliver! Ricoeur gives emphatic priority to the early Marx, and specifically to the concept of praxis, which, Ricoeur argues, articulates with Clifford Geertz's concept of "the autonomous process of symbolic formulation," and thence with Husserlian phenomenology.[39] Accordingly any assessment of Ricoeur's interpretation must be mindful of Marx's ethical orientation toward overcoming reification, and the analogies between this orientation and the Diltheyan hermeneutic. Yet any assessment must at least as emphatically insist that to speak of the process of symbolic formulation as "autonomous," making Marx, Geertz, and Husserl the vehicles of a single message, is to short-circuit any serious consideration of the perspective which Ricoeur has urged us to respect, and for which he has given us the name, the hermeneutic of suspicion.

Such are the strengths and limitations of the approach Ricoeur takes to Marx. There can be little question that an analogous process of reasoning lies at the root of the perplexing turn of events we noted earlier, namely the swallowing up of Freud's distinctive "archeology" within an expanded, all-embracing "teleology."

The Deconstructionist Alternative

If Ricoeur invested such labor in Freud, it is because Freud seemed to him to have hit upon an irreducible truth about the human condition. That truth may be initially stated as the discovery of an irreducible *duality* about what it means to be human. Ricoeur's recognition of this discovery, together with his determination to ground and safeguard it, are attested by his opening remarks on the two languages in Freud and by his long final part, the "dialectic" of archeology and teleology.[40] Yet in practice, both in his textual studies of Freud and in his concluding reflections, Ricoeur winds up by reducing and relativizing this insight. How is one to explain this? The answer would seem to be that a genuine, open-ended dialectic was never truly possible, because of an antecedent commitment regarding *archē* and *telos*. With Husserl, Ricoeur is deeply convinced that whatever the distance between them—indeed precisely because of the great distance between them—the *archē* and the *telos* represent indispensable points of anchorage; and that if an anchorage is to hold firm, it cannot be divided within itself. On such terms, the relationship between the two could not finally be one of irreducible dialectic. It is not without reason that Abrams speaks of a *"circuitous* journey": *archē* and *telos* must finally be one.[41]

It is important at this point to be clear on what can and cannot be said. It remains possible on the Ricoeurian premises to assign psychoanalysis an important place and an important role: the place is that of the second moment; and the role, that of distanciation. It is possible to say that a psychoanalytic reading of experience is not only legitimate, but necessary: for it is indisputably necessary that spontaneous self-awareness be chastened by a point of view which is external to itself. All this would seem to accord to psychoanalysis an irreducible significance. But it is not possible on these terms to entertain the notion that the second moment to which psychoanalysis is assigned might have a sense *in its own right*—that psychoanalysis might be the evidence of *an other sense*. For, at the end of the day, the sense of the second moment is defined by its role, which is that of differentiating and enriching the *archē*, and contributing thereby to the *telos*; and that role cannot be accomplished unless the sense of the second moment is finally that of the first and the third. On these terms it is fore-ordained that Ricoeur's dialectic will eventuate in the subsuming of one member by the other.[42]

Conversely, it follows that if there *is* to be a genuinely irreducible and open-ended dialectic, such as Ricoeur himself initially saw psychoanalysis as requiring, then the second moment will have to be accorded a significance—which is to say, *a capacity for signification*—in its own right. There will have to be an "other sense." Pursuit of that sense, which pretty well defines Derrida's approach to Freud, is certain by its very nature to draw the reader along unaccustomed paths. We do well to remember, therefore, that it is pursuit of a sense, not nonsense—albeit an *other* sense—and that it arose, like the reading of Husserl, by a certain internal necessity. It is an effort to attest to a distinctive, disruptive truth.

To regard a material object as significant in its own right, to become fascinated with a thing apart from any rational context—this is to make of the thing a fetish. Fetishism is a loaded term; it is virtually interchange-able with the reification which Marx, according to Ricoeur, was most de-termined to avoid. But that in itself suggests that we may be on to something. Let us see, then, where the notion leads us.[43] For the fetishist, certain material objects do assume extraordinary importance. But in the closest relation to this phenomenon is another, namely that certain words or word-portions, certain fragments of language, achieve similar impor-tance: witness the Wolf Man's private language and Schreber's secret voices.[44] And well might one say that this fetishism of language stands "in the closest relation" to the fetishism of material objects; for what receives such extraordinary attention is precisely *the material aspect of the language itself*, viz. sound, similarity of sound, homophony or pun. The word is treated as a thing. Here we find ourselves at furthest remove from the Husserlian ideal in which the material aspect of language, upon becoming ensouled with meaning, falls away in favor of a total transparency of sense. Here materiality, so far from withdrawing, occludes all else. And yet by this odd route of homophony, the language of the fetishist achieves its own peculiar coherence. Thus "the *six* in the six wolves . . . is translated into Russian (*Chiest*, perch, mast and perhaps sex, . . . close to *Siestra*, sister, and its diminutive *Siesterka*, sissy."[45]

But surely, it will be objected, the idiosyncratic character of the Wolf Man's discourse disqualifies it from anything more than purely clinical significance. Perhaps so. But by his retreat into this private language, the fetishist enacts a statement with regard to language at large; and that statement may have validity independently of the particular case. For the

fetishist refuses the most fundamental move of the process of acculturation, namely the acceptance of the word as at least a temporary substitute
for, and distanciation from, the reality of the object.[46] There are ironies
here, for it is the fetishist who is commonly regarded as having made a
bizarre substitution, treating a shoe, for example, as if it were divine. But
one might equally well say that it is the fetishist who regards the common
convention of language, viz. accepting words as "temporary" substitutes
for things, as irrational, and refuses to be duped. And through this cleaving to the materiality of language, the fetishist implicitly cleaves to a quite
specific material object. For in any process of acculturation the fundamental movement of detachment is that of drawing the child out of its initial,
infantile relationship to its first, most fundamental object, the mother.
"The detachment is refused, the mother is encrypted, kept safe in an interior vault, a strategy which reinforces the original ties with the object,
amounting to a refusal of mourning."[47]

And yet for all his refusal, the fetishist does fashion a language of sorts.
And so he does not so much refuse, in the end, as seek to have it both
ways, letting go without really letting go. One thus observes within the
language of the fetishist a certain "*undecidability*," a certain oscillation,
which is indeed the very mark of the language's being fetishistic. Each
word, or rather each fragment, is itself, and yet it stands for something
else. Indeed it is the very aspect of the language fragment which makes
it most itself, namely its material particularity, which is also the point of
connection by which it stands for something else. This is because "the
structure, the construction (*Aufbau*) of the fetish rests at once on the denial and on the affirmation (*Behauptung*) . . . of castration. This at-once,
the in-the-same-stroke . . . of the two contraries, prohibits cutting through
to a decision within the undecidable."[48]

Now is there within this aberrant phenomenon something which can
count as an other *sense*? The question is undoubtedly difficult; and, if anything, I wish to dwell on its difficulty. For in answering one makes a decision as to what is to count as sense; and it is not at all clear how one can
determine that without already slanting things one way or the other, in
favor of Husserl or Derrida. For this reason, any decision one makes at
this point must partake of the nature of a wager. Moreover, it is a wager
for which the stakes are large. For, to speak in the Derridean manner, the
question is the camel's nose: *the camel*—Derrida is the outsider, Algerian—
the camel's "no's"—how much is he negating?—*the camel knows*—does he
indeed have some secret knowledge?—*the camel snows*—will we be left behind if we do not follow? It threatens the entire tent, the notion of intention, Husserl's intent—*Husserl's in tent*—for to admit an other sense means
stretching intentionality—*will it then still be in tent?*—*in tension-ality?*

It *is* unsettling to take any of this seriously. For the moment, let us note
a few considerations which might prompt one to follow the Derridean

wager; for a wager, after all, need not be irrational. First, the finding of sense in the materiality of language is not confined to the psychiatric ward. It is a hallmark of modern poetry, at least since the time of Mallarmé. Second, Heidegger, himself influenced by the distinctive voice of poetry, speaks of the need for a less anthropocentric understanding of language. The Derridean turn may well be an extension of Heidegger's dictum that language—language itself—speaks. Third, we glimpsed earlier the possibility that the distinctive, formalist aspect of Husserl's thought might require one "to think representation *as such*, the essence of standing-for short of what is stood-for." Finally, there is the complex of considerations surrounding Freud interpretation: (a) that Ricoeur's interpretation of Freud, which proceeded on Husserlian premises, failed to preserve that which was distinctive about Freud; (b) that Derrida's highlighting of the issue of *archē*, *telos*, and the fate of the intermediate moment helped make sense of this perplexing inability; and (c) that the very "craziness" of Derrida's notion that one might find sense in the materiality of language is, whatever else, *prima facie* evidence that he may be getting closer to the Freudian phenomenon.

The Insistence of the Truth Question

"Three measures of unconscious, two fingers of preconscious and a dash of consciousness—that is what one must at all costs avoid. Eclecticism is always the enemy of dialectic."[49] These words, with which Ricoeur cautions those who theorize about the relationship of Freud and Hegel, are equally applicable to our own reflections on Husserl and Derrida. It is natural to seek some sort of combination. Derrida himself affirms that deconstruction is not self-sufficient, but always "parasitic" upon another text, and in the end I too will propose a combination of sorts. But I would not be doing justice to our common labors, or to the distance we have come in the course of this essay, if I did not seek, in these concluding remarks, to decenter the all-too-easy.

The considerations we enumerated weigh significantly in favor of Derrida. What seems to me decisive, however, is the effect of one of the time-honored criteria for resolving questions of truth, the criterion of comprehensiveness. Put simply, Derrida can include more of Husserl's truth than Husserl can of Derrida's. Phenomenology approaches the notion of "an other sense" armed with the conviction that all sense, to be sense, must finally be coherent, must finally be one. On such premises it is possible to regard deconstruction as an extension and enrichment of the Husserlian notion of intentionality. What is not possible, what phenomenology must decisively refuse, is the notion of an irreducibly *other* sense.

Accordingly the Derridean wager must finally seem from a Husserlian perspective to be senseless, perverse, a pursuit of literary effect for its own sake. But once one shifts perspective it is possible to share Derrida's incredulity before a phenomenology which acts "as though literature, theatre, deceit, infidelity, hypocrisy, infelicity, parasitism, and the simulation of real life were not part of real life!"[50] For Derrida these things are, one must emphasize, a part of *real* life: they are not just secondary matters which could finally, in one's fundamental method, be discounted. This is the basis, I am suggesting, for deconstruction's greater comprehensiveness. So it is that while Husserl cannot make sense of the Derridean proposal, Derrida *can* make sense of the Husserlian refusal. From a deconstructionist perspective, the act which affirms phenomenology's exclusive normativity is simultaneously the act which makes of phenomenology a parallel case, a mirror image, to be set alongside that of Schreber's madness! Such a suggestion will no doubt seem extreme. But having been exposed to deconstruction we are bound to ask certain questions: Can we really be confident that there is no significant analogy between the fetishistic fixation upon the object and phenomenology's absolute, unqualified insistence that there is no sense apart from a (phenomenological) object? And what of the phenomenologist's impassioned insistence upon retaining anchorage at one end and at the other, at *archē* and at *telos*? Husserl states emphatically: "Only if the spirit returns to itself from its naive exteriorization, clinging to itself and purely to itself, can it be adequate to itself."[51] Can we be entirely confident that there is no significant relation between this "clinging" and the fetishist's peculiar clinging, which Derrida terms *cramponnement*: the trying to have it both ways, holding on to the mother while yet seeming to let go; and only feigning letting go, only feigning acceptance of distanciation, in order finally—the *telos*—to hold?[52]

This is the sort of question Derrida raises when, as in *Glas*, he places two quite different texts, the one apparently rational, the other apparently less so, in parallel columns. The effect is to suggest the possible analogies, and indeed the possible interaction, the possible interdependency, between the two. It is to *connect* Husserl and Schreber, Hegel and Genet, the seeming incommensurables. Too readily forgotten when Derrida is identified with a certain notion of "différance" is the fact that he often achieves his ends by breaking down compartmentalizations, unearthing subversive *connections*.[53] By suspecting every act of exclusion, deconstruction orients itself decisively toward comprehensiveness.

Alongside this relative endorsement of Derrida I wish, however, to set a further thesis. For it seems to me that Derrida's own approach finally makes sense only within the context of a fundamental struggle for truth—and specifically within the arena of debate opened up by Kant's transcendental turn, and more recently represented by Husserl's phenomenology. Given present limitations of space, I must argue this thesis in a manner which is largely negative, by indicating the aporias which develop when it is denied. Recently the rejection of "foundationalist" thought has become widespread in the field of religious studies: so much so that it might be difficult nowadays to find any mainstream figure who would *want* to be called foundationalist. "Overcoming foundations has become the watchword and preoccupation of contemporary thought."[54] Now these rejections of foundationalism invariably present themselves as a more sophisticated, more critical awareness. But in all charity it must be said that many such dismissals are not (to use the term Derrida applied to Husserl) truly "vigilant," and thus not truly critical. For they regard the foundationalist project as readily identifiable and patently absurd. An illusion to be dispelled, there is little need for vigilance against it, once it has been disavowed.

This giving up on the foundationalist project, this simple letting go, is worthy neither of the transcendental tradition nor of poststructuralism. It is not worthy of the former because it fails to comprehend that what is true of Kant and Husserl, what virtually defines their common effort, was that their philosophy believed that it could be foundational *because* it was truly critical; and that its being critical was inseparable from its effort after foundations. Husserl cautioned in a moving passage that "Europe's greatest danger is weariness."[55] One senses in certain disavowals of the transcendentalist form of the foundationalist effort the implicit complaint that it is just too difficult.

Nor is the disavowal worthy of the best of poststructuralism, which is exemplary in its determination to be vigilant, or, in the word de Man uses of Nietzsche, to be "rigorous."[56] The best of poststructuralism realizes that what is disavowed cannot be simply disavowed; that it reappears in subtle and unexpected guises; and that it is therefore essential to exercise a certain hermeneutic of suspicion. But the moment one does this, one has already moved away from the pure relativism implicit within much of anti-foundationalism. For the exercise of any form of the hermeneutic of suspicion (with the possible exception of Derridean deconstruction itself) entails one or both of two things: the affirmation of some sort of explanatory framework, with the consequent nonrelativist affirmation that certain things are the case; and an interpretation of motives, which latter entails a nonrelativist assertion about what certain matters meant for certain people.

The greatest obstacle to a careful consideration of Derrida is the reading of him, common among advocates and detractors alike, which understands him as saying that, in the end, all we have is language. Language in this instance is understood as a series of conventions and constructs, a succession of more or less useful metaphors. Once we realize this is all there is, it is said, we are no longer held captive by the chimera of some objective truth; we are free to enter unreservedly into the free play of the signifier. There are indeed passages in Derrida which encourage such an interpretation. In the often-quoted essay on "Structure, Sign and Play in the Discourse of the Human Sciences" he distinguishes "two interpretations of interpretation." The first, represented in that essay by structuralism, "has dreamed of full presence, the reassuring foundation, the origin and the end of play." The second has entered unreservedly into "the Nietzschean *affirmation*, that is the joyous affirmation of the play of the world . . . , the affirmation of a world of signs without fault, without truth and without origin which is offered to an active interpretation."[57]

In a terminology which has become widespread, the first interpretation is still merely "modern," still tied to the Enlightenment; only the second position moves beyond that, to the "postmodern."[58] The lines just quoted might well seem to invite one to the latter; but on the following page Derrida makes his intent quite clear: "I do not believe that today there is any question of *choosing*." Rather, given the difference and the irreducibility of the two positions, "we must first try to conceive of the common ground, and the *différance* of this irreducible difference."[59]

This neglected statement can serve us, I believe, as a point of reference for an understanding of truth. For the statement has two salient characteristics: (1) it refuses to choose, and (2) it seeks for "the common ground." The refusal to choose is not a simple entry into free play; there remains the quest for common ground. Yet the common ground itself is not a "presence," to be invoked and chosen by an easy eclecticism. Similarly, in his study of Husserl's *Origins of Geometry* Derrida arrives at a choice—a wager, if you will—between Husserl's search for univocity and the alternative represented by James Joyce: "to repeat and take responsibility for all equivocation itself."[60] Yet, as Henry Staten rightly observes:

> What is both original and problematic about Derrida's own project is that it does *not* pursue Joyce's path, but remains faithful to the problematic of that "univocity" that Derrida sees as underlying Joyce's equivocity, while yet opening out the univocal language in which he [Husserl] works, the language of philosophy, to that spread of meaning Joyce explored.[61]

The situation may be illumined by reference to the typology with which we began, regarding psychoanalysis. The first three positions were variously efforts to define, and thus to delimit, the spheres in which psychoanalysis would and would not apply. But there was something about psychoanalysis which resisted this setting of boundaries and which was thus unsettling to the Enlightenment mind. Yet this elusive quality is not one which can be explained by the alternative, "postmodern" view. Certainly it is tempting to suppose that psychoanalysis says "something about everything" because it constitutes a hermeneutical framework, a way of looking at things, a series of powerful metaphors. But that leaves unaddressed the question of why this particular set of "metaphors" should be so powerful, so unsettling.[62]

The reason, in simplest terms, is that psychoanalysis has hit on a fundamental *truth*—that there is an irreducible elusiveness and tension at the heart of finite reality; that the sought-for foundation of all things is not univocal. This is the truth—the truth of "undecidability"—which is embodied by the fetishist. Yet it is a truth which holds true for all of existence, all of language. This is why psychoanalysis can say something about everything; and it is why Derrida is fully in earnest in saying there can be no question of choosing. The entirety of *Glas*, with its bell-like movement, swinging between two columns of text, aims to convey and confirm this logic of undecidability.

But this also means that if one resists choosing, it is because undecidability itself is not just a choice but an objective condition, a state of affairs. At this point one must affirm, with whatever caution, that "radical hermeneutics makes a pass at formulating what the French call *la condition humaine*, the human situation."[63] In the passage quoted, Derrida speaks of a "common ground." In *Positions* he speaks of "writing" in the radical sense as "the common root of writing and speech," and of "différance" as "the common root of all the oppositional concepts."[64] The notion of that sort of common root is not impossible, it is merely difficult: difficult in the sense suggested by Heidegger—not the Heidegger of the philosophy of presence, but the Heidegger of "equiprimordiality."[65] It is this way of envisioning the common ground that makes Derrida's position the more comprehensive.[66] Thus Derrida need not exclude Husserl's quest for a univocal sense. After all, Derrida himself is questing for the common ground, which is in a fashion a quest for the univocal. All he needs to exclude (or undermine) is Husserl's own a priori exclusion of the Joycean non-univocal: "the 'non-serious,' the *oratio obliqua* will no longer be able to be excluded . . . "[67] "It remains, then, for us to *speak*, to make our voices *resonate* through the corridors in order to make up for [*supléer*] the breakup of presence."[68] For it is only in taking "responsibility" for *both*, seeking to make sense while listening to one's "nonsense"—seeking "to listen as we talk"[69]—that we gesture toward the common ground.

This reading of Derrida is confirmed in the "Afterword: Toward an Ethic of Discussion" in the English translation of *Limited Inc*. It would be difficult to exaggerate the importance of this interview-essay for understanding deconstruction.[70] Here it must suffice to note two points in this extraordinary text: the discussion of "text" and "context," which is highly pertinent to the notion of contextualization; and the reference to a "finite infinite," relevant to our programmatic typology.[71] The latter phrase is explicitly glossed by *Speech and Phenomena*, in which Derrida writes, "Only a relation to my-death could make the infinite differing of presence ap-

pear. . . . The appearing of the infinite *différance* is itself finite. Consequently, *différance* is itself finite. . . . *The infinite différance is finite.*"[72]

For all that may be said of Derrida's Jewishness, there is still about his
thought something profoundly Western and Greek. He partakes of the
tradition of truth as "unveiledness"—when that tradition is coupled with
the affirmation that the revealing is at the same time a concealing, and
that truth loves to hide itself. These too are Heideggerian themes; and a
great deal of Derrida's thought may be understood as a series of tactics
for taking the concealing with radical seriousness, as Heidegger did not,
while never giving up on the quest for unconcealment. There is more than
a suggestion of the Greek conception of Fate in Derrida's understanding
of discourse as an event in which sense and "nonsense," "chance and necessity, arbitrary and motivated, converge"—witness the way in which he
sees a person's life as encrypted in the proper name which they happen
to have been given.[73] His thought breathes as much of tragedy as of bac-
chanale.[74]

We may perhaps conclude, then, epigrammatically. The "postmodernist" position realized that truth is not something which can be grasped.
Therefore it concluded that the question of truth must be let go. What it
failed to realize is that the *question* of truth is more than a question: it is
a reality. And it is a reality which has hold of *us*.[75]

IV

THE KANTIAN OPENING

We are now in a position to begin our study of Kant. The present chapter will deal with the philosopher's work up through *The Critique of Pure Reason*, while chapter 5 will focus upon *The Critique of Practical Reason*. In view of the path traced thus far, we bring to Kant a threefold agenda. From chapter 1 we have the task of relating Kant the rationalist to the issue of human suffering. In a sense this will be easier than might appear. The rationalist, Leibnitzian tradition to which Kant was heir had coined the very term "theodicy"; and in his early, precritical writings Kant deals explicitly with the issue. In the mature, critical writings, however, treatment of theodicy disappears, or becomes at any rate indirect. The challenge will be to show that, nevertheless, the issue of theodicy continues to be an underlying theme in both of the Critiques.[1]

From chapter 2 we inherit the task of relating Kant to the typology regarding theology and difference with which that chapter concluded. I shall argue that by approaching Kant with this typology, and particularly the position represented by type 3, in mind, we can better understand the inner coherence of his complex thought. Finally, we have from chapter 3 a discussion, still in progress, regarding the question of truth. Following the lead provided by Christopher Norris, I hope to show that Kant is a good deal closer to Derrida on this matter than one might expect—Kant is, after all, as serious about human finitude as he is about the rights of reason—and that Kant's distinctive transcendental method may even help clarify some things which remain obscure in Derrida.

Acknowledging that the distinctions are relative, we can anticipate that the present chapter will address these topics more or less in sequence: beginning with the issue of theodicy, proceeding through the formal, methodological questions raised by the typology, and concluding with an examination of the text of the first Critique a propos of the question of truth. Chapter 5, by contrast, will stress that the three threads of our inquiry are profoundly intertwined; so much so that the reader of Kant may indeed be justified in speaking of a "wound of reason."

Kant and the Sublation of Theodicy

When a philosopher speculates about how the world must appear to an infant, we do well to pay attention. Whether or not we learn anything about children, we shall certainly learn something about the philosopher. For what one regards as earliest, one must in some sense regard as fundamental. Now in his little-read *Anthropology*, a set of lectures he presented and developed across his teaching career, Kant observes: "When an infant is forced to approach certain objects, or merely to change his general state, he feels that he is checked. The impulsion to have his own will and to take offense at that which obstructs him is . . . signalled by the tone which he takes."[2]

Kant's choice of experience is interesting in light of our reading of Derrida, for what he describes is precisely an experience of *opposition*. The child senses the world as obstacle and responds accordingly. Are we then to conclude that Kant's is a philosophy founded upon opposition? Some interpreters have suggested as much; but Theodor Adorno suggests a more subtle approach when he affirms that behind all genuine thinking there lies some spontaneous impulse which is "at once preserved and surpassed."[3] Here we do have a useful formula for reading a thinker in a way that keeps touch with experience without reducing thought to a mere reflection of experience.

Thus we have a hypothesis: that Kant's philosophy is one in which the experience of opposition is "at once preserved and surpassed." And from this it is but a small step to the question of theodicy. After all, the child, given the language, might well say the opposition was evil; one thinks of how children speak of the "bad, old" this or that, and of how adults refine the practice through variants of the expletive "damn!" The question of the extent to which these very human and very spontaneous judgments are justified, the question of how far they are to be preserved and how far surpassed, is only a part of the issue of theodicy. But it is an important part, in that it determines much of how one thinks about the experience of being finite; and thus we shall use it as a point of entree into the larger philosophy.

Turning from the obscure *Anthropology* to what is perhaps the best-known passage in the Kantian corpus, we find the issue refracted in an unexpected way. Persons who know nothing else from Kant are still apt to be familiar with the lines from the second Critique, "Two things fill the mind with ever new and increasing admiration and awe, the oftener and more steadily we reflect on them: the starry heavens above me and the moral law within me." The lines, from the conclusion of the second Critique, seem to bespeak the very essence of the Enlightenment (which is, no doubt, the reason they are so frequently quoted). The law without, the law within; and between the two, a profound consonance. What greater confirmation could there be that reason and morality were at one? What clearer charter for the human vocation within the cosmos?

Let us not move too quickly, however. For those who look more carefully at the Kantian text, a different situation begins to emerge. The much-quoted statement is not meant, after all, as a throwaway line. It appears as the first sentence in the opening paragraph of the conclusion of the second Critique. Obviously the entire paragraph occupies a pivotal position, summing up the significance of what has gone before and setting the terms for the conclusions to follow. Simply by giving the paragraph due attention, we can anticipate a number of themes which will emerge in the course of our own reflections on Kant. The second sentence claims for the two realities a certain *givenness*: "I do not merely conjecture them . . . I see them before me." We shall need to ask whether this implies that Kant himself is appealing to a form of presence. Or, to put the matter another way, we shall need to ask whether, contrary to our anticipations, there may be a form of givenness which is *not* a presence.

The remaining four sentences, which constitute the bulk of the paragraph, take a different turn. No longer setting the two realities in close parallel, the sentences alternate between the two realities, elaborating contrasts between them. "The former begins at the place I occupy in the external world. . . . The latter begins at my invisible self." Certainly there is a common theme to the two, the theme of *infinity*. But the two exhibit the theme in strikingly different ways. My contemplation of the starry heavens

> begins at the place I occupy in the external world of sense, and it broadens the connection in which I stand into an unbounded magnitude of worlds beyond worlds and systems of systems and into the limitless times of their periodic motion, their beginning and their continuance.

As we shall see, this passage is identical in its imagery with an early, precritical work of Kant, an essay on cosmology, in which the imagery is explicitly tied to questions of theodicy. There Kant observes, for example, "the infinitude of the creation is great enough to make a world, or a Milky Way of worlds, look in comparison with it, what a flower or insect does in comparison with the earth." And he then proceeds to quote Alexander Pope, speaking of God:

> He sees with equal eye, as God of all,
> A hero perish, or a sparrow fall;
> Atoms or systems into ruin hurl'd,
> And now a bubble burst, and now a world.[4]

Is it reading too much into the present, later work to think that similar issues may be at work in the second Critique as well?

The fourth sentence, while it continues the theme of infinity, sounds a warning note of contrast. "The latter begins at my invisible self, my personality, and exhibits me in a world which has *true* infinity" (emphasis added). Is the external infinity, whose expanse Kant described so emphatically, not a true infinity after all? What is meant by the implicit contrast between two sorts of infinity? The sentence continues with a further point of contrast, now fully explicit; the inward reality "exhibits me in . . . a world with which I recognize myself as existing in a universal and necessary (and not only, as in the first case, contingent) connection." First, let us appreciate that the point Kant is driving at, the thing he is seeking, is indeed a *connection*—a connection which holds not only within but also, as the sentence concludes, "with all those visible worlds" without. Apparently Kant's own purpose, at any rate, was not to disconnect and divide.

Moreover, the specific connection Kant seeks is one which is "universal and necessary," not contingent. The significance of this contrast is driven home by sentence five, which is the kicker:

> The former view of a countless multitude of worlds annihilates, as it were, my importance as an animal creature, which must give back to the planet (a mere speck in the universe) the matter from which it came, the matter which is for a little time provided with vital force, we know not how.[5]

With these words, the starry heavens have ceased to be cause for exultation. They "annihilate" the importance of the living, struggling human self. Gone is the reassuring consonance between cosmic order and aspiring soul. In its place we confront something nearer the anguish of Pascal—"the eternal silence of these infinite spaces frightens me."[6] We would seem to have, at any rate, the answer to our earlier question as to whether we were unfairly projecting the theodicy question onto this later work. Yet at the same time this sentence, so powerful in its imagery, nestles so quietly within the larger paragraph that it has gone largely unremarked. The very style of Kant's writing would seem to imply that in some fashion the issue had been addressed.

The nature of that address is suggested in the final sentence, where twice again a reference to the infinite occurs. The moral law "infinitely raises my worth" in that it reveals a noncontingent connection, "a life independent of all animality and even of the whole world of sense." It reveals "a destination which is not restricted to the conditions and limits of this life but reaches into the infinite." In terms of our typology, this seems an unequivocal instance of type 1. Finite transcendence "reaches into the infinite"; and it does so by minding a strong distinction, "independent of all animality and even of the whole world of sense." Thus further questions: is this in fact the final word on Kant? and if not, what grounds are there in his thought for another sort of theology?

My own suggestion is indicated by the quotation from Adorno and by the title of this section. As in Kant a certain passion may be "at once preserved and surpassed," so it is also with the issue of theodicy, which is what I mean to indicate by speaking of "sublation." The result, as I propose to show in the following sections, is something which presses in a direction increasingly distinct from that of ontotheology.

Ontotheology and the Great Chain of Being

In order to situate Kant with regard to ontotheology, we need to clarify that term. We need some more specific referent for it. In the process, I want consciously to avoid the temptation to use this term (or related terms, such as "metaphysics," taken in the negative sense) as a stick with which to thump upon my chosen opponents. That is the trap into which one can fall when one is exploring the notion of the postmodern and needs some blanket term with which to designate—and distance oneself from—that other thing, the modern. The result, inevitably, is a sort of oppositional thinking.

We need to recognize that "ontotheology" is a disputed term, that its meaning cannot be taken for granted or established by assertion; and yet we need to hold on to it as a useful term. I propose, therefore, that we begin with a relatively noncontroversial case and work from there. Let us begin by saying that what we mean by "ontotheology" is at least this: any effort or tendency to think of God and the finite order in univocal terms. That would seem simple enough, until one pauses over "tendency." It might well be that a theology which had spoken solemnly and at length about how our language about God is never more than analogical would nevertheless, in practice, *tend* to use the language univocally.

An example is provided by the historian and philosopher Leroy E. Loemker, who speaks of the rationalist tradition as it emerges from medieval scholasticism in the person of Francisco Suarez (1548–1617). Suarez makes great claims for the role of analogy; yet at the same time his thought is held together from top to bottom and from end to end by the glue of certain Ideas:

> The Ideas mediate between the divine and human thinking. They are the assurance of the truth of our judgments, but also of the identities of quality and form which assure the validity of our perception. This role of essences in assuring the unity of direct perception with the discursive work of the understanding is widely adopted by the metaphysicians of the seventeenth century.[7]

"The Ideas mediate between the divine and human thinking." *Ipso facto*, the Ideas suggest that there is a univocal relation between the divine and the human. More, the Ideas suggest that they themselves *are* the univocal relation between the divine and the human. Further still, the way of thinking Loemker describes establishes a direct connection between ontotheology, as we have defined it, and the notion of truth as correspondence or representation. Which is also to say that it establishes a connection between a notion which many people would deny that they hold (Ideas, with a capital "I," linking the human and the divine) and a notion which many people do in fact have (certain "identities of . . . form" which represent the correspondence between the thing outside our minds and the image in our minds, thus assuring "the validity of our perception"). Thus we find confirmation of Derrida's suspicion that the seemingly innocent notion of truth as representation may carry within it an implicit, quasi-theological appeal to a self-authenticating Presence, which is what is finally being represented.

Conceptually, this position has virtually collapsed the crucial distinction, or difference, between Truth and particular truths. Truth becomes quantitative, the sum total of all valid forms; truth becomes formal, the superform gathering together all particular forms. Truth itself has lost its otherness. The way lies open for what Heidegger calls "the era of the world picture," truth as the comprehensive picture, and for the various projects of instrumental reason.

Historically, the position was "widely adopted by the metaphysicians of the seventeenth century," as Loemker says. Not that these thinkers were impervious to its problems: they were energetic, for example, in trying to prevent a straightforward assimilation of the human to the divine; and their means of seeking to achieve this—to honor the differences and yet maintain some comprehensive order—was generally some sort of *hierarchy*. Thus there rose to prominence the notion of the Great Chain of Being.

> The Chain of Being is the idea of the organic constitution of the universe as a series of links or gradations ordered in a hierarchy of creatures, from the lowest and most insignificant to the highest, indeed to the *ens perfectissimum* which, uncreated, is yet its culmination and the end to which all creation tends.[8]

Arthur O. Lovejoy observes that "next to the word 'Nature,' " the Chain of Being was "the sacred phrase of the eighteenth century."[9] Unquestionably the key figure in this regard is Leibnitz; and it is in the school of Leibnitz (initially, as mediated by Christian Wolff) that Kant had his early philosophical formation. So our project of situating Kant vis-à-vis ontotheology points quite naturally to a consideration of Kant's relation to

Leibnitz. But Leibnitz is himself a thinker of some complexity and the effort to clarify Kant by way of Leibnitz may wind up illumining shadow with darkness. Moreover, we have resolved to begin with a simple, relatively indisputable instance of ontotheology and to get clear on that before proceeding outwards to the more disputed cases. Accordingly, I propose to adopt as stand-in for Leibnitz a vigorous piece of writing which self-consciously takes up the cudgels on behalf of ontotheology, or at any rate on behalf of the Great Chain of Being. Alexander Pope's "An Essay on Man" tackles frontally the issue of theodicy, and it has the further virtue of having been penned by a master of the English tongue.

Lest any one miss the metaphysical character of the poem, Pope advertises the point in capital letters—"ORDER is Heaven's first law . . . " (IV:49).[10] The conservative implications of such an appeal did not escape Pope's readers, nor were they intended to; Pope could curry favor. Yet it would be too easy to label Pope's position as metaphysical, identify metaphysics with a defense of the status quo, and dismiss the whole enterprise out of hand. I argued in the introduction that there is a certain irreducible truth to metaphysics, which I tried to indicate by the term "contextualization"; and I mean to stand by my argument now, even though Pope is in some ways unpleasant company. For one function of the notion of "ORDER" is surely to gesture toward an all-embracing scheme of things, *whatever* that scheme may be. And remarkably, a great deal of Pope's argument, so far from being an effort to lay that scheme out and defend it point by point, is instead a vigorous reminder of how *little* we know about such things. In this sense there is about Pope's argument a modesty, even a sort of agnosticism; and it is when he is arguing in this vein that he is on his strongest ground.

Thus Pope cautions, in a passage one may associate with both Kant's starry heaven and Kant's impetuous child, "Ask for what end the heavenly bodies shine, / Earth for whose use? Pride answers, 'Tis for mine" (I.131–32). What we find disagreeable is not for that reason evil, our wishes do not shape reality; it is a point on which Pope sharpens his satirical wit. "While Man exclaims, 'See all things for my use!' / 'See man for mine!' replies a pampered goose" (III.45–46). And a generation which has witnessed ecological devastation and consumerist self-indulgence has even more reason than did Pope's to acknowledge the justice of the poet's jibe: "Destroy all creatures for thy sport or gust, / Yet cry, If Man's unhappy, God's unjust" (I.117–18).[11]

To the skeptic who would object that any rational system is shattered by the reality of evil, Pope, himself no stranger to pain, responds that our human efforts to draw the limits of good and evil are themselves no less presumptuous, no less shattered by a larger reality. The tenacious validity of the metaphysical impulse springs from what one might call a sort of *positive* agnosticism. It is agnostic in a manner best captured by the classic

line (from Shakespeare now, not Pope), "There are more things in heaven
and earth, Horatio, than are dreamt of in your philosophy"—a line which
is most often used against metaphysics, against "philosophy." But, *nota
bene*, that very line turns on a positive affirmation—"there *are* more
things . . . "—an affirmation about mysterious matters, an affirmation
which must be regarded, in its impulse and in its sense, as metaphysical.
Without such affirmation, Hamlet's very rejection of "philosophy" would
have no sting. This then is metaphysics in its legitimate office, as a critique
of human presumption, as an intimation of a larger reality and thus as an
act of contextualization.

Plenitude and the Otherness of Time

Thus when Pope speaks of a "vast Chain of being, which from God began"
(I.237), the proper role of this image within the poem's argument is to
contextualize us, to place us in a setting which exceeds our comprehension—as is powerfully apparent from the passage in which the first major
reference to the Chain occurs:

> See, through this air, this ocean, and this earth,
> All matter quick, and bursting into birth.
> Above, how high progressive life may go!
> Around, how wide! how deep extend below!
> Vast chain of being, which from God began,
> Natures ethereal, human, angel, man,
> Beast, bird, fish, insect! what no eye can see,
> No glass can reach! from Infinite to thee,
> From thee to Nothing! . . . (I.233–41)

The language is powerful; and the intent, clearly, is like that of the voice
which speaks to Job from the whirlwind. But in the book of Job what is
primary is the voice, the fact of being addressed; and the address is in the
form of questions ("Where were you when I laid the foundation of the
earth?" [38:4]). The statements of the form "Behold . . . " follow after and
have as their object specific earthly creatures, Behemoth, the hippopota-
mus, and Leviathan, the crocodile (40–41). Pope's passage, in contrast,
begins with the magisterial "See . . . !"; as a result, the words that follow
are beset by ambiguity. No doubt the poet's intent is to demonstrate that
"The bliss of Man (could Pride that blessing find) / Is not to act or think
beyond mankind" (I.189–90). But the very passage which would enforce
this limit oversteps it, laying out a vast panorama ("Natures ethereal,
human, angel, man") which in principle surpasses human knowing, and

bidding us rhetorically to "see." Who then is the subject who knows all this? and who is the subject who is invited to see?

This points to a dilemma besetting the entire argument. Pope would have us understand " 'Tis but a part we see, and not a whole" (I.60). But the device by which he seeks to bring home this, the great Chain, is in fact a whole, indeed *the* whole; its entire significance springs from that fact. Nor are these difficulties from which God, the creator of the Chain, is exempt. At the very beginning, as if to set the terms from all that follows, the poet dwells upon the difference between divine and human knowing.

> Through worlds unnumbered though the God be known,
> 'Tis ours to trace him only in our own.
> He, who through vast immensity can pierce,
> See worlds on worlds compose one universe
> . . . .
> May tell why Heaven made us as we are.
> But of this frame the bearings, and the ties,
> The strong connections, nice dependencies,
> Gradations just, has thy pervading soul
> Looked through? or can a part contain the whole? (I.22–32)

Yet that same transcendent God is ever on the verge of being reduced to the status of a member, albeit the greatest member (as it were, the founding member) within the Chain. Here again the word "infinite" plays a part: when Pope describes the Chain as extending " . . . from Infinite to thee, / From thee to Nothing! . . . " (I.240–41), there is nothing to suggest that God is not to be identified with that (capitalized) Infinite. Indeed, it would seem a rupture in the Chain, were God not. And all the more is this the case in view of the fact that alongside the negative theology, which we have thus far emphasized, there coexists in Pope's "Essay" a positive theology, which would direct our reflections in a course of ascent, rising toward the divine from the human. Toward its conclusion, the poem praises the person who

> . . . looks through Nature up to Nature's God;
> Pursues that Chain which links the immense design,
> Joins heaven and earth, and mortal and divine; (IV.332–34)

To be sure, Pope means this to be the work of a vision informed by love, and thus perhaps also assisted by grace. By the time of "Epistle III," the Chain itself has become "a chain of love" (III.7). But in what sense is grace really essential, given the basic move of ontotheology: given, that is, that the whole has long been defined as a hierarchical Chain, and that the

Chain as such is a metaphysical concept open to inspection apart from grace?

The problem rises, in short, from the very thing which makes Pope's "Essay" such a clearcut case of ontotheology: the fact that it places all of reality within the bounds of a "world picture." For at the very moment that we contemplate the picture, we, the ones who respond to the admonition "See . . . ," step beyond it. At the least, we take a position analogous to that of God; and very likely, we trade places with God, placing God within what we ourselves have transcended. Indeed, this trading of places is ontotheology's most fundamental move. It is made implicitly, not to say stealthily, but it effectively defines what we mean by ontotheology. One consequence is that God becomes a being alongside (albeit at the pinnacle of) other beings: what Tillich so vigorously condemns. But for our purposes it is the reversal itself, the ultimate denial of the finite/infinite difference, which is the defining gesture of ontotheology.

These issues become acute as the "Essay" engages in earnest its assigned task of theodicy. To set the background, it is useful to distinguish among three devices which the rationalist tradition enlisted in its ongoing effort to deal with the problem of evil. The first, which we have observed in Pope, is the appeal to the *larger picture*. In its modest form, this is to remind us that we are not privy to the larger scheme of things; more ambitiously, it adduces various considerations in favor of the thesis that the larger scheme is in fact benevolent. A second, favored by Leibnitz but less operative in Pope, argues that in any finite system the achievement of certain goods precludes, in practice, the achievement of certain other goods. If I use a tree as firewood to warm me tonight, I cannot complain when it provides no shade to cool me tomorrow. In a finite creation there are limits as to what can possibly go with what, limits of *compossibility*.

Now both these strategies draw to some extent upon a certain strength of metaphysical reflection, which I have termed its positive agnosticism. But to many even within the rationalist camp, these devices came to seem insufficient. When one confronted the hard cases, something more seemed required. Thus Lovejoy observes of Leibnitz that "as the author of a theodicy he is concerned to justify crocodiles." (Again Leviathan raises his redoubtable head.) Leibnitz reckoned that there had to be some additional explanation of why such creatures, "and all the other possible links in the Chain of Being, down to the lowest," should actually exist.[12] It was for this reason that rationalism sought to supplement the previous two principles with a third, which Lovejoy denominates "*the principle of plenitude*."

The stakes in this conceptual move may be clarified by reference to Plato, where the principle first appears. To position oneself in Plato's thought, it is important to bear in mind that for Plato in a real sense the problem was not one of demonstrating the existence of the Ideas. These came with the rationalist territory; postulate noncontingent truth and you have in some sense postulated the Ideas. No doubt there were questions which needed ironing out, but for the rationalist the real problem lay at the other end of things—why should there be a material reality? why should there be time? It was the existence of these—which is to say, their otherness, their being other than pure Idea—which had to be accounted for. To this end Plato offers in the *Timaeus* the following account of God:

> He was good and the good can never have any jealousy of anything. And being free from jealousy, he desired that all things should be as like himself as they could be. This is in the truest sense the origin of creation and the world.[13]

Thus, as Lovejoy nicely observes, "the concept of Self-Sufficing Perfection, by a bold logical inversion, was—without losing any of its original implications—converted into the concept of a Self-Transcending Fecundity."[14] God, not hoarding the goodness to God's self, allowed it to be shared, which is the origin of non-absolute reality.

At once powerful and attractive, this vision of the origin of things spread widely through Western thought. The variety of its uses is reflected in the breadth of Lovejoy's definition of it:

> I . . . shall use the term to cover a wider range of inferences from premises identical with Plato's than he himself draws; i.e., not only the thesis that the universe is a *plenum formarum* in which the range of diversity of conceivable *kinds* of living is exhaustively exemplified, but also any other deductions from the assumption that no genuine potentiality of being can remain unfulfilled, that the extent and abundance of the creation must be as great as the possibility of existence and commensurate with the productive capacity of a "perfect" and inexhaustible Source, and that the world is the better, the more things it contains.[15]

To Leibnitz it was of use in his conceptual wrestling with the crocodile. The absence of even this difficult being would occasion a gap in the plenum of creation, a lessening of the goodness of the whole. Similarly for Pope "all must full or not coherent be" (I.45). But here the problems begin. For, as the Derridean connotations of the term suggest, the principle introduced to "supplement" the rationalist effort soon begins to undermine it. Thus one finds in Pope the astonishing affirmation:

> And if each system in gradation roll,
> Alike essential to the amazing Whole,
> The least confusion but in one, not all
> That system only, but the Whole must fall. (I:247–50)

Nudge one peg out of place and the entire edifice collapses. This is con-
servatism become paranoia, a domino theory of the cosmos. It illumines
the fact that the Chain is after all a chain, which is only as strong as its
weakest (or most rebellious) link. But it also reflects the logic of the principle of plenitude, which requires that every nook and cranny be filled,
every station occupied. Moreover, recalling our earlier issue of theology,
we may note that insofar as it is the principle of plenitude which makes
of the Chain a (complete) chain, it provides a powerful impetus toward
regarding God as an element within the Chain, one link among others,
albeit the first. For if the Chain can be threatened by the loss of the *least*
of its elements, one will not be much inclined to surrender its greatest
member. One will want the divine reality included securely within it. And
that will mean of course that the Chain will have ceased to perform its
original role of being a dependent *reflection of* the divine goodness, becoming itself the inclusive reality.

As Barth would be quick to remind us, the shift is of more than the-
oretic importance. So long as a fairly clear distinction is maintained between finite and infinite, with plenitude performing its function within the
realm of the finite, there is, in principle at least, an independent criterion
of the good. Rationalism might or might not succeed in its effort to argue
that the plethora of finite beings provides, by virtue of its very abundance,
some analogue to God's greatness and goodness. Regardless whether that
argument succeeds, there still remains the prime member of the intended
analogy, namely the goodness of God, against which the various claims
regarding creation can be assessed. But it is in the nature of the principle
of plenitude that, once posited, it cannot readily be contained. If plenitude
is good, why should it be good only so far, say up to the bounds of finitude, and not beyond? And once plenitude comes to comprise both finite
and infinite—or once it becomes itself the infinite—then it is difficult indeed to hold it to any criterion, or to get any critical leverage upon it.
That I take to be the concern behind Barth's polemical typology: the plenum becomes, if not its own god, then certainly its own good. The logic
here is familiar from chapter 1: a gesture which is at first defiant (in this
case, the trading of places) is soon overwhelmed by its own implicit system.
Faust becomes the sorcerer's apprentice.

I wish to argue that struggle over the principle of plenitude provides
one important thread running from early modern rationalism to contemporary debates over postmodernity, making the latter seem less an aber-
ration and more the final flowering of something long latent within the
tradition. Leibnitz seems almost to have anticipated this; he saw it in the
pantheism of Spinoza and struggled to defend his own Christian ortho-
doxy against it.[16] Hegel, for his part, may virtually be defined as the res-
olute application of the principle of plenitude to the finite and to the

infinite: the finite does not achieve fullness without the infinite; but also, the infinite does not achieve fullness without the finite. Moreover, it was Hegel's achievement to deliberately return the rationalist tradition to the issue within the issue, the otherness of time. On Hegel's terms, that otherness is not denied; quite the contrary, it is affirmed as being required by the plenitude. Time, by its own processes, by its historical unfolding, comes to constitute the all-encompassing fullness.

On Hegel's terms, that is so; whether it is so in truth is, of course, the question that Kierkegaard pressed. Our own contemporary position on the matter—quite apart from the various pro forma dismissals of Hegelian philosophy—is by no means clear, as I shall try to show in the following chapter, where we will examine various popular metaphors of "process" and "self-realization." Nietzsche, to conclude for the moment with him, had the genius's capacity to hammer out two equally devastating, and totally conflicting, positions on the matter, and to maintain them unresolved. At one moment he proclaims aloud what had been implied but not acknowledged—that the plenum is the only good, that it is to be affirmed and embraced for its own sake, that it is in this sense "beyond good and evil." Then at the next moment he implies that it is the very notion of a plenum which we must fight free of—that absence and lack are inexpungible.

Kant and the New Cosmology

Our title recalls a commonplace dear to historians of philosophy: that much of Kant's thought, particularly in its earlier phases, was a struggle to come to terms with the revolutionary achievements of Newtonian physics and Copernican astronomy. But it would be a mistake to portray Kant as merely reacting to something which was thrust upon him as a *fait accompli*. He himself made an important contribution to that science—there is at least one historian who laments Kant's critical philosophy as the evidence of a great scientist gone to seed. If we understand that contribution, we will have a start at understanding the philosophy.

In 1775 the young philosopher published a longish essay in Latin under the enterprising title "Universal Natural History and Theory of the Heavens."[17] The work is of additional interest in that its conclusion contains his most extensive early treatment of theodicy. The result is a juxtaposition—cosmology and theodicy—which seems fairly natural, if one recalls the "starry heavens" passage from the second Critique. Now I have said the Newtonian astronomy did not arrive on Kant's doorstep a *fait accompli*. In retrospect, the sphere within which Newton took his laws to be applicable seems surprisingly restricted:

Newton confined his attention to the solar system, which he regarded as
entirely isolated from the rest of the universe. Moreover, even within the
solar system he used his theory of gravitation only to explain how the or-
bital motions of the planets and satellites are maintained and not how these
motions may have originated.[18]

Not only did the great theoretician, for all his brilliance, leave the theories
restricted as to their application; he likewise left them ungrounded as to
their origin. It was possible to speculate (or fear) that the apparent law-
fulness of this world might ultimately be a quirk or illusion. Now the restrictions as to application were restrictions within the realm of science,
whereas the lack of grounding was a specifically philosophic issue. In the
long run, it was the latter which was to concern Kant more, leading him
into the critical philosophy. Yet along the way he managed to hammer out
the first viable account of the origin of our own galaxy, the Milky Way;
to fashion an explanation of its current shape which is still basically accepted; and to hypothesize that the other nebula, the most distant heavens, were of the same nature, so many additional Milky Ways. Virtually
none of this had been done before. It was Kant, and Kant at an early stage
in his career, who managed to incorporate the postulates of Copernican-
Newtonian astronomy into a new view of the universe which was unwavering in its consistency and unrestricted in its scope. In the words of one
observer, it was Kant who "first truly discerned the evolutional process of
Nature in its universal range, and gave it corresponding expression."[19]

For us, living in a time when the achievements of modern astronomy
are taken for granted, it is difficult to appreciate the effort of thought
which was required in order to extend the application of Newton's theory
beyond the boundary at which Newton had halted. The great scientist had
shown that his physics was not confined to the earthly realm; the solar
system obeyed the same principles. But beyond the solar system stretched
"the heavens," and the very ambiguity of that term suggests the problem.
Indeed, the effect of recent advances in astronomy, the move "from closed
world to infinite universe," had been in many respects to *reinforce*, via the
notion of infinity, the traditional association between the far reaches of
the universe and God. In such a context, it was no simple matter to extend
the domain of the earthly physics to the cosmos at large. To do so was to
impose upon the highest realms of the great Chain, perhaps upon the
divine reality itself, laws proper to a lower realm. It was an act of presumption to which Newton felt hardly more inclined than Pope.

Thus on historical grounds as well as philosophic, it is of interest to
determine just how it was that Kant made his bold extension. It is upon
this question of the Archimedean point that we shall focus, rather than
upon the particulars of his theory (e.g., the fact that he posited two com-
plementary forces, attraction and repulsion, or that he envisioned the uni-

verse emerging gradually from a dispersed gas). But when one raises the question of method, the answer is by no means clear. Much of what Kant himself tells us about his method stands foursquare within the onto-theological tradition, shedding little light on why it was that this particular philosopher should have managed to transgress the traditional bounds. In the Preface, for example, Kant notes the harmonious relationships which exist between various things within the natural world, and proceeds to argue that such harmony can be explained only on the supposition that the diversity of things sprang from "a common origin, namely, an Infinite Intelligence."[20] This is an instance of reasoning from the observed world to a purported origin, a certain *archē*. As we might anticipate from our earlier reflections on the notion of *archē*, there is nothing in that sort of reasoning which would disturb the traditional cosmology.

Matters proceed somewhat differently, however, when one turns to the essay's final section. The section begins in a familiar manner, contemplating the grandeur and harmony of the universe, which "fills us with silent wonder"; and further wondering at the fact that "such magnificence and such greatness can flow from a single law" (135). The second paragraph continues the theme of *archē*: "If, then, all the worlds and systems acknowledge the same kind of origin . . ." There ensues a reference to the powers of attraction and repulsion—and then, in obtrusive parallelism with the opening clauses, there appears a further clause, "*if, in presence of the infinite, the great and small are small alike . . .*"[21]

Now undoubtedly such a sentiment is not uncommon in the Christian tradition, particularly the pietism in which Kant was raised. But as Kierkegaard would remind us, it is one thing to repeat a pious phrase and quite another to absorb its implications. What Kant proceeds to do does bear comparison with Kierkegaard, in that he takes up a notion deeply rooted in piety and follows out its full implications, with results which prove disastrous for ontotheology. Nor does the following-out require great subtlety; in a sense it is very simple. Simply to affirm with a sort of childlike earnestness that "in presence of the infinite, the great and small are small alike" is to call the entire Chain into question. For if there is one thing a hierarchy requires, it is relative distinctions. Even if they propound it in its most moderate, chastened form, even if they make efforts to honor the otherness of God, and to recognize discontinuity at the upper end, still the Chain's proponents have to assume that the higher levels are relatively closer to God, *relatively nearer* the infinite. Without that, the Chain cannot function. Without that, there is no ascent heavenward. But it is just this point which Kant drives home—"all that is finite, whatever has limits," he writes, " . . . *is equally far removed from the infinite.*"[22]

By way of anticipation, we may say that what has happened is that rationalism's suppressed question, the question of the otherness of matter, the otherness of time, the otherness of *finitude*, has reasserted itself.[23] It has reasserted itself as being so distinct that it does not even begin to transmute, even at its highest point, into the infinite and the eternal. Yet this same turn of argument, so antithetical to the Chain, is what makes Kant's cosmological breakthrough possible. In the sentence we have been examining, Kant makes the connection explicit:

> if, in the presence of the infinite, the great and small are small alike; have not all the universes received a relative constitution and systematic connec-tion similar to what the heavenly bodies of our solar world have on the small scale . . . ? (136)

This, I believe, is the Archimedean point. This is the turn of thought which enabled Kant to conceive the utmost reach of "the heavens" as not fundamentally different from our earth, in respect to the laws by which it is governed. On the terms which Kant has explicitly prepared, to speak of *fundamental* difference is to speak of one difference and one difference only, namely the difference between that which is finite, however grand, and that which is infinite.

Beyond Ontotheology

In chapter 1 we sketched a typology of relationships between finite and infinite. In terms of that schema, the decisive conceptual move in Kant's cosmology clearly corresponds to type 3: great emphasis is placed upon the distinction between finite and infinite, with the result that all other distinctions (i.e., all distinctions *within* the finite sphere) are radically rel-ativized. They are relativized to such an extent that no particular reality within the finite sphere can be said to be inherently closer to the infinite than any other.

In the early pages of the essay Kant frames a debate which demon-strates his sensitivity to the theological stakes in this matter. He begins with a straightforward declaration of the essay's aim, which is (spatially) "to discover the system which binds together the great members of the cre-ation in the whole extent of infinitude," and (temporally) "to derive the formation of the heavenly bodies themselves, and the origin of their movements, from the primitive state of nature by mechanical laws" (17). He then proceeds to the issue of atheism; which is no small matter in a society where the doctrines of the church might still be enforced by the state. The objection is that,

> if the blind mechanics of the natural forces can evolve so glorious a product out of chaos, . . . then the proof of the Divine Author which is drawn from

the spectacle of the beauty of the universe wholly loses its force. Nature is thus sufficient for itself; the Divine government is unnecessary; Epicurus lives again in the midst of Christendom. (18)

Kant would seem to have undermined certain proofs for the existence of God.

Kant responds that "the defenders of religion, by using these proofs in a bad way, perpetuate the conflict with the advocates of Naturalism by presenting them unnecessarily with a weak side of their position" (19). The religionists have failed to do their own cause justice; they have defined themselves over against the naturalists in a manner which is needlessly oppositional, to the detriment of their own argument. The character of this distortion Kant now proceeds to set forth in a trenchant analysis which bears quoting in full:

> It is usual to signalize and emphasize in nature the harmonies, beauty, the ends of things, and the perfect relation of means adapted to them. But while nature is thus elevated on this side, the attempt is made on another to belittle it again. This admirable adaptation, it is said, is foreign to nature; abandoned to its own general laws it would bring forth nothing but disorder. These harmonies show an alien hand which has known how to subdue to a wise plan a matter that is wanting in all order or regularity. (19)

Within the present essay, this is Kant's principal critique of the traditional theology; with it, he cannily brings to light the unavowed anxiety which we noted in Pope. Yet the critique proceeds along lines which the (polemical) typology would lead one to expect. In effect, Kant associates the traditional position with type 1. True to type, it affirms a certain coherence within the finite realm, which provides the basis for proceeding conceptually from finite to infinite. Thus is nature elevated, as Kant says, on the one side. But at the same time—also following type—the position cannot succeed without the introduction of a further premise, roughly a distinction between "nature-subjected-to-law" and "sheer nature" or "matter." For the position to accomplish its task of overcoming the gap between finite and infinite, it must implicitly open a gap, *generating an opposition within the finite order*. Figuratively speaking, one has to "push off" against the lower element, refusing it as inherently chaotic or subversive, in order to propel the ascent toward God. In clear contrast, Kant allows that matter may bear certain laws inherent within it; he thus avoids setting matter and law in opposition.[24] At another level, Kant similarly dispels the notion that one must choose between honoring God and honoring (the "lower" aspects of) nature. Nature is granted a certain coherence and God is honored for being able and willing to bestow upon the finite realm an integrity of its own.

In the sections which follow I will try to indicate how something along the lines of the type 3 position runs through Kant's later, critical thought. Before leaving the essay on cosmology, however, I wish to turn to Kant's reflections on theodicy, for it is there that the full significance of his position is made plain. Immediately after asserting that "all that is finite . . . is equally far removed from the infinite," Kant reflects: "Now it would be absurd to represent the Deity as passing into action with an infinitely small part of His potency." Rather, "is it not *necessary* to represent the system of creation as it must be in order to be a witness of that power which cannot be measured by any standard?"[25]

With these words Kant admits into his own argument an appeal to the principle of plenitude. As we have seen, one needs to be well aware of what one is doing when one makes this appeal. It is therefore worth watching Kant closely at this point. I will distinguish five steps. (1) Consistent with the strong distinction Kant has just made between the finite and the truly infinite, the operation of the principle is *confined to the realm of nature*. Thus the tendency for the principle to engulf the divine reality is precluded at the outset. Yet (2) solely within the finite realm, the operation of the principle can amount to a sort of reflection of the truly infinite, a sort of "witness of that power which cannot be measured by any standard." Thus on the basis of a thinking through of the distinction between finite and infinite and of the principle of plenitude, Kant arrives at (3) a *radicalization* of the conception of nature.

We have seen the effect of this radicalization in Kant's extension of the existing science, but it is in the reflections on theodicy that Kant, pressing the very limits of language and of ontology, explores fully the implications. To provide a reflection of the divine, nature itself must be without limit, either spatial *or temporal*. Going well beyond Pope's rather atemporal perspective, Kant holds that at any given moment it is impossible for nature to display an order which is in any way an adequate reflection of the divine. Rather, that reflecting requires time—indeed all of time: nature's own eternity, as it were. Kant thus shifts the terms of discussion from an instantaneous order to an extended process of ordering. Just how extended, Kant makes clear: "millions and whole myriads of millions of centuries will flow on, during which always new worlds and new systems of worlds will be formed . . . " (145). One hesitates to say which is the more extraordinary, the fact that nature is extended so far—or the fact that nevertheless, despite that unimaginable extension, Kant resists the ontotheological impulse to soften the distinction between nature's particular infinity and the divine infinite.

Kant's seriousness about the distinction becomes increasingly evident as the argument proceeds. Each natural being, however great, is finite and thus perishable (149); the perishability of the least reality is simply evidence, in more accessible form, of the perishability of the greatest (150).

In applying the rule of perishability as in applying the laws of science, Kant is extraordinarily consistent. And in the one case as in the other, the source of his consistency is the overarching distinction between nature and the truly infinite:

> And, I say it again, the greatness of what has to perish, is not the least obstacle to it; for all that is great becomes small, nay, it becomes as it were a mere point, when it is compared with the Infinitude which creation has to exhibit in unlimited space throughout the succession of eternity. (151–52)

The impact upon the Chain is radical. All hierarchy is relativized; any member, even the highest, will sooner or later become (in a phrase impossible for Pope) "a superfluous member in the chain of beings" (151). It is this un-Pope-like relativization which Kant intends when he says, quoting Pope, that God "sees with equal eye, as God of all, / A hero perish, or a sparrow fall."

Let us return now to the enumeration of the steps involved in Kant's distinctive use of the principle of plenitude. Given that in accordance with the principle all possibilities must be realized and given that this dictum applies to the greatest of realities as well as the least, there follows a sort of theodicy. Specifically, it follows that (4) any loss at any particular place and time will be offset by a corresponding gain elsewhere. Each day new plants and animals appear to replace those which have died; so too, in identical fashion, "worlds and systems perish" and are replaced (149). Nature proves to be a Phoenix (154), demonstrating "her riches by a sort of prodigality" (150). Such is "the plan of the Divine revelation" (154): it is a "big picture" indeed, and (5) Kant, still faithful in this respect to the tradition of ontotheology, invites the reader to derive from the spectacle a certain sense of balance and harmony, and thus a certain equanimity (e.g., 151).[26]

By giving this section the title "Beyond Ontotheology," I mean to indicate a direction rather than a definitive accomplishment. Clearly, this early, "precritical" Kant retains important ties to the tradition in which he was schooled. What is surprising is not that this should be so, but that already, in a work which has little obvious connection with the critical turn, he should have introduced a mode of thought which runs so distinctly counter to the tradition (while yet drawing on traditional piety), and that he should have faced so unblinkingly the consequences of it. In a sense it is a grand vision of order in the classic tradition. But in another sense, which Kant repeatedly makes explicit, it envisions an endless give and take *between* creation and destruction, *between* order and chaos. Unsparing in its embrace of "millions and whole myriads of millions of centuries," it is, from the pen of this thinker of Enlightenment, a remarkably "postmodern" vision—a vision akin to Nietzsche's "eternal return."

Opening the First Critique

Kant's "Copernican revolution in epistemology" has been portrayed by M. H. Abrams as a shift from conceiving the mind under the metaphor of mirror, seeking to reflect reality, to that of a lamp, providing an active illumination of reality. While the former image descends from Plato, the latter view of mind is found in the thought of Plotinus—where it is applied specifically to the divine. From conceiving the mind as active, not just a passive recipient, it is indeed a small step to conceiving of it as *creative*: creative of knowledge, perhaps even creative of reality. As the history of thought since Kant attests, issues of idealism and nihilism are close at hand the moment one takes this "Copernican turn."

How does Kant himself introduce the fateful notion? Between the first and second editions of the *Critique of Pure Reason* there occurs an important tactical shift. The opening paragraph of Edition A asserts,

> Experience tells us, indeed, what is, but not that it must necessarily be so, and not otherwise. It therefore gives us no true universality; and reason, which is so insistent upon this kind of knowledge, is therefore more stimulated by it than satisfied. (A 1–2)

To carry through the argument thus introduced Kant must persuade his reader of at least two things: first, that there is within our experience (but not totally reducible to our experience) a knowledge which is endowed with universality and necessity; and second, that this universal, necessary knowledge is generated by the knowing subject. Conceptually speaking, the argument has two hairpin turns. Readers who are not offended by the confident rationalism of the first are generally repelled by the seeming subjectivism of the second. By the time of Edition B, Kant has a more persuasive approach:

> There can be no doubt that all our knowledge begins with experience. . . .
> But though all our knowledge begins with experience, it does not follow that it all arises out of experience. For *it may well be that* even our empirical knowledge is made up of what we receive through impressions and of what our own faculty of knowledge . . . supplies from itself. *If* our faculty of knowledge makes any such addition, it may be that we are not in a position to distinguish it from the raw material, until with long practice of attention we have become skilled in separating it.
> This, then, is a question which at least calls for closer examination . . . [27]

Here Kant asserts rather little, he simply poses a possibility. But it is an unsettling possibility; for if it is true, if some part of our experience is supplied out of "our own faculty of knowledge," then we can by no means be confident to what extent and in what way our experience corresponds to reality. The burden of proof has suddenly shifted. Now it is up to those who do *not* join with Kant, at least in exploring the question, to show how they can escape appearing naive and doctrinaire.

My own impression is that Kant's argumentative shift from the first edition to the second nicely illumines the nature of critical thought. It is not so much a matter of *asserting* this or that (about the activity of the subject, about a Copernican revolution), though assertions must eventually be involved. It is more fundamentally a matter of *raising certain troubling questions*, and holding onto them in all of their troubling character. The questions are troubling because we naturally tend to assume that if there is anything we know, it is that which we ourselves have done. But this *is* an assumption, and what Kant has done is simply to have pointed to the fact that, as regards the most basic constituents of experience, we cannot rest content with assuming that we naturally, spontaneously, know what is and is not our own doing. In Derridean terms, Kant has called into question the subject's natural, spontaneous assumption that it is more or less present to itself. For "if our faculty of knowledge makes any such addition, it may be that we are not in a position to distinguish it."

In this respect the Kantian suspicion is closely allied with certain basic conceptual moves in Freudian psychoanalysis. The subject is no longer at home with itself; and the subject's experience becomes less clearly compartmentalized—it shifts toward what we earlier called a condition of undecidability. This is the phenomenon which we highlighted earlier, in the fourth type of our four-part typology regarding Freudian psychoanalysis. Now I wish to propose the thesis that, notwithstanding all the talk about Kantian foundationalism, the effect of Kant's thought is to locate us in a condition of undecidability, and to give us a way of coping. The effect is, in the language of our introductory chapter, an act of contextualization.

If there is anything to the proposal, the next, natural question is, "How does Kant do this? what makes the contextualization possible?" Here I will propose a further thesis, that what makes the contextualization possible is a certain concept of God; and that, in seeking to understand the logic by which this works, we will find that we have been well prepared by our study of the role of the infinite in Kant's early cosmogony. For, acknowledging the very real differences between the "precritical" essay and the present "critical" work, there still is, I believe, a crucial theological link between them. In the pages which follow, my two theses will be addressed in reverse order. The present section will seek to bring into view a certain implicit conception of the divine; the concluding section of the chapter will spell out the effect as a logic of contextualization.

Now it is scarcely news to observe that there is a concept of God in the first Critique. At several junctures Kant considers a quite traditional concept of God, the God of ontotheology, and finds the arguments for the existence of such a God to be at best inconclusive. And when, on the strength of considerations formulated in the second Critique, Kant does venture to posit God's existence, many readers have charged him with a slackening of the critical rigor of his earlier work. In making the present proposal, I have no desire to reopen that familiar debate. The religionist's temptation is to proceed too quickly to the specific, explicit statements about God, as if seeking the theological bottom line. We shall do better to attend to the logic of the first Critique as a whole; and, if an implicit concept of God should appear, to attend patiently to how the concept functions within his thought, rather than hasten to claim some sort of theological vindication.

In an excellent dissertation entitled "Divine and Human Subjectivity in Kant," Joe Harold Hicks distinguishes between theism and "trans-theism," the latter being the conception of a "deity transcending any determinate form."[28]

> Put most briefly, the trans-theistic concept in Kant is that of God as absolute intellectual spontaneity. God is here conceived as radically indeterminate primordially or in himself—i.e., unconditioned by any determination to a certain essence or form. God is the antecedent spontaneous source of all determining—including self-determining—form. Accordingly, God is not even Being, for to be is to be determinate.[29]

Through an extended series of analyses, Hicks traces the appearance and reappearance of this conception in the first Critique as a concept of "intellectual intuition," in the second Critique as "holy will" and in the third Critique as "archetypal intellect."

To see what is at stake here, we may match our earlier examination of the Introduction of the first Critique with a discussion of the opening lines of the body of the text. *The Critique of Pure Reason* begins with three sentences:

> In whatever manner and by whatever means a mode of knowledge may relate to objects, *intuition* is that through which it is in immediate relation to them, and from which all thought gains its materials. But intuition takes place only in so far as the object is given to us. This again is only possible, to man at least, in so far as the mind is affected in a certain way.[30]

The passage proceeds in the manner of genus and species, first offering a generalization, then making a distinction. The initial sentence makes a statement about all knowledge whatsoever: all knowledge bears a primary relationship to intuition. Sentence two provides the basis for a distinction (and reflects Kant's own conviction that his position is not simply subjectivist); the sentence affirms that intuition requires the givenness of an object. Sentence three signals by a phrase, "to humankind at least," that it is indeed making a distinction; and then makes it, albeit in rather general terms. Human knowing (and other knowing of its kind) is distinguished by the fact that in it "the mind is affected in a certain way."

These opening lines are characteristic of the first Critique at large in that they bear what I believe we may fairly call, in Derridean fashion, the trace of a crucial distinction. But the distinction, being no more than a trace, is continually being effaced, as it is in the present passage, where the entire momentum is in the direction of laying out the specifics of human reason, delineating human reason in its own right—forgetting the distinction. One commentator who joins Hicks in resisting this anthropocentric impetus is Merold Westphal: "My own suggestion is that the heart of Kant's fundamental ontology . . . insofar as it is presented in the first Critique, is to be found in the Aesthetic's distinction between finite, receptive intuition, and divine, creative intuition." Westphal further observes:

> Using synonymously the honorific phrases "intellectual intuition" and "intuitive understanding," whose connotations would be something like "direct and comprehensive insight into the nature of reality," Kant calls attention to a necessary advance (analytic, I believe he would say), namely that knowledge so conceived is possible only if it is creative, and thus only for God.[31]

Westphal's reading of the first Critique finds support in the work of John Sallis, who notes that if it is true, as Kant says, that "intuition takes place only in so far as the object is given to us," then it is possible in principle to distinguish two forms of knowing "corresponding to the possibility that the giving may proceed from the side of the subject or from the side of the object. In the first case the subject would give itself the object; in the other case the object would give itself to the subject."[32]

Of all the commonplaces of modern philosophical discussion, none is more common than the depiction of Kant's "Copernican revolution" as a move to anthropocentrism. (Never mind that Copernicus's own revolution was precisely a paradigm shift *away from* geocentrism and thus away from the anthropocentric.) It is this philosophic commonplace, as much as anything, which has thrown modern theology off track. Thus the importance of arguing, *per contra*, that to have maintained a vigilant awareness of the distinction or difference between a (possible) divine way of knowing and the human way of knowing—and thus to have overthrown (or more sub-

tly, to have undermined) philosophy's implicit and longstanding anthropocentrism—is the real import of the Kantian revolution.[33]

The *Coram Deo*

Let us then follow Sallis's four-point delineation of the contrast. The first
of the two alternatives, a knowledge in which "the subject would give itself
the object," postulates an act in which the knowing of the object and the
creating of the object would be one and the same. Such is the mode of
knowing proper to God—should God exist. The reservation is important
because, in Sallis's terms, one associates such knowing with the divine "in
an emphatically empty way."[34] Neither demonstrating nor presupposing
the existence of God, one is simply saying this is the sort of knowledge
which befits the *notion* of God.

Even with such reservations, Sallis is able to describe this mode of knowing with some specificity. He does so on four counts, each of which affirms
in one way or another that divine knowing is characterized by *immediacy*;
that in the divine knowledge there is no shadow of separation or inadequacy. Thus there is no separation of subject from object, for in the case
of the divine "the object does not exist beyond (independently of) the
intuition."[35] Second, as regards intuition, this "original intuition is such
that from its very inception the object is posed in its *full presence*." The
intuition "is spared that indetermination which, testifying to a withheld
reserve, announcing . . . a certain *absence*, would shatter the mirror of full
presence."[36] Third, as regards intellect, there is no "reflection." That is to
say, there is no second moment following after intuition to clarify, correct,
or critique that which was distorted or lacking in the intuition, for the
simple reason that in this mode of knowing there *is* nothing lacking or
distorted in intuition. Now for Kant (and for many others) the whole aim
of intellect, the whole desire of intellect, as it were, is to know things as
they are. In the present mode of knowing, things are given to intuition
as they indeed are. In this sense it becomes possible to speak, in a paradoxical but crucial phrase which Kant himself employs, of an "*intellectual
intuition*."[37] Which is simply a way of saying (Sallis's final point) that there
is no separation or division between intellect and intuition. This is a knowing in which "intuition and thought . . . are fused into an essential unity."[38]

It is no accident that such a notion should seem difficult to entertain;
for intuition implies a certain *receptivity*, it implies that something is taken
in, whereas intellect entails an active spontaneity, a certain *positing*, as in
a judgment which takes the leap of affirming or positing that such-and-
such is in fact the case. It is thus paradoxical indeed to speak of a knowing
which simultaneously posits and receives. In our own kind of knowing
receptivity and activity are quite distinct; for this reason they are often

conceived as two discrete stages—first the mind takes sense data in, then it works it over. And yet for all that, the notion of intellectual intuition is little more than a gloss on the original description of a mode of knowing in which "the subject would give itself the object."

Once this hypothetical, divine knowing has been described under the theme of unity, it is a relatively easy matter to describe the human mode of knowing under the heading of a "fourfold fragmentation." For human knowing, subject and object cannot be one and the same; "as mere effects, mere modifications of the subject's receptivity, sensations cannot be regarded as corresponding to anything in the object itself" (26). Moreover, "in place of the thing in its singular unity there is given to human intuition only sensations"; and these "constitute only the 'matter' of appearances; they are devoid of form, utterly fragmentary, utterly lacking wholeness and unity (cf. B 129–30; A 99)" (27). Third, thought too, like intuition, suffers a certain partiality or disunity. While still a positing, it is insuperably dependent upon the sensible for content; it is thus "a positing *relative to* a 'given'" (27). And so, finally, there is "separation between receptivity and [positing or] spontaneity" (27). These are the contrasts which Sallis considers to be so fundamental as to establish the "interpretive horizon" for the entire Critique (12, 18). Sallis thus provides striking confirmation of the line of argument espoused by Hicks.

Granted, then, that the notion is present and operative in Kant, what role does it play? Hicks speaks of a twofold role, as limit and as ideal, and makes a persuasive case that the interplay of these two functions is a consistent thread running throughout the three Critiques. But everything depends on just *how* the two functions interrelate. The easiest and most natural formulation would be to say as ideal, the notion acts as a lure, an ideal of perfect knowledge to be pursued; and that as a limit, it reminds us of how far we have yet to go. It may never be possible to speak of human knowing as constituting, in godlike fashion, the very being of what it knows; but it would seem that one might speak of humankind as moving in that direction, through the progress of science and through the fashioning of a world which is increasingly penetrated by human values and aspirations. In the classical period, this is the direction indicated by Plotinus and the metaphor of the mind as light. In the modern period, it is the direction taken by the Enlightenment and by the idealists, who understood themselves to be simply following through on Kant's "Copernican revolution."

To make the idealist interpretation work, however, one has to assume that Kant reversed himself, and indeed reversed himself in the direction of ontotheology! One has to assume that the logic governing the indeterminate God of the first Critique is fundamentally different from that governing the infinite of Kant's essay on cosmogony. There Kant distilled his argument in a poetic exclamation, "Infinity! What measures thee? . . . To thee all numbers bow" (146). There Infinity was a reality in the face of which all finite hierarchies faded into insignificance: a reality, therefore, which could not be approached by any series of finite steps. For all the differences between precritical and critical philosophy, that reality seems much closer to the one delineated by Sallis's contrasts than does the divinity of the idealists, which must be in some sense and to some degree approachable, if not attainable—in some degree subject, in Kierkegaard's phrase, to a process of approximation.

In briefest terms, the Plotinian, idealist reasoning is as follows: (1) insofar as human knowing is active and creative, it is godlike; (2) insofar as it is godlike, it in some fashion approaches the divine. It is a line of reasoning which is very compelling, very attractive, and, once the initial premise has been given, very natural as well. It has inspired much of Romanticism in the various arts, quite apart from its impact in philosophy and theology.[39] Yet it is a prime instance of what Kant has termed the transcendental illusion.[40] Like most instances of the illusion, however, it makes, indirectly, an important point. For the extraordinary thing about Kant's thought, and the thing that makes it extraordinarily difficult, is that it *does* affirm the first proposition and yet does not affirm the second.

Remember that when the notion of a spontaneous, creative activity on the part of the subject is introduced in Edition B, it comes as a disturbing possibility, intimating there may be something going on in the knowing process of which we are not naturally aware. It is ironic that this neglected something should be, on Kant's hypothesis, the subject's own activity. But that only serves to drive home the point; it shows the subject does not have transparent knowledge, even with regard to the subject's own self. Now if one considers the disturbing character of Kant's initial question with the contrast case of divine "intellectual intuition" constantly in mind; and if the contrast is maintained consistently, without postulating some moment of presence, the result does not support the idealist assertion of some relative convergence between the human and the divine. For the comparison is simply not a relative comparison—at least not for those who know in a human manner. We finite knowers possess no overarching gauge by which to reckon nearer or further with respect to the divine. To have such a gauge would be the same as to have, in that respect at least, a sure knowledge of things as they are, an intellectual intuition. Conversely, maintaining the contrast case as a contrast case, thus being ever mindful that our knowledge is *not* that of an intellectual intuition, means renouncing the notion of such a gauge, and thus renouncing any process of approximation to the divine. This is the reasoning which permits Kant to affirm the first of the enumerated theses, yet not the second. Precisely *because* the subject has been active, and not simply a mirror, the situation has become clouded. And precisely because that activity is thoroughgoing—godlike in the sense that there is nothing that is known that escapes it—*everything* is for us mortals clouded. For us mortals, Kant is saying something about everything. As a result, there is for us no unmediated knowledge, no point of absolute contact, no presence.

What prevents this Kantian position from getting a hearing is the assumption that it must necessarily lead to relativism or nihilism. Commonsensically it would indeed seem that if our knowledge cannot "approach" to absolute knowledge, it can have no objectivity. But it is through such assumptions that common sense consorts with ontotheology. Calling this assumption into question, causing it to "tremble," opens the way for a renewed appreciation of Kant. The trembling may be sensed in what is the clearest point of contrast between Kant's transtheistic god and the god of ontotheology: namely, the fact that the former can perform its function (in Kant's thought) without needing to exist. In Sallis's phrase, this god is thought "in an emphatically empty way." In Kant's terms, it can be *thought* but not *known*. It is Kant's Archimedean point; but its position, unlike that of the god of ontotheology, is a position which we finite knowers cannot in any sense occupy. An Archimedean point which does its work without necessarily existing and without being occupied by those who use it, its function is to render our thought truly critical. To think critically, however, is not to be confused with thinking negatively, though those who charge Kant with an implicit relativism tend to do just that. To think critically about our knowledge is to think of it as specifically human knowledge, neither more nor less.

It is this mode of thinking which I wish to designate as thinking *coram Deo*. The Deus of such thinking, Kant's transtheistic concept of God, does indeed function as both limit and ideal, but in such a way as to transform our concept of both. It is a limit, indeed an insurmountable one, yet it does not simply negate or frustrate the human; it helps us better understand, and affirm, the human as human. And it is an ideal, but not one which we can approximate, even asymptotically, as a type 1 position might suggest. Rather it is an ideal in its "insistence," in the manner in which it disturbs us and presses itself upon us—in much the way that the truth question is, as we have seen, a question which cannot be disavowed.

V

THE OTHERNESS OF
THE ETHICAL

" *'You must love the Lord your God with all your heart, with all your soul, and with all your mind.'* This is the greatest and the first commandment" (Matt. 22:37–40). We consider it a truism that the one thing which cannot be compelled is love. Yet there it is, explicitly at the heart of the Christian gospel: "You must love . . . " "This is the . . . commandment." How can this be? Perhaps it is possible only if there should be a difference between commanding and compelling. Perhaps it is possible only if there should be a peculiar sort of command which does *not* compel, which speaks neither of punishment nor reward—a command which, like Barth's Gospel, "does not expound or recommend itself . . . does not negotiate or plead, threaten, or make promises," but rather "withdraws when it is not listened to for its own sake."[1]

Such a command might indeed be a gift to Christian theology. For, quite apart from the particulars of Freudian, Marxist, or Nietzschean analysis, Christian theology has always labored under a certain suspicion. The suspicion is aroused by blatant efforts to sell the Christian message, to make of it a commodity—Jesus as "the best fire insurance." But in principle the suspicion applies to our more sophisticated forms as well. For as Buber reminds us, loving another means loving that other *for his or her own sake.* But if the gospel is a gospel of salvation, and if, then, we love God in order to be saved, is this not an insidious hypocrisy? Does Christian "charity" not become a sly, roundabout way of saving one's own eternal skin?[2]

This is why Christian spirituality has consistently had at its core a process of *askesis.* In the background of the present chapter is a reading of Kierkegaard, whereby Kierkegaard becomes guide to the theological pertinence of Kant. While the Kierkegaard reading cannot be developed in its own right here, it is important to say that it is one for which "the ethical" is more than a momentary station on the way to "the religious."

The ethical becomes the crucial *test*, the needle's eye through which all else must pass.[3]

The present chapter examines the second Critique in light of these concerns. The first section treats the requirement that the distinctive reality of the ethical not be subverted to other, extrinsic ends. The second section introduces an existential dimension by describing the price a concrete, struggling human being may pay in the effort to honor the ethical. The third dwells upon the peculiar sort of reality which the ethical, understood as categorical imperative, represents. In the fourth the notion of *reward*, which insistence on the autonomy of the ethical has steadfastly bracketed, is surprisingly reintroduced, under the heading of the Highest Good. By the same gesture issues of theodicy also reemerge, but in an importantly different manner. Pursuing the consequent, altered approach to theodicy, we will draw out implications for two key issues of theological method: the role of existentialism (the fulcral type 2 of our typology) and the critique of the idealist diamond.

Opening the Second Critique

Critics often complain of a Kantian "rigorism." The effect is to impute to Kant's moral theory something rigid and puritanical. The critics point in particular to the first theorem of *The Critique of Practical Reason*, which denies that any principle presupposing "an object . . . of the faculty of desire" can provide a proper basis for moral conduct.[4]

But Kant does not arrive at this position arbitrarily. Within the theorem itself he indicates that the problem with principles which are predicated upon human desires is that they are "empirical." With this term Kant recalls a distinction made at the outset of his study, between two kinds of imperative:

> imperatives determine either the conditions of causality of a rational being as an efficient cause only in respect to its effect and its sufficiency to bring this effect about, or they determine only the will, whether it is adequate to the effect or not. In the former case, imperatives would be *hypothetical* and would contain only precepts of skill; in the latter case, on the contrary, they would be *categorical* and would alone be practical laws.[5]

This is no minor distinction. It is not too much to claim that at stake is the question of whether there can *be* a second Critique at all.[6] By their nature, imperatives of the first sort are predicated upon a calculation of cause and effect. They are "empirical" in that they operate in a manner which has already been described in the study of understanding in the first Critique. Doubtless there is some difference between saying "Given that there exists effect B, there probably existed cause A" and saying "Given that you wish to achieve result B, you should probably perform act A." But if *that* is all the difference that remains between a study of pure reason and a study of practical reason, or between empirical knowledge and morality, then it is hard to see what all the fuss regarding the distinctive character of morality is about.

In addressing this central (one might well say, "foundational") question, Kant proves to be the advocate of a strikingly contemporary hermeneutic of suspicion. He refuses to accept as ultimately decisive the classical distinctions between "lower" and "higher" objects of desire. In Theorem II he insists: "All material practical principles [i.e., all principles which "presuppose" an object (material) of the faculty of desire] are, as such, of one and the same kind and belong under the general principle of self-love or one's own happiness" (20). This said, he then proceeds to drive home the implications of a fundamental sameness. Anticipating Freud, he rejects a hierarchy of desires based on whether the satisfaction has its "origin in the senses or in the understanding" (21). Indeed he mocks those who, positing ever higher, ever more refined and ethereal objects of desire, "imagine matter as so subtle, so supersubtle, that they almost get dizzy considering it" (23). In a passage which may have influenced Kierkegaard, and which is in any case worthy of him, Kant berates

> our syncretistic age, when a certain shallow and dishonest system of coalition between contradictory principles is devised because it is more acceptable to a public which is satisfied to know a little about everything and at bottom nothing, thus playing the jack-of-all-trades. (23)

Like Kierkegaard, Kant presses an either/or: "Either, then, no higher faculty of desire exists, or else pure reason alone must itself be practical" (23). That is to say, either pure reason, in treating practical matters, does no more than calculate cause and effect, assessing the alternatives in terms of probable satisfaction, in which case the talk of morality and of some distinctive and "higher" exercise of reason comes to nothing—or reason, when it engages in practical matters, does so in a way which has its own integrity, its own autonomy, i.e., in a way which is distinctly other.

This, then, is the point. When morality makes its appearance in Kant's philosophy, it does so under the aspect of otherness. The overriding question in the opening pages of this Critique is not one of rigorism, more or less; it is not whether to plunk for this or that particular form of morality. Rather, to borrow the language of the third Critique, the question is whether the exercise of reason in practical matters is sufficiently distinctive to constitute a different "realm"; or whether it is simply a secondary variation on the exercise already adequately described within the first Critique.[7] Kant answers that it can be distinctive if, in practical matters, reason can ground its activity entirely in a *form*—a form derived from reason itself—rather than relying upon some object, as happens when one predicates one's activity upon the thing desired, i.e., upon a goal or *telos*.

The Wound of Reason

The specific form Kant proceeds to derive is of course the categorical imperative. "So act that the maxim of your will could always hold at the same time as a principle establishing universal law" (30). Regarding the charge of rigorism, note that there is nothing within the imperative which requires inordinate self-denial. The imperative may be regarded as a formula for fairness and justice, which need not entail renunciation of pleasure and satisfaction. Indeed, the only requirement is that the formal imperative should be the "basis"—in the sense not so much of "foundation" as of fundamental test. Ample room is allowed for a whole range of cases which would meet the test *and* be pleasurable as well. To pleasure of this innocent variety, neither Kant nor the imperative object.

Still and all, while there is no problem in principle, there remains a problem in practice. Ronald Green has written an illuminating study of the religious implications of Kant's moral theory. Green distinguishes among (1) *theoretical reason*, which is the particular domain of the first Critique; (2) hypothetical or *prudential reason*, which is theoretical reason exercised with an eye toward (short-term or long-term) reward; and (3) *moral reason*—the distinctive exercise which is the concern of the second Critique.[8] Adopting these terms, we can say that what Kant's categorical imperative requires is merely that moral reason *have priority* over prudential reason. It does not require that the voice of prudential reason be stifled. To the contrary: because moral reason remains so formal in its prescriptions, there *needs* to be that concrete, pragmatic perspective as well.

Thus once again there is no conflict—in principle. But difficulties do arise the moment one enters upon the tenacious ambiguity inherent in everyday life. As a case study Green offers the imaginary account of an officer who is "commanding a platoon of soldiers in a guerilla war." Bracketing for the sake of argument the question of the justice of the war, Green focuses upon one particular incident. The platoon finds itself "in the environs of a small peasant village whose inhabitants the guerillas resemble. . . . "[9] Green continues:

> Imagine the worst to occur. . . . Approaching the village, the officer perceives a group of figures, apparently armed, moving menacingly in his direction across the fields. Nervous and naturally concerned for the safety of

his troops, he orders his men to open fire. Drawing near, he discovers a
group of injured and dying peasants with only their work implements and
no weapons at all.[10]

If the officer is a person of conscience, he is bound to experience moral
pain as he contemplates the result of his decision. The source of his anguish, abstractly expressed, is the fact that moral reason requires of him
strict impartiality (i.e., it requires that he not rate his own well being or
that of his men any higher than that of the peasants who, he knew, might
be in the area)—while simultaneously prudential reason demands that, so
far as possible, he care for himself and the men in his charge.

Green depicts the "friction" of war, how easily the unintended can happen. Here we have a case of anguished choice in face of irreducible ambiguity, the recurrent theme of existentialism. One would not expect a
close connection between the pain of such situations and the abstract matters which Kant the rationalist treated in the *first* Critique. Yet connections
there are, and the more one looks, the closer they seem. First, the ambiguity with which the soldier was struggling is an instance of what we, reading Kant via Derrida, have called *undecidability*. The partially discernible
figures, the unfamiliar terrain, each sound signaling perhaps an approaching enemy: in that situation there is no presence, no clear point of reference. Yet this is by no means an isolated case. Encountered in a novel by
Sartre or Camus (as well it might be), it would be read as depicting the
ambiguity and the necessity of choice which inhere in the human condition, even down to so simple an act as that of perception. In Kantian
terms, all human cognition involves an act of synthesis. For struggling
mortals, no intellectual intuition.

Ambiguity is thus the first link between the situation of the soldier and
the human situation as portrayed by Kant already in the first Critique.
For a further link, consider the point to which Green most draws attention. The soldier, like every moral agent, has two guides: moral reason,
requiring impartiality, and prudential reason, with its eye for the main
chance. He has two faculties which are qualitatively different and he has
a capacity for free decision. But that's it. *There exists within his rational
makeup no further agency or criterion which can tell him how to arbitrate between the two.* For prudential reason, the bottom line is the survival of
those elements which are necessary in order to achieve the desired goal.
For moral reason, impartiality is the sine qua non; it is what is required
categorically. Neither criterion reduces to the other; they are *equiprimordial*. Now "equiprimordial" is the term we used to clarify the relation of
sense and intellect, matter and form, within the first Critique. We saw how
equiprimordiality accounted for the impossibility of presence, rendering
untranscendable (if I may be allowed such a term) the fact of human finitude. In the present case those same themes reappear in a more exis-

tential key; equiprimordiality again entails a situation of untranscendable finitude. Viewing matters through the eyes of one engaged and responsible, we see the harsh logic by which finitude gives rise to moral anguish.

The neglected fact is that the reason of which the two Critiques treat is one and the same. It is simply viewed a propos of different activities. Finite in the one case, human reason proves finite in the other as well. Neither the flights of speculation nor the depths of engagement offer egress from the human condition. Moreover, there exists *between* the two activities of reason a similar condition of equiprimordiality. Though we cannot pursue the topic in the present context, we may note the crucial consequence that in order to account for the tensions and divisions within human experience, *one does not need to set reason over against something else.* In the fine phrase of Pierre Thévenaz, "what one says of reason, one ought to say of the human being, and vice-versa."[11] The divisions are already there *within* reason itself, by virtue of its being simultaneously moral and pragmatic. In the abstract, that is marvelous versatility; concretely, it spells pain and conflict. As a result "the wound of reason" acquires a further sense. No longer a disruption which reason visits upon an otherwise harmonious humanity, it becomes instead *reason's own wound*, a wound which reason bears within itself: from reason wounding to reason wounded.

A final connection between first Critique and second has to do with the understanding of the self. Here again a point which remained abstract in the first Critique becomes existential in the second. Behind the platoon leader's question "Did I do the right thing?" lurks another which is still more unsettling—"What sort of person *am* I, after all?" The question is troubling indeed. Yet Kant holds that there exists no straightforward intuition of self to provide the answer; and his taking this position is not simply a function of epistemological reserve. It has to do with his very notion of the subject. In Hicks's terse formulation, "the practical will is no more than the theoretical understanding, unmediatedly determinative of itself as subject."[12] Translating "unmediatedly determinative of itself" into existentialist terms: what there is, is first freedom (though Kant would add, freedom confronted by the imperative) and as a result of freedom, inescapable responsibility. The determination is unmediated: no other subject or thing is there to blame.

Undoubtedly, Kant's talk of "mediation" can seem opaque. Once clarified, however, it proves telling. The subject *determines* itself directly, unmediatedly. The person makes his or her own decisions; such is freedom. But the subject does not *know* itself directly; it knows itself only by way of the acts it performs in the world. Moreover the acts themselves are not accomplished in unmediated fashion; it is an aspect of human finitude that our acts must proceed by way of a complex network of cause and effect, where results are no more than probable and causes are multiple.

Our acts are mediated, in short, by a world which is irreducibly ambiguous. Thus the situation we have seen, in which the moral agent must decipher her nature from the tea leaves of her actions.

Finally, the screw of suspicion must be given one last turn. For it is not enough that the moral agent tally up the actions and say, "In the larger scheme of things, I've more good acts than bad, so I can't really be such a bad person after all." Such assurances may assuage "the easy conscience of modern man,"[13] but they do not placate Kant any more than Freud. Honesty requires recognition that "lower" purposes take on the guise of the "higher"; and that, as the writers of fiction have long observed, one can pass a lifetime performing "good" acts, all for an ulterior purpose, such as thinking well of oneself. In such cases the entire house of cards, the entire history of good appearance, can be threatened by a slip of the tongue, an isolated act, which suggests some unacknowledged truth. To be consistent in self-scrutiny, thus, the soldier must reflect, "I had been behaving well enough before this happened—but maybe all that good behavior is just me trying to curry the favor of those around me. Maybe this time for once, under pressure, the truth came out."

A dramatization of this question is provided by popular culture, in an episode from the television series "L. A. Law." After a succession of short-lived affairs, one of the principal characters surprises his friends and perhaps himself by getting married. Some time later he is unfaithful to his wife, "just once." When she learns of his infidelity, he assures her that "it was an isolated incident." She responds, "No, Arnie, it's who you are," and she divorces him. What one person regards as an isolated incident, another sees as the moment of truth. Officials caught in wrongdoing like to speak of having made "an error of judgment." That way of putting it is designed to isolate the issue, precluding it from being taken as an index of the person's moral character. Congressional confirmation hearings have the task of deciding whether particular statements and acts are to be disregarded, or taken as revelatory of "who you are." Recent discussions of the activities of Martin Heidegger and Paul de Man during the fascist period show how painful such examination can be.[14] Finally, an example from our own collective history, having to do with who we are as Americans, is the decision to drop the atomic bomb on Japan. The parallels with Green's case are unsettling. Were those distant figures, those citizens of Hiroshima, a threat to us? Would their implements become weapons, as some of them said? The clash of moral and prudential issues is vivid in Paul Fussell's essay, "Thank God for the Atom Bomb" and in Michael Walzer's response.[15]

A well-conditioned reflex tells us "not to be so hard" on ourselves. But deflecting the question may only force underground the troubling awareness that as rational beings we despise hypocrisy and require, as sine qua non, *some* form of authenticity or consistency. The troubling implication is that, simply as rational, moral beings, we *are* hard, we are "rigorous." Some unmeasured amount of the pain of contemporary culture may derive from our relentless effort to reduce the voice of conscience, the voice of the otherness of the ethical, to psychological dynamics. The evasion is identified by the fact that even in the effort at diminishment, we are not consistent. We apply a quasi-Freudian reductionism to those with whom we disagree, while reserving for ourselves the gentler ministrations of a humanistic psychology. Cynicism for others, compassion for ourselves: such is the psychology of "Christendom." "The majority of men are subjective toward themselves and objective toward all others, terribly objective sometimes, but the real task is in fact to be objective toward oneself and subjective toward all others."[16] In such straits, it may be that Kantian "rigorism" is but the promise of honesty.

Imperative as Contextualization

Theology in our century has sought to thread its way between the pitfalls Tillich helpfully described as those of heteronomy and autonomy. In the effort to trace that path, the notion of a categorical imperative would seem of little value. As late as the third Critique Kant wrote, "The moral law, as the formal rational condition of the use of our freedom, obliges us by itself alone, without depending on any purpose as material condition."[17] To the contemporary ear, the words breathe an air of stern heteronomy. One mistake of this common assessment is that it separates Kant's moral from his transcendental thought; it ignores, if you will, the alchemy which is peculiar to transcendental thought. Conversely, nothing better illustrates the significance of the transcendental than its impact in the area of morality. In a powerful study entitled *L'Impératif catégorique*, Jean-Luc Nancy, one of the contemporary French philosophers most closely associated with Derrida, sets forth a line of thinking paralleling that argued here.[18] In the present section I shall take advantage of this complementarity by mingling my own reflections with Nancy's.

"The injunction," Nancy writes, "is more and less than an order." It is less in that "it does not threaten, it does not compel action—and the imperative as such is totally deprived of the power to carry out" (20). It is, in this regard, a still, small voice: threatening no punishment, offering no reward (17). Were it to do either, it would betray itself, forsaking moral in favor of prudential reason. Yet by the same token—because it is categorical and not hypothetical-prudential—the imperative is also *more* than an order. It "humbles" reason, it "imposes itself the way a *fact* imposes itself." Nancy goes so far as to liken Kant to Nietzsche in that the imperative presents itself as a given, like a constraint of nature (83). Yet even at so distant a point we cannot speak of heteronomy; for while it is indeed a sort of fact, it is a *factum rationis*, a fact *of reason* (21). That is to say, it is born from within reason by reason's own laws. Being transcendental, it belongs to "the condition of the possibility of a reason which professes to be, in its own right, practical" (19). In current discourse, a holistic view of the human being is a generally acknowledged desideratum; less appreciated is the inherent difficulty of achieving holism without eclecticism. But the elements of the whole cannot be thrust together arbitrarily. "Eclecticism is always the enemy of dialectic," recalling Ricoeur. This is the context in which Nancy makes, for his own part, the observation that one and the same reason is interrogated in the two critiques. In the second Critique reason, pure reason, is examined as regards its actions. But "to act *as pure reason* is to make law" (19).

The reason transcendental reflection escapes the alternatives of autonomy and heteronomy is that it reveals law and freedom are equally nonderivative.

> Thus the law is *addressed to* a freedom, and is not *founded by* that freedom. Conversely, freedom consists not of following one's own law . . . but of initiating something by oneself: it is a freedom to inaugurate, in advance of any law. And yet it is this very freedom which is, from the very beginning, engaged by the law. In short, there are always two "origins" here, which do not overlap and each of which seems endlessly, in its turn, to take precedence over the other: the address by the law and the free beginning. (30)

Admittedly this is not the way the resolution of autonomy and heteronomy is normally imagined. Quite naturally one longs for a solution which would "transcend the alternatives" and produce . . . produce what? On reflection, the very notion of transcendence—not to be confused with the transcendental—and *a fortiori* the notion of "transcending alternatives" suggest that unity has the final word. In such a case, would otherness really have been recognized? Wouldn't the balance have tipped toward autonomy, indeed autonomy of an especially ambitious sort? It would be autonomy paying lip service to otherness while limiting the field to an other existing solely *within* reason, as an other which reason "gives to itself"! Such an act of "auto-presentation" is precisely what the idealist diamond depicts. The provisional other of the second stage is reabsorbed, early or late, into the third and final stage. Indeed one can say that for the idealist the whole *point* of the process is to make it apparent—to the subject—that the process has been one of, precisely, auto-presentation (99).

For Nancy the imperative cannot be reduced to such unfolding of "truth as *homoiôsis*."[19] That understanding of truth is ruled out from the very beginning, i.e., from the point of supposed *archē*. For, as we saw in the long quotation of a moment ago, the very character of the imperative as categorical implies that law and freedom are equally nonderivative; it implies what we have called a condition of *equiprimordiality*. It implies that there is no single *archē*, no antecedent oneness for the self to recover. This has implications at the level of concrete judgment making. It means our decisions are not certified by some underlying fit, correspondence, or unity. They are rather surrounded—contextualized—by a condition of undecidability. Yet this does not negate the making of concrete decisions. Just as Derrida affirmed that undecidability provides the condition for the possibility of concrete decisions, so Nancy avers that "uncertainty is constitutive of judgment" (45).

"Transcendental," I have suggested, is a term Kant introduces in order to clear space for the possibility that that which determines or conditions may be fundamentally *different* from the determined or conditioned. That proposal is borne out here: on Kantian premises, truth is no more a matter of *homoiôsis* than it is a matter of presence. That upon which truth is grounded is different from truth; as Heidegger would have it, truth itself is not true.[20] Or as Nancy puts it, to state "the true on the true" is impossible. But this does not mean there *is* no truth. It is a matter of our being contextualized. Thus Nancy writes, "the imperative does not belong to the nature of the subject; it belongs to that which, while resembling a subject, absolutely exceeds the rule of the subject" (18). With the imperative as with truth, the point upon which we need to meditate is that there emerges *from* "*within*" the subject that which "exceeds" the subject, contextualizing it. Having said that pronouncing "the true on the true" is impossible, Nancy proceeds to strike the crucial balance by adding "the true on the true is impossible *in truth*." He then observes, "it is by this 'in truth'—ever enigmatic, a sort of vertiginous darkness at the heart of the *skepsis*, a blindspot in the middle of the eye—that truth is drawn out of itself" (94). To Anglo-Saxon ears the rhetoric seems overwrought, but the essential point is one which is confirmed in every act of human judgment. For every such act is, on Kant's account, a *compositio*. It is a bringing together of disparate realities, a particular intuition and a particular concept. "If the *ratio* is the same for all, judgment varies according to the individual" (46). The act of judgment proceeds with no intellectual intuition to guide it, no "truth as *homoiôsis*" to undergird it. So it can be said that "the Kantian critique, because it is constructed upon the act of judgment, is the *opus philosophicum incertum* par excellence" (46).

Accordingly, the situation envisaged by the second Critique proves consistent with that described by the first. Nancy argues, contra Emmanuel Levinas, that the goal is not to exalt the ethical over against the theoretical, but rather to sharpen, to bring to crisis, certain issues inherent to thought and discourse as such (125). To play upon Nancy's words, there is within truth a "gaping obscurity," but the obscurity is there "*in truth*." There is a wound, but there is also truth; for the wound is reason's own. In this connection Nancy says that the law "abandons" us. "The categorical imperative is perhaps no more than a transformation of the tragic truth that destiny is essentially an abandonment. The law abandons—to itself" (29). The imperative, remember, "is both more and less than an order" (20). It binds absolutely, yet is "merely" transcendental. It leads to nothing "real"—neither punishment nor reward.

Only by confronting the otherness of the ethical can one begin to envision a way beyond autonomy and heteronomy. It is in this sense that "the ethical" is a test. It sets before us the meaning of a truly human, truly finite transcendence:

> It is Kant's famous fourth question, on which Heidegger concentrated his analysis of finitude. That question should, therefore, be posed as follows: what sort of being is it which is founded, fixed in its very truth by a *received order*? What ontology—if it is an ontology—is implied by such a radical dependence—which is yet a dependence upon nothing, upon nothing which has power and upon nothing which can be verified, represented or presented (112)?[21]

The Return of Theodicy

Ethics textbooks point to Kant as the paradigmatic case of a "deontological" ethic. Derived from the Greek *deon*, "duty," "deontology" denotes that theory of ethics "which holds that at least some acts are morally obligatory regardless of their consequence for human weal or woe."[22] The contrasting position, exemplified by Aristotle and Aquinas, derives from the conviction that each being has an inherent nature which it naturally strives to fulfill. Children have an impetus toward realizing their full humanity, just as seedlings have a penchant toward becoming trees. Each being is possessed of an inherent purpose or *telos* which provides the point of reference for moral judgments. This "teleological" ethic affirms what Kant denied, viz. that the moral worth of an act may be judged by the concrete result it seeks to achieve.

The contrast could hardly be clearer. We, for our part, have devoted three fairly laborious sections to showing why Kant stands on the one side of the divide rather than the other. It comes as a jolt, therefore, when Kant blithely proceeds to spend a substantial portion of the second Critique discussing the *verboten* topic, the ends which various actions aim to achieve. More perplexing still is the fact that Kant introduces and in some sense affirms the notion most dear to the classical teleological tradition, that of a "Highest Good" uniting all lesser goods within itself.[23] It really does look as if Kant were playing both sides of the street; as if the arch-advocate of consistency were ignoring his own admonitions. Many have charged that at this point Kant does indeed tumble into incoherence. Some follow Schopenhauer in charging Kant with hypocrisy. However "high" the "Highest," Kant's talk of a Highest Good is taken as evidence of an implicit promise of happiness, of reward, hidden within the Kantian ethic "like a secret article, the presence of which makes all else only a sham contract. It is not really the reward of virtue, but yet is a voluntary gift, for which virtue, after work accomplished, stealthily holds its hand open."[24]

The criticism has a familiar ring. It echoes the suspicion regarding Christian faith with which the present chapter began: Christianity claims to act out of love of God and love of neighbor, then it holds out its hand for eternal reward. So we have succeeded in one thing, at any rate. We have shown that the Kantian ethic reflects both sides of the argument. It contains a discussion of the Highest Good, the eternal fulfillment which critics claims must vitiate the notion of selfless charity, *and* it contains in Kant's deontological ethic an exemplary statement of why such considerations should *not* be a factor. Kant's own thought is thus a microcosm of the debate, which is one of the most crucial for Christian theology. But how can the inclusiveness be consistent? A common defense is to appeal to Kant's own distinction between an action's basis and its object. The mere fact that an action is apt to secure a certain object does not mean that it was necessarily chosen *in order to* get that object. It is still possible that the particular course of action was chosen because of a certain rule.

The defense is valid in principle; but in an age of suspicion it seems disingenuous. Hence the importance of determining why Kant should have courted the charge of inconsistency in the first place. What were his positive reasons for introducing all the talk about objects and ends? The explanation lies, I believe, with what might be termed, as counterpoint to Kant's putative rigorism, his *moral realism*. By this I mean his sober awareness of the sort of being the human agent really is. Kant is a rationalist, no doubt; but a rationalist of a peculiarly chastened sort. He knows full well that while the formal imperative (and the will which is determined to act according to the imperative) must be the basis for an act's morality, they are not enough to assure the act's accomplishment. To accomplish the act, the will must needs enlist the cooperation of *desire*; and for that, right principles are not enough. If desire is to be stirred, there must be an object. On this point Kant, for all his rationalism, never wavers. He is acerbic toward those who repeat the Stoic dictum that virtue is its own reward; he will not permit the object of moral action to be dissolved in tautology. The test is the concrete human agent. That agent's acts have a material aspect. Therefore there must be a material object.[25]

Nor is that all. If Kant speaks of the object of human action, it is not just as a concession to desire. Rather, *reason itself requires an object*. Reason itself must acknowledge that (except insofar as it remains totally formal, reflecting only upon itself) it does not bear its object within itself. Again Kant distinguishes himself from the Stoics, exhibiting a greater realism. In marked contrast to the Stoic ideal of self-sufficiency, Kant's moral agent is avowedly *a being of needs*.[26] Moreover the need is not confined to the "lower" realm: *need proves to be inherent in human reason per se*.

Something like the Stoic view of the perfection of Reason, both human and divine, is at the root of the classical notion of impassability. Given recent rethinking of impassability, the present issue must be of decisive importance for Christian theology.[27] Significantly, Kant's way of securing the crucial point is by way of contrast. He postulates the notion of a very different sort of agency, which he denominates a Holy Will. For *that* sort of agency, to will something would be equivalent to accomplishing it. There would be none of the mediation which we have seen to be so inherent to the human; no detours through a causal order which is other than the Will, no harnessing of desire. Which is to say that not only would there be no external mediation, no mediation between self and world— beyond that there would be no internal mediation, no mediation between various aspects of the self. For the human, in contrast to such a Holy Will, there *is* such mediation—because two aspects of the self, the one formal and the other material, are equiprimordial. Neither is absorbed by the other; the internal difference is irreducible.

Clearly we encounter here a mode of reasoning which recalls the use of Intellectual Intuition in the first Critique. In both cases human finitude is set in bold relief by virtue of the contrast between it and (the concept of) an infinite reality. In both cases the effect of the contrast is to relativize the hierarchies and oppositions which we tacitly assume, and to dissolve the apparent presences. It is because of this clarity, this awareness of what the human agent is *not*, that Kant refuses to view the problems of moral agency in gnostic fashion, as if a quasi-infinite will or reason were tragically enmeshed in human matter. This argument by way of rigorous contrast, which we are entitled to regard as further instance of the *coram Deo*, is the premise of Kant's moral realism.

Having reached this connective point, let us pause to review. As a way of doing so, we may consider at several levels the *distinctiveness* of Kant's position. (1) To begin with, the deontological position is itself a bit peculiar. It bucks the tendency, shared by classical philosophy and common sense alike, to judge the morality of an act by the intended result. And Kant is more than an instance of the deontological position, he is its virtual founder and paradigm case; it is hard to find a clearcut case before him, and those who come after are obviously in his debt. That already places him in a distinct minority. But then (2) he proceeds to incorporate elements of the opposing, teleological position. He speaks warmly of the role in philosophy of the classical conception of the Highest Good.[28] This isolates him even within his own camp, for the Highest Good is a notion which many deontologists feel themselves bound to resist. And yet (3) Kant's rationale for introducing the notion of the Highest Good and his understanding of its status are not those of *either* a traditional teleologist or a traditional deontologist. It is as if Kant meant the Highest Good to comprise within itself the conflict between the teleological and the deontological. It is as if Kant had positioned the notion in such a way that it might be shaped by the very struggle.

However that may be, we find ourselves at a point where Kant's distinctiveness has begun to teeter toward sheer oddity. The charge of inconsistency must now be faced. At issue is the programmatic question of our own study—whether reason, as reason, is capable of respecting its other. Kant's transcendental method is, on my understanding, a process whereby reason, operating in accordance with its own laws, comes to recognize itself as being no more than equiprimordial. (What reason needs to claim for itself in response to the hermeneutic of suspicion is equiprimordiality, neither more nor less.) How does reason accomplish this gesture of self-contextualizing acknowledgment? Within the transcendental context, reason must of course adhere to its own laws. It cannot deny itself, at pain of ceasing to be itself; for reason is nothing if not consistent. Because the fidelity of reason to its own laws is so primary, the deontological character of Kant's position must remain primary. (Not that there cannot be other considerations, but rational consistency is the first and crucial test. Whatever other considerations there be, they must pass by way of this requirement.) But precisely as an exercise of its capacities, human reason *can* have an (empty) concept of a self-sufficient reason, i.e., an Intellectual Intuition and a Holy Will; and reason can recognize that it itself is *not* that. This is thinking *coram Deo*.

From this chastened capacity, several consequences flow. (1) As the contrast exhibits in harshest terms human reason's finitude and dependence, human reason is able to recognize that, quite apart from the influences of desire and the like, it is itself, as reason, "a creature of need." It is able to recognize that the moment it seeks to do anything more than simply reflect upon itself (which is, to repeat, a meaningful and yet empty and formal exercise), it requires an object outside itself. It also follows that (2) the object in question must ultimately be one single object. For if reason were to remain ultimately divided among a variety of objects, there would be no guarantee of consistency. Thus *on his own premises* Kant arrives at the concept of a Highest Good (as well as a thorough-going anticipation of Kierkegaard's insistence that "purity of heart is to will one thing").

Finally, (3) reason itself requires that the Highest Good be *at least possibly realizable*. This important point is illumined by the commentary of Alan Wood.[29] The argument runs as follows. It is not reasonable to pursue an end which cannot possibly be realized. If the Highest Good were in no way capable of realization, pursuit of it would be rationally absurd. But

not to pursue it would be morally reprehensible. As Kant explains in the
Lectures on Philosophical Theology,

> Our moral faith is a practical postulate, through which anyone who denies
> it can be brought *ad absurdum practicum.* An *absurdum logicum* is an incon-
> sistency in judgments. There is an *absurdum practicum,* however, when it is
> shown that if I deny this or that I would have to be a scoundrel
> [*Bösewicht*].[30]

Note that Kant gets to this point (cf. the theological criterion of "ortho-
praxy") by pressing reason's own requirement, the requirement of consistency. Is there to be an inconsistency between reason and morality?
Recalling the story of the platoon leader, the question may be put as
whether there is ultimately—in the final, final reckoning—a contradiction
between prudential reason, which demands that success at least be possible, and moral reason, which cleaves to the imperative. To this question,
it is Saul Bellow who has given the best response: "it depends upon the
universe, what it is."[31] It does indeed depend on whether the world is
finally such as to make a mockery of our deepest moral requirement.
What Kant offers in this regard is, as Ronald Green observes, "a very
small opening." But it is an opening. He demonstrates that the nature of
things is *not necessarily* implacably hostile. He shows that it is not inherently
absurd to believe that reality *may* be such as to permit realization of the
Highest Good. It is just possible that the murderer will not finally triumph
over the innocent victim.[32] A very small aperture, this Kantian opening.
But given that the alternative is for reason to deny itself, to become unreasonable—a course which can equally be termed "unreasonable" or "in-
authentic"—it is enough. The possibility, however uncertain, is enough to
warrant continuance in the human struggle to act in a rational, moral
manner.

By way of conclusion, let us retrieve Adorno's dictum that behind all
genuine thinking there lies some spontaneous impulse which is "at once
preserved and surpassed." In the foregoing reflections, which bring us to
the portal of the actual postulates of practical reason, we may discern the
return within Kant's properly critical thought, of the precritical theodicy
issue. The angry protest Kant attributed to the child (who stands for all
persons and thus in some degree for Kant himself) has indeed been surpassed. The surpassing is attested by the fact that the issue returns, initially, in an entirely *formal* manner, viz. as a question of consistency. It
bears the imprint of its long detour by way of reason. But there is also
the preserving. For despite its having been submitted to a strict formal
test, despite its having passed through that needle's eye, the issue as it
reappears has not been *reduced to* something merely formal. *It returns under
its material aspect as well.* For reason, as we have said, is able to recognize

itself as no more than equiprimordial. It is able to recognize that the material desires have also their rightful claim. A propos of his moral realism, we noted Kant's denial that virtue can be its own reward. Now we may say that in taking that stand, Kant the rationalist kept faith with the protesting child.

We are indeed creatures of need. Gratification may be postponed; the object of gratification may be transformed, for the sake of inclusiveness and impartiality, in a highest end. But that end, when and if it arrives, had better be material. And it had better be good.

Rational Existentialism

The objection may be voiced, however, that even if Kant's critical thought can with effort be construed as a sublation of theodicy, it remains unclear that doing so is worth the effort. Abstractions such as "teleological" and "deontological," the long, laborious process of relating second Critique to first—what have these to say to the anguish of our time?

In response I shall argue that even when it is most immediate and intuitive—and in fact, especially when it is so—the theodicy question bears within itself an internal knot, an impacted complexity, which but for the help of Kant we might not be able to decipher. We have seen that classical theodicy relies upon two conceptual pillars (which were then supplemented by the principle of plenitude): the "big picture" and (in Leibnitz particularly) the limits of compossibility. Now the exasperating thing about the appeal to the big picture is that it does have a formal validity. In principle, it can never be refuted. For whatever the counterevidence which is brought to bear, the apology can fall back to an ever-enlarging picture, an ever-expanding time frame. Kant himself provided a (precritical) example when he appealed to "millions and whole myriads of millions of centuries." Who can gainsay that in *that* perspective, today's evil may turn out to have been for the good?

Logically, no one can. Yet *nevertheless* the modern protest does deny just that! This is what is so remarkable. The characteristically modern formulation of the theodicy question insists on drawing the line.[33] It insists on saying, "Bugger the big picture, some things are simply wrong!" e. e. cummings has a poem which begins, "i sing of Olaf glad and big / whose warmest heart recoiled at war . . ."[34] It contains a description of torture, and then these lines:

> Olaf (upon what were once knees)
> does almost ceaselessly repeat
> "there is some shit I will not eat"

That is how we want to speak about Nazism and the Holocaust. And, in another key, it is how Ivan speaks to Alyosha in *The Brothers Karamazov*. They have talked at length about the Christian promise of paradise, about the socialist promise of utopia, about a variety of *teloi* and justifications, and about the horrors sanctioned by such appeals. Now Ivan leans forward and says with utmost earnestness, "Listen! If all must suffer to pay for the eternal harmony, what have children to do with it, tell me, please? It's beyond all comprehension why they should suffer, and why they should pay for the harmony." And then:

> "Tell me yourself, I challenge you—answer. Imagine that you are creating a fabric of human destiny with the object of making men happy in the end, giving them peace and rest at last, but that it was essential and inevitable to torture to death only one tiny creature—that baby beating its breast with its fist, for instance—and to found that edifice on its unavenged tears, would you consent to be the architect on these conditions? Tell me, and tell me the truth."
>
> "No, I wouldn't consent," said Alyosha softly.[35]

When the question is put this way, our response is intuitive. Some things are simply intolerable, regardless of the larger context. Some things are wrong, even if the largest conceivable good be thrown in the balance against them. Of some things the wrongness is, in brief, deontological. And if the technical term seems intrusive, consider the implicit basis upon which Ivan takes his stand. Can that basis be better expressed than by the familiar Kantian requirement that persons be respected as ends in themselves and not simply treated as means?[36]

The few certainties left us in an age of skepticism are in large part negative. It is well that we should draw from the impulse of protest all the guidance that we can, provided we bear in mind that such certainties, however intuitively experienced, do not attest to a simple presence; not even a negative presence, as the existentialist protest might suggest. Given this reservation, we may decipher within the negative gesture at least two affirmations.[37] For one thing, *some* sort of positive moral statement is being made. Existentialism, to continue with that specific historic movement as our paradigm of protest, has always been of two minds about this. It has emphasized ambiguity and relativity, rebuffing any attempt at rational justification, to the point that avoidance of the rational has come to seem an essential part of the program. And yet if there is *no* gesture in the direction of rational justification, the suspicion grows that the existentialist protest may amount to nothing more than a cosmic temper tantrum. It seems no more justified than the sulking of Kant's unhappy child.

"Heidegger goes on ad nauseam about anxiety and death. What's the man's problem? Everybody dies, that's the way it is. He should stop sniveling and grow up." When existentialism lays itself open to such taunts, it is a loss for theology.[38] Much of the finest theological work of the century is unimaginable apart from the conceptual support provided by existentialism. One thinks of Bultmann, Tillich, Reinhold Niebuhr, and even Barth. These thinkers and others shared a conviction that existentialism implied certain quite positive affirmations. Granted, the movement does focus upon the individual, as is so often urged against it. But is this focus to be taken as if it were making thereby an empirical assertion, as if it were saying that social relations did not exist? Is not the focus rather a way of affirming a certain *value*—viz. the dignity and significance of the human person? Similarly when critics observe the existentialist celebration of freedom and object that it is exaggerated, are not the critics missing the point? Is it not the existentialist point, after all, that human freedom—whatever its empirical extent, even if it shrink to the dimensions of a prison cell—is what gives to human life whatever significance and value it does have? But if such implicit claims are indeed there in existentialism, the question then becomes, *how are the affirmations to be sustained, given the movement's own insistence on negativity, absurdity, and ambiguity?* Can the truth and value of existentialism itself be preserved, given the movement's historical tendency to cancel itself out? These are questions to which theology must attend if it is to find its way.[39]

Our reflections return us to the topic of this chapter, the otherness of the ethical. Whatever else it may be, existentialism is a protest against ontotheology. And when one looks at ontotheology, particularly ontotheology in its most self-revealing gesture, the gesture of theodicy, one may well be struck by its placid assumption of the *homogeneity* of the ethical. The assumption is most visible in the dictum "what is, is right." An untroubled homogeneity between the is and the ought, between ontology and ethics. But it is suggested as well by Leibnitz's calculations of compossibility, where the good of the individual and the good of a larger whole are subsumed within a single conceptual currency, to be weighed and compared. Conversely, if you do draw the line, i.e., if you do insist that one particular good (the life of "that baby beating its breast with its fist," for instance) is *not* to be swept aside for any end, however great, then you are performing the existentialist gesture. You are defending a concrete, human value—and acknowledging that there is a rent in the order of things, a radical heterogeneity within "the good."

By implication, the existentialist assertion is not that values are utterly nonexistent, but that they are irreducibly *heterogeneous*. To quote Kant, "the maxims of virtue and those of one's own happiness are wholly heterogeneous."[40] Witness the plight of the platoon leader, claimed simultaneously by the value of survival and the imperative of impartiality. *Tertio non datur*: no single currency tells us how in the concrete case to measure the one against the other (advocates of exchange value notwithstanding).[41]

The difficulty fully warrants the classical vocabulary of ambiguity, anxiety, the absurd. Yet it is a situation rooted *within* concrete human reason. Accordingly, the existentialist lament cannot be dismissed as simpering or posturing.

Heterogeneity is a second affirmation inscribed within the modern protest. And on this count, too, Kant provides a grounding in reason without which the protest tends inevitably to shoot itself in the foot. Specifically, a Kantian approach prevents the protest from succumbing to dualism, existentialism's inveterate tendency, by substituting for dualism the distinct, though profoundly related, notion of *equiprimordiality*. We encountered equiprimordiality in the first Critique, where it defined the relationship of reason and intuition. In the second Critique it reappeared in the relationship of reason and desire, and of moral and prudential reason. Further study could show how the relationship between the subjects of the two Critiques is similarly one of equiprimordiality—a matter of importance, as there has been a constant tendency to favor one of the critiques over the other. For our purposes we may simply observe that the recurrence of equiprimordiality is no accident; the transcendental method may virtually be defined as a device for sniffing it out. The method is, that is to say, a device for recognizing and respecting the irreducibly differentiated character of finite reason, i.e., of a reason which understands itself in contrast to (the concepts of) an Intellectual Intuition and a Holy Will. The transcendental method is reason's effort to think its other (in the merely formal manner appropriate to reason) and, *recognizing* its knowledge as no more than formal, to respect the otherness.

Cutting the Idealist Diamond

Derrida's own discussion of existentialism occurs in an essay entitled "The Ends of Man."[42] Derrida uses the plural, "ends," to draw attention to an ambiguity in ordinary usage, which speaks of "end" in the sense of termination, death, and in the sense of *telos* or goal. Here as elsewhere, Derrida suggests, ordinary language is suffused with metaphysics. It is a favorite ploy of Western philosophy to begin by underscoring the reality of human finitude (in this sense, existentialism is representative); but then to profess to find, in and through that finitude, some *telos* or goal which promises contact with the infinite. The infant does and does not hide itself, the meditating executive does and does not let go, the fetishist does and does not surrender to language.

Barth no less than Derrida holds that in this matter as in many, the inner workings of Western thought are made most explicit by Hegel.[43] Hegel held that "consciousness . . . is the truth of the soul."[44] To understand what it might mean in a Hegelian context to call consciousness "the truth of the soul," we must consider Hegel's notion of truth. For Hegel, as Derrida observes, truth is "the presence or presentation of essence as *Gewesenheit*, or *Wesen* as having-been." Essence or *Wesen*, that is to say, is known only retrospectively, after the fact; it is known as "having-been." One can even say that for Hegel the essence of a thing *is* its having-been (i.e., its having-been in this or that particular way). But now comes the characteristic Hegelian turn. For in the act of being recognized, essence is "*taken up*" (*Aufgehoben*), by which Hegel understands that it is presented, made present.[45] And obviously that act of making present must occur within a reality which is, itself, present. What is this encompassing reality? For Hegel it is by implication the infinite. Thus the equivocation:

> This equivocal relationship of "taking up" doubtless marks the end of man, man past, but by the same token it also marks the achievement of man, the appropriation of his essence. *It is the end of finite man*. The end of the finitude of man, the unity of the finite and the infinite.[46]

Thus the Western stratagem which Hegel makes explicit is to begin by avowing seriousness about the reality of finitude, only to conclude by rendering ambiguous the difference between finite and infinite.[47] This question of how strong a distinction one is to make between finite and infinite has stood at the heart of our argument since the argumentative typology was presented at the end of chapter 2. Throughout the Kant exposition the question has continued with us; the effort at thinking *coram Deo* has been a way of rendering the question acute.

Moving by imperceptible degrees from finite into infinite is a characteristic move of ontotheology. We began by using the term "ontotheology" cautiously, as it is a broad brush much used for tarring.[48] Thus we started out with a single rather obvious instance, the "Essay on Man." We asked what it was about Pope's position that qualified it as ontotheology. If our answer were to be compressed into a single sentence, we might say that the essay is ontotheological in that it is a gesture of contextualization which fails to contextualize. As evidence, recall that Pope repeatedly invoked a big picture, ostensibly to limit human knowledge, and then proceeded to transgress those very limits. In Hegel, on Derrida's account, the same thing happens. Hegel's distinction is in boldly affirming that it is *meant* to happen. Thus the sequence: the human *appears* to be placed, contextualized; in Hegel's language, the human essence is named. A gesture of contextualization is thus made—but only in order that the contextualization may then proceed to fail with regard to that peculiar reality which *does* the contextualizing. By no accident, contextualization fails with regard to that reality which had (and had not) undertaken contextualization, namely consciousness. By no accident, that failure, that bringing of contextualization "to an end," succeeds in revealing consciousness itself to be "the truth of the soul."

So the distance from Pope to Hegel is not so great. To be sure, the one thinker seems blissfully atemporal while the other is resolutely dynamic, historical. But Metz has shown how those who surrender themselves to an alleged march of history lose touch with history as it is known and suffered, history in its concreteness and contingency. In the first chapter of the present book, the chapter in which Metz was discussed, I declared open season on a figure of thought which I at that time called "the idealist diamond." In the course of the subsequent chapters I have made few explicit references to the diamond, lest the exposition appear tendentious. (The figure made a brief appearance in chapter 3 in connection with Dilthey, Ricoeur, and theological hermeneutics. Thereafter there was only the occasional reference to *telos* and *archē*.) Now, with most of the exposition behind us, the polemic may be resumed. Observe, to begin with, that there are structures within the Hegelian system which resemble nothing so much as Pope's Great Chain of Being—simply laid on its side. Pope ascends, Hegel presses forward, each pursuing his appointed end. And each does so by pushing off *against* some rejected element within the realm of the finite. Kant smokes this out with regard to the traditional Chain when he observes that those who elevate nature at one moment actually denigrate it at the next. They implicitly assume that (sheer) matter is inherently rebellious, without law; they assume that finitude is to be subdued. Hegel simply carries the logic to its conclusion, saying finitude must end. For Hegel, essence is the finite, but specifically the finite as having-been. And while such finitude is affirmed in the gesture of being "taken up," the gesture remains ambiguous. For within the gesture itself there resides that other aspect of the finite which is *not* mere having-been but *the making-present of* the having-been. That is, after all, what Hegelian consciousness does. Thus however much it may "affirm" essence and the finite, the making-present (or in Derridean language, the putative presence) must understand itself *in contrast to* mere having-been. It must push off against the (lesser) finite in order to know "the truth of" itself. Can that truth be other than the infinite?

Chain and diamond thus exhibit a similar logic, which is that depicted by type 1 of our typology.[49]

Viewing the matter historically, it should be remembered that while the overcoming of metaphysics has been much talked of recently, it is not a notion of recent vintage. Kant called the metaphysical enterprise into question, and did so more radically than the skeptics and the empiricists. Subsequent idealism paid Kant homage for this, for it understood itself as "taking up" the Kantian critique, understanding it as the critique of an illusory objectivity—and then transcending it as "mere" critique. This idealist reading of history is not far from the way the history of philosophy continues to be taught in many quarters. Our own historical self-understanding continues to be shaped by the idealist view. Derrida's contribution in this regard is to have given us a deeper understanding of what is entailed by a critique of metaphysics. He shows that idealism's critique of presence proves half-hearted in comparison to its critique of opposition. As this point is made, one senses that much of the thought subsequent to Kant may not have been an overcoming of metaphysics, as advertised, but the reemergence of metaphysics under another form. From this perspective the landmarks begin to shift. Kant no longer appears as a philosophical base camp on the way to subsequent heights. His philosophy becomes at least potentially a blessed break between "metaphysics-1" and "metaphysics-2."

If we ask how it is that Kant wedges open his breathing space, we are returned to equiprimordiality. By way of counterexample: Derrida remarks of Sartre that notwithstanding the Sartrean dualism, the rhetoric of division and conflict, Sartre nevertheless translates Heidegger's *Dasein* with the implicitly unifying term "human-reality." Sartre's choice of translation reflects the fact that in his thought "the unity of man" is never questioned "in and of itself."[50] In Kant's philosophy, by contrast, human awareness finds itself "always already" located in a context of differentiation. Putting the matter in terms of the idealist diamond, human awareness is always already east of Eden, always already at the second "stage"—which is therefore no mere stage at all. I have written at length about how fundamental this stratagem is for Kant's whole way of thinking. I hope to have conveyed my conviction that such a stratagem guarantees, insofar as any conceptual device can guarantee, that the gesture of contextualization really will contextualize. Here I simply observe that the effect of the stratagem with respect to the three-part story is to contextualize our thinking within the second part. In effect Kant cuts the idealist diamond, dropping *archē* and *telos* alike.

At this juncture one might ask, "If it was Kant's intent to extirpate every semblance of *archē* and *telos*, why didn't he say so more explicitly? If he shared even half of the Derridean conviction that notions of 'end' are insidious, why did he himself propound such a notion as the Highest Good?" Derrida himself seems to lodge a similar complaint when he asserts that philosophy turns metaphysical "each time that a recourse to the 'Idea in the Kantian sense' is necessary."[51] It is indeed true that few of those who invoke the notion of an Idea "in the Kantian sense" submit their thinking to the rigor of Kant's approach. For them the notion is a way of disclaiming an objectively existent *telos* (such as might be assumed by metaphysics-1) while leaving the door wide open to the sort of "end" which one finds in metaphysics-2 (i.e., in "post"-Kantian thought). But is the same to be said of Kant himself?

We may imagine him responding to Derrida in Derridean terms. For it is as if Kant were already aware that the language of teleology is not banished by fiat. It is as if he already knew that creating an oppositional relationship invites a return of the repressed. Kant seems to appreciate that if the language of *telos* has proven so insistent, it must be because of some legitimate need or reason. The recognition of this need is precisely Kant's moral "realism." In this light the path of wisdom might be to retain the notion of end rather than seek to banish it—but to retain it *determined by* the distinctively, deontologically ethical.

Which is what Kant does. (1) With his opening consideration of whether there can be a second Critique at all, he clearly distinguishes the question of the *grounding* of the ethical, and shows that for finite reason the grounding must be formal, as grounding in the moral law. Only thereafter, and only on this basis, does he then proceed (2) to formulate the "idea" of a material object or end which might be the concrete and comprehensive realization of the moral law within the world. Thus, in a manner like that of the reason of the first Critique, pure practical reason

> likewise seeks the unconditioned for the practically conditioned . . . : and this unconditioned is not only sought as [cf. step 1 above] the determining *ground* of the will, but even when this is given (in the moral law) is also sought as [cf. step 2] the unconditioned *totality* of the objects of pure practical reason, under the name of the Highest Good.[52]

This is a difficult passage. But in the difficulty, the interest lies. For this is precisely the difficulty which idealism proved incapable of sustaining, the difficulty which it refused when it collapsed the crucial *difference* between morality and teleology, between is and ought, between history and biology. Conversely, it is the resistance which Kierkegaard fought to restore from the time that he found his calling as one who would make life more difficult; the calling he sought to fulfill by vigorously distinguishing between the immediacy of the aesthetic and the ideality—cf. the otherness—of the ethical.

Let us linger, then, with the language of "conditioned" and "unconditioned." Kant did believe that the task of reason was to unify, to overcome oppositions, insofar as that was legitimately possible. He further believed that the principal way in which reason was able to accomplish the task of unification, i.e., the task of holding two realities together conceptually, was to understand the one element as determined or conditioned by the other. That is why talk of "condition" and "determination" appears so often in his work. But Kant also knew that distinctions need to be made. To trace his logic, let us again make use of our two-step schema of a moment ago, this time working backwards from step 2. So long as discussion is confined to the relationship between the concept of the Highest Good and various particular goods, the Highest Good may be said to be unconditioned. It is "that purpose which needs no other as a condition of its possibility."[53] In this context the Highest Good may be called the final end; but it may equally well be called "the *first* end, the *original* end . . . , the end from which all others are *derived*."[54] It may be *archē* as readily as *telos* (though by the same token it is no more *telos* than *archē*). In any event, one can indeed say that, within the context of step 2, Kant does generate something like the entire diamond. However (and this is the all-important "however"), the Highest Good so derived is *only* a conception, only an idea. In Kantian language it can be thought but not known. It is not known as a presence, because it *is not* a presence; it is neither self-justifying nor self-defining. And that is why the notion must be preceded by a step 1 which addresses precisely the task of defining and grounding it. This necessary mediation or indirectness of the notion of the Highest Good is of cardinal importance because it thwarts the human, all-too-human impulse to give content to the notion by looking to what one happens to find fulfilling; by hitching one's wagon to whatever "inevitable march of history" is currently in vogue; by joining in the mindless marching song, "long live life."[55] For Kant the very conception of a Highest Good, however High it be and however big the picture it claims to represent, is *conditioned by* the moral law. To even conceive of a Highest Good— to say nothing of making it real—one needs must pass through the needle's eye, by the otherness of the ethical.

I take Kierkegaard to be making a similar point when he speaks of "the ideality of the ethical." To hear the existentialist affirming ideality will seem odd; but only because our language has succumbed to a conceptual entropy whereby "existential" devolves to a slightly pretentious substitute for "experiential," and "experience" takes on the cloak of ready-made immediacy. We want an existentialist to treat idea and existence as oppositional; and to come down, of course, on the side of existence. That, after all, is where "human reality" is; that is what is closest to "home." As antidote to this natural tendency, we should recall the critique of Sartre. For all his talk about conflict and a break with metaphysics, Sartre left unquestioned the notion of an underlying human reality. For all his awareness of estrangement, he sought to bring thought home to a state of authenticity. This is what Derrida has in mind when he argues that even Heidegger retains a metaphysic of presence or proximity.

Kierkegaard's surprising affirmation of ideality is one evidence among many that he located the human person in a situation of irreducible equiprimordiality—which is a fair paraphrase for what Kierkegaard means by "existence." The idealist diamond would stabilize this situation by setting it between an *archē* and a *telos*, rendering it merely transitional. We have seen how persistent this impulse is. If we are to succeed in cutting the idealist diamond, it can only be by *reversing* the false gesture of contextualization. It can only be by *placing the diamond itself within the context of equiprimordiality.*

This, in effect, is what Kant has done. Because he did not take the shortcut of exiling the language of *archē* and *telos*, he is able to retain it—but retain it as being specifically *a function of* the struggle of reason and desire, of moral reason and prudential reason. Which is to say, as being a function of equiprimordiality. That difficult discipline or *askesis*, Kierkegaard's and Kant's, may be the only viable response to the disabling suspicion with which this chapter began. Obviously it is not an easy way. *Archē* and *telos* are no longer a supportive presence. But neither are they simply absent. Rather they become an ideal of reason which "unceasingly mocks and torments" us.[56]

The diamond is an ideal, not a reality. The diamond-as-presence is a dream. Dream and ideal alike are conditioned by the wound of reason.

VI

THE ETHICS OF OTHERNESS

Debate over theology and difference did not begin with deconstruction. It is a truism that the modern period represented a turning of attention toward the rich, differentiated complexity of the empirical world. During the Renaissance that complexity could still be regarded in Platonic fashion as being reflective of a higher, eternal order. But with the Enlightenment sentiment grew that allegiance to the reality and integrity of the empirical world required the renunciation, or at least an emphatic bracketing, of any notion of a radically transcendent God. In the polemics of Feuerbach and Nietzsche, the very idea of such transcendence came to be regarded as a sort of conceptual vampire, draining life of its color and vibrancy. Yet these hermeneutics of suspicion were simply the sharpened expression of something vaguely felt in the culture at large.

The Argument Reviewed

Our own argument is at grips with similar misgivings. If Barth is commonly regarded as a prime instance of ontotheology notwithstanding his express disavowal of metaphysics, it is because of the radical distinction he insists on making between God and creation. The modern, enlightenment reflex of distrusting such transcendence remains in place long after the experiences of the century have called into question the ultimate competence of modern consciousness as steward and judge of the finite. The task of chapter 2 was to consider whether the *Römerbrief* might not contain a viable alternative proposal regarding theology and difference. The proposal, summarized in the final type of that chapter's typology, was that acknowledgment of the radical otherness of God might actually have a liberating effect. By such liberating acknowledgment, it was suggested, finite difference and the richness of creation might effectively be *affirmed*.[1]

In order to pursue this theological vision, it was necessary to attend more closely to the thought of Jacques Derrida. For it was by use of certain notions borrowed from deconstruction that chapter 2 had suggested that

Barth might be read as not being naively pre-Enlightenment, but as being rather "post-critical." In chapter 3 we found that deconstruction is not simply negative or nihilistic, but that it has the hardly less unsettling effect of locating us in a situation of "undecidability." In such circumstances questions of truth and of value do not disappear, contrary to some postmodern arguments. Derrida states explicitly that undecidability is that which "*opens* the field of decision or of decidability"; it is the "necessary condition" *for* decision and responsibility. Derrida's " 'quasi'-transcendental" approach to this issue brought us within hailing distance of Immanuel Kant.[2]

Our problem was to find a way of connecting with Kant's thought, establishing a "fusion of horizons." Given that suffering and violence have been so much a part of the landscape of our time, we chose to come at Kant by way of the issue of theodicy. Making our way into his writings, we discovered a certain determinative turn of thought which first appeared in the precritical writings, and which played a decisive, albeit generally implicit, role in the critical writings. This movement of thought, thinking *coram Deo*, forged a clear connection between Kant and the disputed final type from our typology.

Kant's role in chapters 4 and 5 is to demonstrate that thought obedient to this peculiar logic is possible, perhaps even important. But in Kant the notions which function as stand-ins for divinity, viz. Intellectual Intuition and Perfect Will, are strictly confined to the role of conceptual foils. The actual existence of such a reality is neither demonstrated nor assumed. For Kant it remains "undecidable." What we glean from Kant is the following: that a certain movement of thought is possible; that it is there to be appropriated, should theology wish to do so; and that, far from dictating surrender to heteronomy, it might actually advance the cause of enlightenment by providing a fulcrum of radical otherness which would give leverage to critical thought.

It does seem to have provided such leverage for Kant. The effect of the *coram Deo* is to keep one constantly aware of the finite character of human thinking and experiencing. It denies one any form of presence. In this sense Kant locates us in something like the Derridean realm of undecidability. Now one way of spelling this out is by reference to the idealist diamond. I shall offer three summary observations which will set the terms for much of the present chapter. (1) Kant shows (especially in the first Critique) the possibility and importance of thinking in a manner which does not rely upon the real or potential existence of either *archē* or *telos*. Thinking this way is a good deal of what transcendental reflection is about. So understood, Kant's thought is not "foundationalist," as is sometimes charged, but a critique of (metaphysical) foundationalism. (2) Kant shows (especially in the second Critique) that *it is the distinctive ethical requirement*, the otherness of the ethical, which ultimately shatters the presumptive diamond. As Jean-Luc Nancy has stressed in language closely paralleling that of the *coram Deo*, the categorical imperative refuses to be reduced to the level of either calculative thinking or teleological justification. At the same time (3) Kant avoids the trap of a flat, oppositional relationship to the diamond. Talk of *archē* and *telos* is not simply proscribed, as if one could so purify the linguistic domain. In this respect Kant anticipates something of the Derridean subtlety. By virtue of a certain moral realism, Kant recognizes it is no accident that human beings keep conjuring up the images of *archē* and *telos*. The images respond to a practical moral need. Critical thought is not asked to rebuff this legitimate need, but it is charged with the task of keeping firmly in mind that, contra the tug of human desire, that to which the need gives access is no assured metaphysical reality, but simply a postulate or idea. Far from being resolved, the issue of whether those ideas do signify a reality persists as an ever-present question, which is the question of theodicy.

A shorthand version of the three observations might be to say that we have (1) a problem (the diamond must be broken open); (2) a solution (the categorical imperative can do the job); and (3) a qualification (ideas of *archē* and *telos* continue to haunt the human spirit).

Regarding the first point it should be emphasized that simply to have pointed to the diamond as being a problem (to have specified the thought forms it represents and shown how they impede critical reflection, how they suppress the reality of difference) is itself one of our inquiry's primary results. As the first point has to do with what would deny difference, the second treats what fosters it. Kant, Kierkegaard, and Nancy converge in forging a strong, positive link between the responsibility to honor the otherness of the ethical and the task of respecting *différance* or otherness at large. But the effect of this linkage is to turn the modern suspicion on its head. For if modernity has been suspicious of a transcendent God, it has been equally suspicious of the notion of a radical Ought. Both have seemed "heteronomous," alienating, and oppressive; and it is understandable that they should appear in this light. But our explorations indicate another way, another type for the relating of finite and infinite, which reflection must explore if it is to be truly critical.

The third point, however, is the one I want to stress. In order to prevent our own thought from turning oppositional, it is important that we accord the "devil" his due. A step in that direction is to recognize that the tenacity of this thought form does not spring from sheer perversity. The thought form reflects an aspiration and a question which—*as* aspiration and *as* question—is profoundly human, profoundly justified. The trick is to affirm the notions of *archē* and *telos* as aspiration/question—neither more nor less.

As metaphysical assumption, the diamond militates against critical thought. As question, it converges with it. The art of critical thinking consists of countering the former tendency with the latter. It consists of maintaining the aspiration/question/protest *by* recognizing that it lacks metaphysical grounding, by recognizing that it contradicts virtually all that is known as real—and then thinking in the space thus opened up.

The A/theology of Mark C. Taylor

To date, the most fully developed alternative to the line of argument I have been setting forth regarding the appropriate relationship between theology and deconstruction is the work of Mark C. Taylor, whose books and essays have set the terms for much of the discussion of this topic in America. Anyone entering into the conversation must reckon with Taylor's achievement sooner or later. The process was begun in chapter 3, where we touched upon the debate over postmodernity. Now it is possible to give Taylor's work the attention it deserves.

I should say at the outset that while I disagree with Taylor on a few cardinal points, I am in agreement with him on many others. In order to suggest something of the power and complexity of his thought, I shall begin with a chapter-by-chapter exposition of *Erring: A Postmodern A/theology*, his most comprehensive statement.[3] In that work Taylor explores the implications of the historical-cultural phenomenon which he identifies as the death of God. On his view these implications have yet to be fully confronted; the event, in Nietzsche's words, "is still on its way, still wandering."[4] But only by entering without reservation into this valley of disillusionment can one hope to find what may lie on the other side. Or rather, only by realizing there *is* no other side can one begin to embrace and affirm the life which is to be lived within the apparently barren valley: the life of wandering or "erring." This reading of our contemporary situation provides the context and rationale for Taylor's appropriation of Derrida. One legitimate way of thinking about deconstruction is to approach it as a strategy for tracing the radical interrelatedness of all of reality. In Taylor's words it is a way of delineating "identity-in-difference and difference-in-identity" (109). For Taylor, this radical interdependency spells the death of every alleged absolute (thus the full extension of the death of God)—culminating in a recognition of the relativity of death itself (thus the reaffirmation of life that comes with the acceptance of death). It is in this sense that "destruction and creation are inseparable" (143). Because deconstruction so assists us in tracing this devious path, the author believes that "it would not be too much to suggest that *deconstruction is the 'hermeneutic' of the death of God*" (6).

The reader approaching Taylor's book may be relieved to discover that this celebration of errancy exhibits, in its broad outline, a remarkable clarity of structure. Part One, "Deconstructing Theology," is primarily critical, treating the demise of four traditional concepts (God, self, history, and book) in as many chapters. The four chapters of Part Two, "Deconstructive A/theology," then mirror the sequence in Part One, striving in each instance to articulate the new truth which is born with the passing of the old. The argument which Taylor deploys within this framework is prodigious in its range and almost hypnotic in its single-mindedness; yet the material is handled with a playfulness and wit which seeks to embody, in the very act of writing, the meaning of deconstruction.

Significantly for our discussions of Sartre and existentialism, Taylor approaches the death of God by contesting not only traditional theism, but secular humanism as well. The latter is portrayed as a sort of mirror game which usurps the place of God only to confer sacral authority upon the human subject. Secular humanism thus lingers on the "modern" side of postmodernity for want of the recognition that what is at stake is not the replacement of one entity by another, but the dismantling of an entire logic. " 'Master of the exclusions and restrictions that derive from the disjunctive syllogism,' this God rules (and is ruled) by the nondialectical 'logic of simple negation, which is the logic of repression.' "[5] Failing to question this logic, indeed reinforcing it with a vengeance, secular humanism betrays a fatal anxiety: "the 'absolute fear' that grows out of 'the first encounter of the other as *other*.' "[6] Such fear of otherness "*outside*" the self is, in turn, a function of the effort to become totally self-contained and self-possessed, and thus to expunge both Eros and Thanatos, both desire and death—which are the evidences of otherness "*within*."

If selfhood is the obstacle, it follows that the second chapter, with its critique of the self, will be the hinge of the entire project. Taylor begins by observing that through its depiction of God as absolutely unitary and self-possessed, Western culture has set forth a model of what any true subject must (strive to) be. He then proceeds to treat Augustine's *Confessions* as paradigmatic of the Western struggle for self-*presence*, which is thought to be attainable within a privileged moment of time, namely the temporal *present*. But the notion of a privileged moment of time is in fact the denial of time. With this critique, Taylor's target stands fully exposed; and he does not hesitate to wheel out his heaviest artillery, namely Hegel's classic critique of the notion of immediacy, reformulated in terms of the Derridean conception of writing. The effect of this strenuous demystification is to demonstrate that "due to the everlasting interplay of identity and difference and of presence and absence, the present is 'present not as total presence, but as *trace*.' Rather than a *nunc stans*, time is ceaseless transition, perpetual motion, and constant movement (*momentum*)" (50).

Part One concludes with chapters on the "end of history" and the "closure of the book." History is here understood as the effort to impose a shape upon the open-textured fabric of time. It matters little whether the shape be linear or circular, for "both circle and line are *forms of closure* and *figures of plenitude* that serve as *totalizing metaphors*" (70). In the course of his discussion Taylor touches upon the kinship between history and fiction, the role of constructive imagination and the inaccessibility of cold, neutral facts: all points which are familiar to current narrative theology. But on Taylor's view, narrative itself is part of the problem: "since narrative strives toward wholeness or totality, it does not tend to be open-ended or infinitely extendible. Narrativization ties together the separate threads of chronicle by forming a centered structure with a definite beginning, middle and end" (64). Overshadowing the differences between various stories and various tellings of them is the fact that all story is emplotment, and thus " 'a reaction formation against the discovery' " of the immanent reality of death and time.[7] From this contention it is a short step to the following chapter's dismemberment of the notion that the patterns of reality at large might be inscribed in a celestial book.

Part Two of *Erring* begins by engaging Derrida's notion of "writing," which is advanced as nothing less than the successor to the discredited notion of God (though, in keeping with the theme of homelessness, it is not to take the "place" of God). Rather, "the death of God is the sacrifice of the transcendent Author/Creator/Master who governs from afar. Incarnation *irrevocably* erases the disembodied logos and inscribes a word that becomes the script enacted in the infinite play of interpretation" (103). As a way into this discussion, one might think of "writing" as a trope for radical interrelatedness. A mark inscribed in a text is wholly dependent upon the context for whatever meaning and being it may have. This is a "relationalism or relativism" which the author distinguishes from "mere subjectivism"; for "while subjectivism separates and isolates, the relativity of scripture establishes the coimplication" (108). In keeping with this thematic, (the) incarnation is summarily relieved of its particularity (104); and the radical self-emptying which has already befallen the Father is extended to the Son (120).

Indeed the principal function of Taylor's Christology seems to be as transition to the topic which, once again, provides the crucial turn among many turnings, namely the death of the self. With this denouement the imperfect nihilism of secular humanism is brought to term and a new affirmation brought to light. For the self that dies is more precisely "the possessive self" or "the self-possessed subject" for whom "otherness represents the guise of death" (140). Once that death is no longer resisted but actively embraced, a genuine openness to the other becomes possible. Passion then becomes compassion; recognition of relatedness leads to mutual recognition; and as "the subject does not need to repress the other 'within,' it is not driven to oppress the other 'without' " (142, 134, 147).

The death of the self confirmed in chapter 6 is celebrated in chapter 7, which bears the title "Mazing Grace." In terms of the (considerable) dramatic movement of the book, this chapter is surely the climax. The delusions of the "unhappy consciousness" here serve as affective counterpoint to the exultant figure of Dionysius, who " 'stands in the middle of the cosmos with a joyous and trusting fatalism, in the *faith* that only the particular is loathsome, and that all is redeemed and affirmed in the whole."[8] To conclude our exposition of *Erring*, a longer quotation may convey some sense of the play of the text:

> The carnality of Dionysius is the word made flesh. "Carnival" appears to derive from Latin *caro, carnis*, flesh, and *levare*, to lift up, elevate, or raise up. Carnival might be understood as the elevation of the body, the resurrection of the flesh. As the god of "the whole wet element in nature," Dionysius embodies the moisture and fluidity of humor and the seminal sexuality of comedy.[9]

The book ends with a chapter on scripture and, in lieu of a conclusion, an "interlude" which is in effect a further invitation to the dance.

One point of contact between Taylor's argument and our own is indicated by the fact that Taylor calls his last section an "interlude." This anomalous gesture is an effort to keep the book from becoming a "book," where "book" is understood as a three-stage exposition with beginning, middle, and end. At least *prima facie*, Taylor's refusal of such narrative seems interchangeable with our own critique of the idealist diamond. The convergence, which is natural enough, given our common debt to Derrida, is confirmed in Taylor's more recent *Altarity*, which includes an assessment of Hegel. Taylor notes that Hegel turns our attention in the right direction in that his System "is the result of his lifelong wrestling with the problem of difference and the question of the other."[10] But Hegel's approach to those legitimate issues is via a three-stage dialectic: "primal union (identity), loss or separation (difference), and reunion or reconciliation (identity of identity and difference, or union of union and nonunion)."[11] Beginning and ending as it does, this conceptual structure "privileges identity and unity." This fetish of oneness proved all too "decisive for subsequent philosophy, theology, and literary criticism."[12] Taylor's entire chapter on Hegel in *Altarity* is an extended critique of the three-part pattern.[13]

So the similarity between Taylor's argument and my own is substantial. The question is, how far does it go? A useful measure may be found in the three summary observations enumerated in the previous section. The first is indeed the critique of the idealist diamond. But what of the other two, regarding ethics and aspiration? There the arguments diverge. From the perspective I have been developing, Taylor's position must seem at best incomplete. An example is his assertion that "the end of history" for which he calls requires "*the overcoming of unhappy consciousness*" (72). This sounds appealing—but it is a quintessentially Hegelian *telos*. To make Taylor's proposal concrete, let us recall the platoon leader. Torn by questions of selfhood and ought, he is presumably an instance of unhappy consciousness. Certainly he *desires*, and we desire for him, an end to the anguish. But our second summary point requires that that not be done in a way which violates the autonomy of the ethical.

Taylor's own way of making the notion of unhappy consciousness concrete is by citing an encounter depicted in Edmond Jabès's *Book of Questions*. The unhappy figure is a wanderer, an exile, who is addressed by a poet:

> The poet explains to the despairing exile: "Yukel, you have never felt at ease in your skin. You have never been *here*, but always *elsewhere*, ahead of yourself or behind like winter in the eyes of autumn or summer in the eyes of spring . . . "

A person in exile may indeed long for an *archē*, the homeland; the exile may well be paradigmatic of the person who thinks of existence on the model of the diamond. But think of the refugees; think of the political exiles who have wandered homeless in this century. Too often the condition of exile has been testimony to the fact that all *is not* well in the world. When Taylor castigates the exile by way of Jabès, there is the risk that the child of ethical awareness will be tossed out along with the bathos of nostalgia.

That the risk is not fanciful seems to be confirmed by Taylor's own comment on the passage:

> *Always* exiled between beginning and end, the unhappy person nostalgically remembers the fulfillment he believes once was and expectantly awaits the satisfaction he hopes will be. Anticipated satisfaction, however, never becomes fully present. . . . This elusive beyond creates a tension between what is and what ought to be. The persistent opposition between "reality" and "ideality" lends a saddened, nay, melancholy, tone to time. (72)

Taylor does seem to oversimplify. Agreed, the real and the ideal are not to be treated as a metaphysical opposition. But, ethically? Ethically do we not have to say that regrettably there *is* a chasm between the ideal and the real; and that, alas, it *does* lend "a saddened, nay, melancholy, tone to time"? In chapter 1 we adopted as a fundamental point of reference Metz's "memory of suffering." What is that memory about, if not preserving a sense of this very rent, this very wound? Without that fundamental tension, how could Metz maintain his critical thought? How, for that matter, could Ernst Bloch maintain his utopian vision? How could Horkheimer maintain his hope that the murderer shall not have the last word? That is what is in danger of being lost when one joins Taylor in disparaging the "tension between what is and what ought to be." In the language of our own exposition, it is one thing to posit the reality of an *archē* and *telos*; it is another thing simply to long for them. No doubt the longing often leads to positing. But the longing *as such*: is it not very close to the cry of Kant's infant? Is it not, with all its angry confusion of narcissistic self-pity and legitimate indignation, the bearer of our ethical discontent? The overcoming of unhappy consciousness is, as we noted, a Hegelian theme. Perhaps Taylor must be taken, at this point, as one further confirmation of how difficult it is, in actual practice, to get beyond Hegel.

Taylor himself conveys a healthy discontent with the way things are; he means his book to be prophetic. When, for example, he writes that "with the realization of the total reciprocity of subjects, the entire foundation of the economy of domination crumbles" (134), he is a visionary utopian. But how, on his own terms, can he justify his use here of the distinction which he derides elsewhere, the distinction between is and ought? Moreover, one finds a similar waffling in Taylor's use of the distinction between appearance and reality. Playing upon his own name, he asks us to regard writing, or at least his writing, as a sort of tailoring: "The tailor, after all, is profoundly interested in surfaces and completely preoccupied with appearances. His task is to cover rather than strip, to veil instead of unveil" (180). Yet *Erring* could not be the iconoclastic project it is without a constant pressing of the distinction between appearance and reality; or without a constant insistence upon the Derridean reality, against the metaphysical illusion. Repeatedly we are told, for example, that belief in God is *really* a denial of death, that secular humanism is actually theological. And all of this is true, we are told, "appearances to the contrary notwithstanding" (72). Such assertions are hardly the work of one who is "completely preoccupied with appearances."

Unable to dispel questions of the true and the good, *Erring* is equally unable to legitimate its own persistent involvement with those issues. Having made a determined effort to be done with them, the book is evidence of how tenacious the questions are. In a backhanded way, the book lends credence to the autonomy of the ethical. No doubt the tensions of our lives, including our gestures of protest, are all a function of neurosis; no doubt our various conceptions of God are all the product of projection. But after that has been said, after it has been demonstrated and denounced, has one really done more than to have said only "*something* about everything"? Is one really entitled at that point to pronounce the phrase, "nothing but . . ." with its denial of anything other or anything more? Is it not at least possible that there are tensions which we—even we in our deconstructive, hermeneutic-of-suspicion mode—do not succeed in collapsing? Tensions which we cannot dispel and contextualize? Tensions by which we are contextualized?

Contextualization of that sort is what our second and third summary observations had in view. In the remaining pages, which return to Barth's *Commentary on Romans*, I hope to show why this matters theologically.

Barth and the Problem of Ethics

In our previous discussion of the *Römerbrief*, we scarcely looked beyond chapter 1. Barth insists, however, that the book be read as a whole and that "above all, Chs. I–XI must not be separated from Chs. XII–XV."[14] Accordingly, it is to this concluding portion of the commentary that we shall turn. Gathered under the heading "The Great Disturbance," the chapters begin with a section called "The Problem of Ethics." The title is appropriate, as the topic of ethics predominates through all the subsequent sections. It seems clear enough that Barth's text will be pertinent to our second thesis, regarding the importance of the ethical. As for the third thesis, which treats the longing for *archē* and *telos*, Barth's section entitled "The Pre-supposition" begins with a passage from Kierkegaard:

> As the arrow, loosed from the bow by the hand of the practiced archer, does not rest till it has reached the mark; so men pass from God to God. He is the mark for which they have been created; and they do not rest till they find their rest in Him. (438)

No question about it; for better or worse, Barth here makes use of the three-part story. Nor is the passage a fluke, for the "pre-supposition" of which Barth speaks turns out to be God—who is variously termed the "unobservable origin" (426), the "Primal Origin" (454, 465), and "the One" (467).

For deconstructionism in the mode of *Erring*, such passages confirm Barth's status as an exponent of ontotheology. I shall argue, however, that we have here an important instance in which for all the appearance of being precritical, Barth turns out to be critical, indeed critical at a second level, and thus effectively *post*critical. I shall argue that Barth's references represent, if you will, a sort of "second naivete";[15] and that what makes the difference is precisely the role of ethics. In the course of the argument I will also pick up an important exegetical question which has been hanging since our engagement with the *Römerbrief*. At that time we found Barth making a few enigmatic suggestions to the effect that humankind bore some sort of *memory of God*. The passages were puzzling because they seemed to fly in the face of Barthian theology, with its relentless denial of any "point of contact" between the human and the divine. Yet there the passages were, and they seemed to be doing important work in providing warrant for the argument that humankind is actually culpable for denying or ignoring the reality of God. By affirming Kierkegaard (and Augustine) regarding the heart that is restless till it rests in God, Barth challenges us to come to a judgment about this enigmatic aspect of his thought.[16]

Barth's pages treat "*the problem* of ethics," ethics as problem. As Barth declares, "the power and earnestness of Christian ethics lie in its persistent asking of questions and in its steady refusal to provide answers to these questions" (466). It is only *as problem* that ethics can effect or reflect the "great disturbance": Barth makes this point in the opening lines (424). And to what purpose? Precisely in order to set aside at the very outset a dualistic (read "metaphysical," "ontotheological") conception of God.

> The fact that ethics constitutes a problem reminds us that the object about which we are conversing has no objectivity, that is to say, it is not a concrete world existing above or behind our world. . . . The fact that ethics are presented to us as a problem . . . provides us with a guarantee that, when we repeat—sometimes tediously perhaps—the formula "God Himself, God alone," we do not mean by it some divine thing, or some ideal world contrasted with the visible world. (424–25)

Barth's words recall Metz: "The shortest definition of religion: interruption."[17] But Metz's formula omits the crucial middle term. In that regard Kierkegaard is closer to the mark: religion is interruption *by* the problem of ethics. It follows that religion cannot appeal to deconstruction as a sort of gnosis, trusting that deconstruction will have of itself the power to unsettle metaphysics. *Erring* notwithstanding, the ethical tension must be maintained.

What then is the conception of God to which the problem of ethics leads? If by "the formula 'God Himself, God alone,'" Barth does not intend "some divine thing, or some ideal world," what does he intend? The answer is found in this affirmation: "We mean by the formula that unsearchable, divine *relationship* in which we stand as men."[18] "God alone" means . . . a relationship! It means a relationship which is created and sustained by God alone. *That* is the reality which stands beyond dualism, but beyond all quasi- idealist monisms as well.[19] It is what stands beyond metaphysics and ontotheology because, in Barth's words, "*it is not what men comprehend, but that by which they are comprehended.*"[20] These words are a *locus classicus* for the concept of contextualization. Appearing in a climactic passage, they declare the point toward which his thought has been driving. Better, they declare the "presupposition" (438) toward which his thought repeatedly "bends back." At times the presupposed relationship is called "grace" (430, 438), at times "double predestination" (452, 463).

In each instance the thrust is the same. This is a relationship—it is *the* relationship—by which we are contextualized.

Is this relationship an idea? Is it an experience? Barth refuses to categorize. He calls his concepts "existential concepts" (424), yet he begins the section with an "apology for intellectual thought" (426). Intellectual thought treating existential concepts is *dialectical* thought; "only dialectical human thinking can fulfill its purpose and search out the depth and context and reality of life" (425). Barth's point is that to be dialectical, thought must be more than (mere) thought. It must be the thought of a person at grips with the problem of ethics. Thus Barth's marvelous exhortation, "break off your thinking that it may be a thinking of God; *break off your dialectic, that it may be indeed dialectic . . .*"[21] For "genuine thought must always be broken thought" (425–26). Genuine reason must be wounded.

"Break off your dialectic, that it may be indeed dialectic . . ." This is not a formula for pitting reason against action, or action against reason. It is an effort to insure that the *whole* person will "share in the tension of human life, in its criss-cross lines, and in its kaleidoscopic movements" (425). For only when no aspect of the person is held aloof, only when no "high place" remains unsurrendered (428); only then will the human be contextualized. It is in order to accomplish such contextualization that Barth speaks repeatedly of the *ambiguity* of human life. One is thrust into life not to discover some underlying reality, some presence or "securitas" (465), but precisely to confront the ambiguity. "What are we to demand of men? and to what are we to invite and exhort them? Since the truth lies in the ambiguity of human existence, we must exhort them to affirm that ambiguity" (436). "For the vast ambiguity of our life is at once its deepest truth" (437). "Why should it not be that the vast ambiguity of the ebb and flow of time constitutes its vast significance?" (457). Barth hammers away at the "questionableness" of our existence. But note the terms he uses—"the truth lies in . . . ," " . . . is at once its deepest truth," " . . . constitutes its vast significance." Ambiguity is known only indirectly—by one who persists in the active struggle for something more than ambiguity. Contrary to the existentialist penchant, ambiguity is not treated as something which can be known directly or directly proclaimed. Ambiguity itself is not a presence. Barth seems to be aware that the moment ambiguity is so understood, the *grounds* for its being known, viz. the struggle to know truth and find significance, withdraw and disappear.

Like all truth, ambiguity loves to hide. Existentialism, we have seen, has an odd inability to sustain itself. Now we can understand better why this is. For once the announcement has been made and the message has been received that life is irredeemably ambiguous, what reason is there to continue to look for truth? If life is absurd, then everything, including the earnest proclamation of absurdity, loses significance. Existentialism performed gyrations—it was said that one continued "because of the absurd," it was intimated that there was an unexplored richness to the absurd—but its following drifted away. For all its fierce independence, existentialism would seem to have been conceptually and historically a derivative phenomenon. And if that is the case, might one not have to say something similar about the position represented by *Erring*? Mightn't that position be like existentialism in being dependent upon an antecedent condition which it cannot justify or explain, namely the capacity to be disturbed by the problem of ethics? Don't both presuppose a person of conscience: a person moved by an ought which is "ideal" in the sense that it is not undercut by ambiguity, but presses its claim in the face of that ambiguity? Such is the ought of which Nancy says that it is not ambiguous but also that it is not real: the ought which is "categorical."

Barth seems to have something like this in view when he says that "the absolute character of Christian ethics lies in the fact that they are altogether problematical" (465). To be absolutely problematical, it is not enough that ethics affirm the ambiguous or the problematical; it is not even enough that ethics affirm them absolutely. Ambiguity must be conjoined with—better, it must *collide* with—some firm requirement. "An action which represents really and genuinely the disturbance of men by God . . . must possess a universal validity . . . " (468). Only by way of such universality can ethics refer to God; only so can it refer to "the One in the particular." Barth says explicitly that "here Kierkegaard" (and by implication existentialism generally) "needs to be corrected from time to time by reference to Kant" (468). Precisely so. Similarly, having struck an existentialist note by asserting that ethics is protest, a refusal of "the judgement of the 'Many,'" Barth adds, in Kantian fashion, that "not for one moment dare we refuse to accept the judgement of 'All'" (469). Barth has been called an irrationalist; but it is an odd irrationalism which points away from Kierkegaard toward Kant. My own understanding is that in Barth the rational ethical requirement of universality, the categorical imperative as the requirement of universalizability, is not denied. It is reaffirmed and reinforced, as the effort to witness to God, the One in the particular. Similarly, Kantian "rigorism" is not denied; "the action which is properly ethical must not be directed towards some . . . happiness or unhappiness" (468). "Pure ethics require—and here we are in complete agreement with Kant—that there should be no mixing of heaven and earth in the sphere of morals" (432). Ethics is deontological.[22]

To summarize, the pure ethical requirement remains fully in force—in a world of unrelieved ambiguity. Thus we can say that there is for Barth a *primary question* and a *secondary questionability*. First and primarily, there is the "earnest, inexorable question, What shall we do?" (465) Then, indispensably but secondarily, there is our own uncertain questionability. It is by bringing *both* of these to view—asking "more and more questions" not only to show our questionability, but also and most importantly to press the ethical question—that Christian ethics fulfills its mandate to be "altogether problematical."

Dialectic and Repentance

Adorno concludes the *Minima Moralia* with a critique of occultism. What he has to say on the subject is pertinent to our reflections:

> The tendency to occultism is a symptom of regression in consciousness. This has lost the power to think the unconditional and to endure the conditional. Instead of defining both, in their unity and difference, by conceptual labour, it mixes them indiscriminately.[23]

"To think the unconditional," i.e., to acknowledge the question posed by the Ought, in all its categorical otherness; "to endure the conditional," i.e., to live without "securitas," acknowledging the questionability of our existence; and not to escape by trying to confuse the two. Adorno's statement reads like a formula for the situation Barth depicts.

The description also recalls the situation of the platoon leader. In addition, it connects with our discussion of Barth in chapter 2. There we noted Barth's distinctive appropriation of the Hegelian term *Aufhebung*: "by the Gospel the whole concrete world is dissolved and established" (35). We also noted that the linking of *Aufhebung* with *Begrundung*, translated as "dissolved and established," was a recurrent trope in Barth's text (30, 36, 38, 46, 51). Now we find him saying that "the problem of ethics disturbs our conversation about God, in order to remind us of its proper theme; dissolves it, in order to give it its proper direction; kills it, in order to make it alive" (426). We can thus say that in this specific respect, the problem of ethics stands in the place of the Gospel. Conversely we can say, in language more Kierkegaard's than Barth's, that the religious disturbance proceeds by way of the ethical. But it is only *by way of* the ethical; in this sense the role of the ethical remains transitional. Not that it at any point disappears: "the ethical problem has nowhere been left out of account" (427). But it is transitional in that its whole purpose is to press us toward "an act of thinking which, because it dissolves both itself and every act, is identical with the *veritable worship of God*" (436–37, cf. 428).

The "veritable worship of God" requires an act of *repentance*. Repentance is "the 'primary' ethical action upon which all 'secondary' ethical conduct depends" (436). It is an act, yet in describing it Barth affirms that "we are brought back to thought" (436). This is not a chance remark; there is the closest parallel between the "dialectical human thinking" of

which Barth speaks in the opening pages of this chapter (425) and the act
of repentance toward which the problem of ethics presses.

> Genuine thinking is always strange to the world and unsympathetic. For
> thinking is not a biological function. To think is to formulate the question,
> the answer to which is itself the possibility of the very existence of any
> biological function. (425)

His most characteristic description of this strange mode of thinking is to
say that it is not "direct" or "straightforward" (425), but *"broken thought."*[24]
The denial of directness, recalling Barth's earlier denials of "direct observation" (29), "direct communication" (41), or "direct experience of God"
(52), casts light on why those denials were so important. For before God,
coram Deo, a human gesture which *is* direct (or rather, a gesture which
believes itself to be direct) is a gesture which still has confidence in its own
sufficiency. It is an act which lacks repentance.

Lacking repentance, it does not attain to God. But once broken, once
repentant—it then becomes *ipso facto* a gesture toward God. In the imagery Barth uses repeatedly, the human must "bow." In that bowing, "the
secondary ethical action of self-recollection is bent backwards to its origin"
(444, cf. 454). It is bent backward to its Primal Origin! This, if I read
Barth correctly, is the context, indeed the only context, in which it becomes possible or permissible to speak of a "memory of God" and of God
as *archē* or Origin. When he says, for example, "Relativity is our relationship to our Primal Origin, our being related to it" (465), this is not to be
taken as a metaphysical formula capable of direct appropriation. Rather
it is shorthand for a process which proceeds indirectly, by way of the problem of ethics and the response of repentance; and which thereby gestures—in its failure, in its brokenness—toward the Origin. Moreover, I
take it that Barth would regard this to be the real "Problem in the problem" (463) when one speaks of ontotheology and metaphysics. There simply *is* no link between the Origin and the human, other than the grace of
God which overcomes us from the one direction and the human act of
repentance which gestures back toward God from the other. To think that
there is some independent link is, in what Barth would regard as the
deepest sense of the word, "metaphysics." There is no independent metaphysic, and so too there is no independent *problem* of metaphysics or
ontotheology. To the problem of metaphysics as to the problem of ethics
there is in the end only one solution, which is that of repentance.

This is not a way of thinking which is likely to appeal to contemporary
consciousness, whether modern or postmodern. But surely it is a way
which may lay a certain claim to being critical and/or postcritical. Moreover, if Barth is correct, there is a fundamental sense in which it is *not*
constrictive. There is a sense in which it is, to use one of Barth's favorite

words, a way of freedom, opening space for the free play of human activity in all its creaturely variety.

> From the dialectic of this rule, that is to say, from the Rule in the rule—
> *Sola Deo gloria!*—the great contradictions emerge, world-denial and world-acceptance, enthusiasm and realism, the wisdom of faith and the wisdom of life. But *sub specie aeterni* they are resolved into one comprehensive and unified view of life. This comprehensive view of life has never, however, had any concrete existence in itself, no man possesses it, for it is not what men comprehend, but that by which they are comprehended. (465)

In the language of our typology, this is a logic by which a strong difference between finite and infinite does not negate, but rather fosters, the richness of finite difference. Once we surrender the fantasy that truth is something we can comprehend, a high place we can occupy; once we recognize that truth is that by which we are comprehended, contextualized; once we are thus set on a common footing with our fellow human beings—it becomes possible for us to allow space for the neighbor, for the enemy, for the other. (In a high place, after all, space is at a premium; there is little room for hospitality.) It then becomes possible to acknowledge Barth's moving exhortation—"Are we not all patients in one hospital? Do we not stand under one accusation? . . . What, then, can we do, but be of the same mind one toward another?" (465).

"Do we not stand under one accusation?" The exhortation is another form of the *coram Deo*; the tone is more confrontational, but the logic is the same. And indeed it is never an easy turn of thought to attempt to view matters "sub specie aeterni," under that radical perspective by which all hierarchies are shaken, all contradictions resolved, yet resolved in a manner which remains ungraspable (465). It is a perspective which unflinchingly insists that the human calling is less to grasp than to be grasped. But that does *not* make it a perspective in which one ceases to think. Quite the contrary, its rigorous and relentless character requires a particular exertion of thought. But it must be thought which has heard the challenge, "break off your dialectic, that it may be indeed dialectic."

In a remarkably similar passage, Adorno cautions against the thinker who "uses the dialectic instead of giving himself up to it."[25] We must "break off" our thinking because there exists no direct link between the creation and God, no hidden correspondence to be discovered. There is no Great Chain to ascend, no comprehensive form to understand. That is the hiatus, the strong distinction. But precisely because there is that strong distinction, that "abstract contrast" (425) guarded by rigorous thought, therefore the lesser differences become possible. It becomes possible to let the lesser differences be, without making them more or less than what they are. The violence done to creation has sprung time and time again from the human effort to become, ourselves, the link between finite and infinite. We have sought to make of our own finite transcendence a bridge beyond; we have tried to find in our finite reality some reassuring correspondence with the absolute. But no such form or correspondence exists. Rather that to which we are to correspond is our "veritable situation," which is the absence of such a link, an absence which compels humankind to bow to the One who is wholly other (444). The distinction remains rigorous—and therefore the creation is free to be what it is: various, many-faceted, a festival of innocent difference. Creation is released from the requirement that it deliver a saving presence. And we are freed to live without that anxious, idolatrous demand. Recalling a passage from Adorno quoted in our first chapter:

> Reconcilement would release the nonidentical, would rid it of coercion, including spiritualized coercion; it would open the road to the multiplicity of different things. . . . Reconcilement would be the thought of the many as no longer inimical.[26]

It is along these lines that a case for type 3 can be made. We could pursue the argument further. We could look into the particulars of Barth's ethics, noting, for example, the role of the otherness of other persons (442, 454), and the shaking of every earthly hierarchy (462ff.). But the lines of that argument are fairly clear. I propose to conclude, therefore, with a few remarks on the status of reason.

Thinking through the Wound

At one point Adorno sketches a sort of genealogy of reason. "Mind arose out of existence, as an organ for keeping alive. In reflecting existence, however, it becomes at the same time something else. The existent negates itself as thought upon itself. Such negation is mind's element."[27] To negate oneself, as thought upon oneself: such is the nature of thought. Whether interpreted as negativity, resistance, or asceticism, this difficult gesture is familiar to the classical Western tradition. That tradition, as Husserl reminds us, was born of a resistance to the natural standpoint. If it affirmed another order, viz. the order of the ideal, it did so with the purpose of gaining critical leverage over against the invisible tyranny of common sense. But once affirmed, that other order became itself an instrument of acceptance and affirmation, a metaphysical obstacle to critical thought. Thus was required a further critique, epitomized by the hermeneutic of suspicion, which would question the unquestioned ideal by exposing within it the role of eros, *bios*, and oppression.[28]

It is almost as if thought itself were an implicit gesture of repentance.[29]

It is almost as if reason were striving in its innermost reality to respond to Barth's call—"an act of thinking which, because it dissolves both itself and every act, is identical with the 'veritable worship of God' . . . " (436–37). The Logos of reason, that classical notion which seems so supremely rationalist, so supremely metaphysical—might that Logos be, after all, the *crucified* Christ? And reason's proper negativity: might it be not the negativity-as-power which has entranced modern thought, but the peculiar, gracious No which is the negativity of the cross? However that be, it is clear that reason as hermeneutic of suspicion, no less than reason as metaphysic, betrays itself as reason when it becomes a security. If romanticism is spilt religion, as T. E. Hulme has said, then cynicism is spilt suspicion. It is suspicion without determinacy, discipline, or energy of thought, a ready-made enlightenment which perceives "nothing but" eros, *bios*, oppression; and which in so doing surrenders its birthright as being, qua reason, "something other." The theological usefulness of Kant, Adorno, and Derrida derives, it seems to me, from their vigorous advocacy of this active—vigilant, critical—otherness of reason.

To praise reason's otherness is not to deny the pain, disruption, and alienation it may cause. I have tried to keep that pain (some of it avoidable, some of it not) before us in the course of this argument. I have tried to learn from the splinter in the eye. One recent commentator asserts that there is in culture and in critical reflection an "ascetic imperative."[30] Freud was well aware that critical awareness requires reflection, and that reflection requires a degree of distancing and sublimation.[31] In contrast, much of postmodern thought encourages the notion that critical awareness can be achieved without such effort, by the very absence of such effort. Thus, for example, the promise that immersion in the electronic media bestows *ipso facto* an awareness inherently superior, at once playful, critical, and free.[32] The complacencies of ready-made enlightenment continue unabated, unabashed.

Here as elsewhere, it seems to me, the touchstone is the problem of ethics. In *Erring* Taylor sketches a three-step historical process (despite his own strictures against legitimating stories with a beginning, middle, and end). First theism, with God as transcendent subject; then humanistic atheism, with the human as absolute subject; finally deconstruction, in which the very notion of a subject is dissolved. Taylor intends the story to illustrate thought as negativity, a standpoint dissolving itself. But there is at least one important respect in which it remains metaphysical. Pope, when he professed to discern the Chain of Being within the human individual, was drawing on a venerable tradition. It is the tradition of "man as microcosm," which held that the human subject can find within herself or himself the structural clue by which to understand the universe and God. In *Erring* subject and structure are dissolved—and so is God. Thus despite the book's assertion of difference there remains a fundamental continuity, even a fundamental sameness, between the condition of the erstwhile human subject and the condition of God. There is a reasoning "from like to like."[33]

Such reflections highlight the distinctive role played by the categorical imperative. In effect it fulfills the intention of "metaphysics at its best"— the intention which is present, however offset and thwarted, in the reasoning from microcosm to macrocosm; the intention which runs like a subterranean stream, whatever the consequences, through thinkers as divergent as Pope and Taylor. For it is in the imperative that we confront an "other" which is profoundly a *part of* ourselves, while yet relativizing the entire reality *within which* we find ourselves. The imperative plays the role which Martin Luther (another commentator on *Romans*) assigned to the Law. Time and again Western theology has sought to replace "the traditional Lutheran concept of accusation by the *law* with the idea that . . . it is the *world* which convinces" us of our limitations, lostness, and destiny for death.[34] The result has been metaphysics, and generally not metaphysics at its best.

The alternative would seem to be something like the imperative. The imperative which in and through its very difficulty serves, in Paul's phrase, as pedagogue—tracing a dialectical path toward "the veritable worship of God."

NOTES

Preface

1. Barbara W. Tuchman, *The Proud Tower: A Portrait of the World before the War, 1890–1914* (New York: Macmillan, 1966), 463; cf. Stefan Zweig, *The World of Yesterday* (Lincoln: University of Nebraska Press, 1943).

2. "To express my own hypothesis, the most basic of such terms and relations is, in fact, those references to the self of the theologian and to the objects within that self's horizon which any given model discloses," David Tracy, *Blessed Rage for Order: The New Pluralism in Theology* (New York: Seabury Press, 1975), p. 23. Similarly see James Brown, *Subject and Object in Modern Theology* (London: SCM Press, 1955).

3. Paul Ricoeur, *The Conflict of Interpretations: Essays in Hermeneutics*, Don Ihde, ed. (Evanston: Northwestern University Press, 1974), pp. 440–67.

4. See Hans Frei, "The 'Literal Reading' of Biblical Narrative in the Christian Tradition: Does It Stretch or Will It Break?" in Frank McConnell, ed., *The Bible and the Narrative Tradition* (Oxford: Oxford University Press, 1986), pp. 36–77.

5. Theodor W. Adorno, *Negative Dialectics*, trans. E. B. Ashton (New York: Seabury Press, 1973), p. 23.

6. Emmanuel Levinas, *Totality and Infinity: An Essay on Exteriority*, trans. Alphonso Lingis (Pittsburgh: Duquesne University Press, 1969), pp. 36, 43.

7. See in particular Claude Welch, *Protestant Thought in the Nineteenth Century: Volume 1, 1799–1870* (New Haven: Yale University Press, 1972), pp. 47–48; Louis Dupré, *A Dubious Heritage: Studies in the Philosophy of Religion after Kant* (New York: Paulist Press, 1977).

8. John D. Caputo, *Radical Hermeneutics: Repetition, Deconstruction, and the Hermeneutic Project* (Bloomington: Indiana University Press, 1987), p. 97.

9. Susan Meld Shell, *The Rights of Reason: A Study of Kant's Philosophy and Politics* (Toronto: University of Toronto Press, 1980); see also Richard Lee Velkley, "Kant as Philosopher of Theodicy" (Ann Arbor: University Microfilms International, 1978).

10. On the Kant-Derrida connection, see Irene E. Harvey, "Derrida, Kant and the Performance of Parergonality" in *Derrida and Deconstruction*, Hugh J. Silverman, ed. (New York: Routledge, 1989), pp. 59–76; Christopher Norris, *Derrida* (Cambridge: Harvard University Press, 1987), pp. 142–71; Kevin Hart, *The Trespass of the Sign: Deconstruction, Theology and Philosophy* (Cambridge: Cambridge University Press, 1989), pp. 207–36; and Rodolphe Gasché, *The Tain of the Mirror: Derrida and the Philosophy of Reflection* (Cambridge: Harvard University Press, 1986), passim.

1. Introduction

1. Theodor Adorno, *Minima Moralia: Reflections from Damaged Life*, trans. E. F. N. Jephcott (London: NLB, 1974), p. 54. Cf. Maurice Blanchot, *The Writing of the Disaster*, trans. Ann Smock (Lincoln: University of Nebraska Press, 1986): "To think the disaster . . . is to have no longer any future in which to think it" (1); "can one maintain any distance at all when Auschwitz happens? How is it possible to say: Auschwitz has happened?" (143).

2. Adorno's abstract formulation is confirmed by Paul Fussell's historical and textual studies in *The Great War and Modern Memory* (London: Oxford University Press, 1975). See also Edith Wyschogrod, *Spirit in Ashes: Hegel, Heidegger and Man-Made Mass Death*: "During World War I a new process burst upon the historical horizon, a multifaceted state of affairs which later included such features as nuclear, biological, and chemical warfare and death camps. I call this social, political, and cultural complex the *death event*." Wyschogrod continues, "Colliding with antecedent systems of meaning, the event henceforth dominates cognitive, ethical, and aesthetic signification. In the case of contemporary man-made mass death we are in the eye of the storm and so cannot hope to constitute it both retrospectively and as a whole" (New Haven: Yale University Press, 1985), pp. xii, 15.

3. Modris Eksteins, *Rites of Spring: The Great War and the Birth of the Modern Age* (New York: Doubleday, 1989), p. 174.

4. Simone Weil, *Waiting for God*, trans. Emma Craufurd (New York: Harper & Row, 1951), p. 120.

5. See Christopher Lasch, *The Culture of Narcissism: American Life in an Age of Diminishing Expectations* (New York: Norton, 1978), and *The Minimal Self: Psychic Survival in Troubled Times* (New York: Norton, 1984). On the phenomenon of psychic numbing see Robert Jay Lifton and Richard Falk, *Indefensible Weapons: The Political and Psychological Case Against Nuclearism* (New York: Basic Books, 1982), pp. 10–12 and passim.

6. Max Horkheimer and Theodor W. Adorno, *Dialectic of Enlightenment*, trans. John Cumming (New York: Herder & Herder, 1972), p. xiv.

7. *Minima Moralia*, p. 65.

8. Adorno rounds off his *Minima Moralia* with a set of "theses against occultism" (238–44).

9. G. W. F. Hegel, *Phenomenology of Spirit*, trans. A. V. Miller (Oxford: Clarendon Press, 1977), p. 6. Empty depth is the "night in which all cows are black": it is a depth which is, in Hegel's terminology, "indeterminate," lacking in difference. If, as I shall argue, Hegel's thought represents a challenge with which we still must wrestle, it is in large part because he recognized the indispensable importance of difference—but then sought to contain it within "determinate" bounds. See Jacques Derrida, "From Restricted to General Economy: A Hegelianism without Reserve" in Derrida, *Writing and Difference*, trans. Alan Bass (Chicago: University of Chicago Press, 1978), pp. 251–77; also Mark C. Taylor, *Altarity* (Chicago: University of Chicago Press, 1987), pp. 3–33.

10. Derek Sayer, *Capitalism and Modernity: An Excursus on Marx and Weber* (New York: Routledge, 1991).

11. See Robert Howard, *Brave New Workplace* (New York: Viking, 1985), pp. 139–67.

12. For a vigorous and appreciative reading of Hegel by a member of the Frankfurt School, see Herbert Marcuse, *Reason and Revolution: Hegel and the Rise of Social Theory* (Boston: Beacon Press, 1941).

13. Johann Baptist Metz, *Faith in History and Society: Toward a Practical Fundamental Theology*, trans. David Smith (New York: Seabury, 1980), p. 6. In the present chapter, references to *Faith in History and Society* will be included parenthetically within the text. On Metz, see particularly Rebecca S. Chopp, *The Praxis of Suffering: An Interpretation of Liberation and Political Theologies* (Maryknoll, N.Y.: Orbis Books, 1986), pp. 64–81.

14. See Horkheimer and Adorno, *Dialectic of Enlightenment*.

15. Metz, *Faith*, p. 33. One must also exercise a certain hermeneutic of suspicion with regard to promises to "overcome the subject-object split." Adorno cautions that it is just this which wealth and privilege have always promised to deliver (in

a manner much more concrete than that of any religious-philosophical theory). From time immemorial, social privilege has grounded itself upon the conviction that "wealth shall vouch for the possibility of reuniting what [social violence has] sundered, the inward and the outward" (*Minima Moralia*, p. 185). See Adorno, "Subject and Object" in *The Essential Frankfurt School Reader*, ed. and intro. by Andrew Arato and Eike Gebhardt (New York: Urizen Books, 1978), pp. 497–511.

16. Max Horkheimer, "The End of Reason" in *Frankfurt School Reader*, Arato and Gebhardt, ed., p. 31.

17. Martin Heidegger, *Basic Writings*, David Farrell Krell, ed. (New York: Harper & Row, 1977), pp. 249–55.

18. Any critique of capitalism must begin by taking the full measure of this extraordinary phenomenon. Michael Harrington begins his defense of socialism by calling capitalism "the greatest achievement of humankind in history." *Socialism: Past and Future* (New York: Arcade, 1989), p. 4.

19. The phrase is borrowed from Marx by Marshall Berman as title of his book, *All That Is Solid Melts into Air: The Experience of Modernity* (New York: Simon & Schuster, 1982); see p. 15. I do not wish to encourage an oppositional stance toward capitalism, but to signal an important issue which is receiving increasing attention. See Ben Agger, *Fast Capitalism: A Critical Theory of Significance* (Urbana: University of Illinois Press, 1989); David Harvey, *The Condition of Postmodernity: An Enquiry into the Origins of Cultural Change* (Oxford: Basil Blackwell, 1989); and Frederic Jameson, *Postmodernism, or, The Cultural Logic of Late Capitalism* (Durham: Duke University Press, 1991). Cf. *Writing the Politics of Difference*, Hugh J. Silverman, ed. (Albany: State University of New York Press, 1991).

20. Cf. the remarkable chapter on "Capital, Civil Society, and the Deformation of Politics" in Richard Dien Winfield, *Overcoming Foundations: Studies in Systematic Philosophy* (New York: Columbia University Press, 1989), pp. 171–216.

21. Marc Boasson, *Au Soir d'un monde: lettres de guerre* (Paris: Plon, 1926), p. 311. Quoted in Eksteins, *Rites of Spring*, p. 223.

22. Adorno, *Minima Moralia*, p. 53.

23. Ibid., p. 63.

24. Ibid. Cf. Michael Ryan, *Marxism and Deconstruction: A Critical Articulation* (Baltimore: Johns Hopkins University Press, 1982), pp. 216–21 and passim.

25. Metz, *Faith*, p. 173. Metz's point is that for the culture at large evolution has ceased to be a limited scientific hypothesis, becoming instead a "pseudo-religious symbol" (172). If Metz's fastening upon the term "evolution" seems puzzling, one might consider Barbara Tuchman's remark that Darwin's trip aboard the *Beagle* was "the most fateful voyage since Columbus." For "Darwin's findings in *The Origin of Species*, when applied to human society, supplied the philosophical basis for the theory that war was both inherent in nature and ennobling"—a notion which exercised enormous influence throughout the Western world (*Proud Tower*, p. 249). Two useful studies of the ideology underlying everyday language are Raymond Williams, *Keywords: A Vocabulary of Culture and Society* (New York: Oxford University Press, 1976, revised 1983), and Peggy Rosenthal, *Words and Values: Some Leading Words and Where They Lead Us* (New York: Oxford University Press, 1984).

26. Metz, *Faith*, p. 75, quoting *Unsere Hoffnung*, published by the synod of German bishops (1:3).

27. Ibid., p. 128. For this important point Metz credits Adorno, *Negative Dialectics*, p. 385.

28. Ibid., p. 60, emphasis added.

29. See, e.g., ibid., p. 81, n. 23; Chopp, *Praxis*, p. 43.

30. My other major reservation is that even in the chapter on "the dangerous memory of the freedom of Jesus Christ," the Christology is at best undeveloped.

31. Metz, *Faith*, p. 65. Metz's particular target is the "transcendental" theology of Karl Rahner (64).

32. Ibid., p. 50; also p. 79, notes 3 and 8.

33. The phrase was suggested to me by a passage in Peter Sloterdijk's *Critique of Cynical Reason*: "I believe that Critical Theory has found a provisional ego for critique and a 'standpoint' that provides it with perspectives for a truly incisive critique—a standpoint that conventional epistemology does not consider. I am inclined to call it *a priori pain*" (Minneapolis: University of Minnesota Press, 1987), p. xxxiii. Also Moltmann, *Trinity and the Kingdom*, p. 49.

34. Adorno, *Minima Moralia*, p. 50. Cf. Blanchot, *Writing of the Disaster*, 145: "*Learn to think with pain*"; also cf. Henri J. M. Nouwen, *The Wounded Healer: Ministry in Contemporary Society* (Garden City, N.J.: Doubleday, 1972), passim.

35. One also thinks in this connection of Freud, who knew much about human brokenness; who also, in his late theory, envisioned existence as a struggle between two giants, Eros and Thanatos; and who placed a cautious hope in reason. Knowing well the vulnerability of the human intellect vis-à-vis the instincts, Freud nevertheless believed that "there is something peculiar about this weakness. The voice of the intellect is a soft one, but it does not rest until it has gained a hearing." See *The Standard Edition of the Complete Psychological Works of Sigmund Freud: Volume XVIII: Beyond the Pleasure Principle . . .* and *Volume XXI: The Future of an Illusion . . .* , James Strachey, ed. (London: Hogarth Press, 1955, 1961), XXI: 53.

36. Heidegger's "destruction" of Western metaphysics is itself dialectical; see the brief discussion of Heidegger's relation to the Western tradition in the section entitled "Tradition in Question."

37. The term "instrumental reason," which is less misleading than "theoretical reason" in this context, is borrowed from the Frankfurt School; see Max Horkheimer, *The Critique of Instrumental Reason: Lectures and Essays since the End of World War II*, trans. Matthew J. O'Connell et al. (New York: Seabury Press, 1974). Also see Horkheimer in *Frankfurt School Reader*, Arato and Gebhardt, eds., p. 28.

38. Cf. Jürgen Habermas, *Knowledge and Human Interests*, trans. Jeremy J. Shapiro (Boston: Beacon Press, 1971).

39. The difficulty of Derrida's various discussions of deconstruction derives in part from the author's determination to *do* deconstruction at the same time that he talks about it. Those encountering Derrida for the first time might wish to begin with two exceptions to this practice: the interviews (particularly the first two) in Derrida, *Positions*, trans. Alan Bass (Chicago: University of Chicago Press, 1981), and the extremely important "Afterword: Toward an Ethic of Discussion" in Derrida, *Limited Inc*, trans. Samuel Weber and Jeffrey Mehlman (Evanston: Northwestern University Press, 1988), pp. 111–60. A fairly accessible example of the deconstructive reading of a text is "Plato's Pharmacy" in Derrida, *Dissemination*, trans. Barbara Johnson (Chicago: University of Chicago Press, 1981), pp. 61–171.

As regards the secondary literature, one might start with Jonathan Culler's brief essay in John Sturrock, ed., *Structuralism and Since: From Lévi-Strauss to Derrida* (Oxford: Oxford University Press, 1979), pp. 154–80; and then proceed to Christopher Norris's longer but still introductory *Derrida*. Also valuable is the translator's preface to Derrida, *Of Grammatology*, trans. Gayatri Chakravorty Spivak (Baltimore: Johns Hopkins University Press, 1974), pp. ix–lxxxvii. Among the longer studies, special mention should be made of Rodolphe Gasché, *The Tain of the Mirror*. Those approaching deconstruction from a background in English-language philosophy will find assistance in Henry Staten's *Wittgenstein and Derrida* (Lincoln: University of Nebraska Press, 1984).

40. Derrida, *Positions*, p. 26.

41. Ibid., p. 41; note, however, that the dismantling of hierarchy is not to become an end in itself (p. 42).

42. "Thus one could reconsider all the pairs of opposites on which philosophy is constructed and on which our discourse lives, not in order to see opposition erase itself but to see what indicates that each of the terms must appear as the *différance* of the other, as the other different and deferred in the economy of the same." Derrida, *Margins of Philosophy*, trans. Alan Bass (Chicago: University of Chicago Press, 1982), p. 17. Here as elsewhere there are striking parallels between Derrida and the later Wittgenstein: see Staten, *Wittgenstein and Derrida*.

43. *Of Grammatology*, pp. 1–26; cf. *Dissemination*, pp. 84–94.

44. P. 6; cf. Adorno, "Subject and Object," in *Frankfurt School Reader*, Arato and Gebhardt, eds., p. 500: "Peace is the state of distinctness without domination, with the distinct participating in each other."

45. Peter Dews, "Adorno, Poststructuralism and the Critique of Identity" in Andrew Benjamin, ed., *The Problems of Modernity: Adorno and Benjamin* (London: Routledge, 1989), p. 15.

46. For a more direct demonstration of Adorno's theological pertinence, Wayne Whitson Floyd, Jr.'s *Theology and the Dialectics of Otherness: On Reading Bonhoeffer and Adorno* (Lanham: University Press of America, 1988) is indispensable.

47. "Deconstruction in America: An Interview with Jacques Derrida," ed. James Creech, Peggy Pamuf, and Jane Todd, *Critical Exchange* 17 (Winter 1985), p. 12; published by The Society for Critical Exchange, Miami University, Oxford, Ohio.

48. John Henry Newman, *The Idea of a University*, I. T. Ker, ed. (Oxford: Clarendon Press, 1976), p. 232.

49. Derrida, *Positions*, pp. 12–13, 52.

50. Martin Buber, *I and Thou*, trans. Walter Kaufmann (New York: Charles Scribner's Sons, 1970), 63–64.

51. "To 'deconstruct' philosophy, thus, would be to think—in the most faithful, *interior* way—the structured genealogy of philosophy's concepts, but at the same time to determine—from a certain *exterior* that is unqualifiable and unnameable by philosophy—what this history has been able to dissimulate or forbid . . . By means of this simultaneously faithful and violent circulation between the inside and the outside of philosophy—that is of the West—there is produced a certain textual work that gives great pleasure" (Derrida, *Positions*, pp. 6–7; emphases added). Cf. *Margins*, p. 135.

52. Cf. the recent collection of essays edited by Silverman aiming "to return deconstruction . . . to the history of philosophy": *Derrida and Deconstruction*, p. 4.

53. Martin Heidegger, "Modern Science, Metaphysics, and Mathematics" in *Basic Writings*, p. 274.

54. Ibid., p. 279.

55. See particularly the two volumes edited by James M. Robinson and John B. Cobb, Jr., in the series "New Frontiers in Theology": *The Later Heidegger and Theology* (New York: Harper & Row, 1963) on the thought of Heinrich Ott; and *The New Hermeneutic* (New York: Harper & Row, 1964) on Gerhard Ebeling and Ernst Fuchs. One of the finest efforts in this direction is Peter C. Hodgson, *Jesus—Word and Presence: An Essay in Christology* (Philadelphia: Fortress Press, 1971).

56. Martin Heidegger, *Being and Time*, trans. John Macquarrie and Edward Robinson (London: SCM Press, 1962), p. 47.

57. Derrida, *Margins of Philosophy*, p. 130.

58. This problem seems to me to beset even as excellent a book as Joseph Stephen O'Leary's *Questioning Back: The Overcoming of Metaphysics in Christian Tradition* (Minneapolis: Winston Press, 1985).

59. Derrida, interview from *Le nouvel observateur*, trans. David Allison et al., in David Wood and Robert Bernasconi, ed., *Derrida and Différance* (Evanston: Northwestern University Press, 1988), p. 81.

60. Derrida, "From Restricted to General Economy: A Hegelianism without Reserve," *Writing and Difference*, pp. 251–77.

61. See Robert J. Schreider, *Constructing Local Theologies* (Maryknoll, N.Y.: Orbis, 1985).

62. See Van Harvey, *The Historian and the Believer: The Morality of Historical Knowledge and Christian Belief* (New York: Macmillan, 1966).

63. For this distinction between two Enlightenments, see Jon Sobrino, "Theological Understanding in European and Latin American Theology," in Sobrino, *The True Church and the Poor*, trans. Matthew J. O'Connell (Maryknoll, N.Y.: Orbis, 1984), pp. 7–38.

64. Adorno, *Minima Moralia*, pp. 88–89. For a measured and influential critique of "foundationalism" in theology, see Nicholas Wolterstorff, *Reason within the Bounds of Religion Alone* (Grand Rapids: Eerdmans, 1976).

65. Cf. James S. Hans, *The Question of Value: Thinking through Nietzsche, Heidegger and Freud* (Carbondale: Southern Illinois University Press, 1989), pp. 56, 125 and passim.

66. Adorno, *Minima Moralia*, p. 112.

67. Failure to recognize this aspect of metaphysics is, to my mind, the crucial shortcoming of Dietrich Bonhoeffer's otherwise exemplary *Act and Being*, trans. Bernard Noble (New York: Harper & Row, 1961). A new translation of this work is forthcoming from Fortress Press.

68. Obviously the term "the tradition" denotes a reality which is multiple and complex.

69. Adorno, "Was bedeutet: Aufarbeitung der Vergangenheit" in Adorno, *Erziehung zur Mündigkeit: Vorträge und Gespräche mit Hellmut Becker, 1959–1969*, G. Kadelbach, ed. (Frankfurt am Main: Suhrkamp Verlag, 1971); cited by Christa Burger, "The Disappearance of Art: The Postmodernist Debate in the U.S.," *Telos* 68, p. 103, n. 36.

70. Russell Jacoby, *Social Amnesia: A Critique of Conformist Psychology from Adler to Laing* (Boston: Beacon Press, 1975), p. xviii.

71. Heidegger, *Holzwege* (Frankfurt am Main: Klostermann, 1950), p. 42; cf. L. M. Vail, *Heidegger and Ontological Difference* (University Park: Pennsylvania State University Press, 1972), p. 44.

72. Dietrich Bonhoeffer, *Ethics* (New York: Macmillan, 1955), p. 372; quoted by Wayne Whitson Floyd, Jr., in "The Search for an Ethical Sacrament: From Bonhoeffer to Critical Social Theory," *Modern Theology* 7:2 (January 1991), p. 187.

73. Augustine, *De Genesi Ad Litteram*, Imperfectus Liber, 1: 3.

74. Susan Buck-Morss, *The Origin of Negative Dialectics: Theodor W. Adorno, Walter Benjamin, and the Frankfurt Institute* (New York: Free Press, 1977), p. 55.

75. Cf. the twofold method described in the final section of this chapter.

76. The latter passage is spoken by God in the "Prologue in Heaven," the former by the angels in the final scene as they bear Faust's soul aloft; thus the two passages bracket the action of the play. Marshall Berman writes, "This is the meaning of Faust's relationship with the devil: human powers can be developed only through what Marx called 'the powers of the underworld,' dark and fearful energies that may erupt with a horrible force beyond all human control. Goethe's *Faust* is the first, and still the best, *tragedy of development*" (Berman, *All That Is Solid*, p. 40).

77. To counter this triumphalist celebration of the given as right and natural,

Adorno asserts that "whatever is in the context of bourgeois delusion called nature, is merely the scar of social mutilation" (*Minima Moralia*, p. 95).

78. The argument here advanced is indebted, directly and indirectly, to Hegel's dialectic of master and bondsman, *Phenomenology of Spirit*, pp. 111–19. That dialectic, which gained influence in French thought through the teachings of Alexandre Kojève, has amply demonstrated its capacities as an instrument of social criticism in the work of Jean-Paul Sartre and Franz Fanon, among others. See Kojève, *Introduction to the Reading of Hegel*, Allan Bloom, ed., trans. James H. Nichols, Jr. (New York: Basic Books, 1969); Sartre, *Anti-Semite and Jew*, trans. George J. Becker (New York: Schocken Books, 1948); Fanon, *Wretched of the Earth*, trans. Constance Farrington (New York: Grove Press, 1963). A perfect expression of "it could have been otherwise" is Milan Kundera's title, *The Unbearable Lightness of Being*. It is fitting that the phrase should come from an exiled Czech.

79. *The Complete Essays and Other Writings of Ralph Waldo Emerson* (New York: Modern Library, 1940), p. 52. Emerson and the transcendentalist movment are emblematic of an American receptivity to idealist modes of thought.

80. Paul Ricoeur, *Freud and Philosophy: An Essay on Interpretation*, trans. Dennis Savage (New Haven: Yale University Press, 1970), p. 43.

81. Ibid. Cf. Paul A. Cantor, *Creature and Creator: Myth-making and English Romanticism* (Cambridge: Cambridge University Press, 1984).

82. Derrida calls for "a *departure* from the Heideggerean problematic," particularly from the Heideggerean notions of "*origin* and *fall*." He reflects, "I sometimes have the feeling that the Heideggerean problematic is the most 'profound' and 'powerful' defense of what I attempt to put into question under the rubric of the *thought of presence*" (*Positions*, pp. 54–55).

83. Derrida, *Writing and Difference*, p. 251.

84. Proceeding this way may help prevent the critique of presence from becoming an end in itself.

85. After surveying the work of a variety of figures in contemporary hermeneutics, David E. Klemm proposes that theological hermeneutics be understood as reflecting a "second negation, the overturning of otherness. . . . The otherness of the other is a figure of the unity within the diversity of being, which is seen as issuing from a common source and aiming at a common end," Klemm, ed., *Hermeneutic Inquiry. Volume I: The Interpretation of Texts* (Atlanta: Scholars Press, 1986), p. 51. For a critique of this paradigm in religious studies, particularly Eliade, see Tomoko Masuzawa, "Original Lost: An Image of Myth and Ritual in the Age of Mechanical Reproduction." *Journal of Religion* 69:3 (July 1989), pp. 307–25, esp. 320–25.

86. See Lowe, *Evil and the Unconscious* (Chico, Calif.: Scholars Press, 1983), pp. 107–24, and "Dangerous Supplement/Dangerous Memory: Sketches for a History of the Postmodern," *Thought: A Review of Culture and Idea*, 61: 240 (March 1986), pp. 34–55.

87. This matter will be treated more fully in chapter 5.

88. Buck-Morss, *Origin of Negative Dialectics*, p. 49; emphases Buck-Morss's. The passage, like most of Buck-Morss's text, includes a number of helpful notes.

89. Yirmiyahu Yovel, *Kant and the Philosophy of History* (Princeton: Princeton University Press, 1980), p. 302; I have altered the author's emphases.

90. Ibid., p. 306.

91. For drawing my attention to this paradigm shift in the construing of the history of philosophy I am indebted to a remark made by Professor Alexander von Schoenborn of the University of Missouri in conversation.

92. See Adorno's extensive critique of Kant in *Negative Dialectics*, pp. 211–99.

93. Bonhoeffer, *Ethics*, p. 372.

2. Qualitative Difference

1. Indeed to give the discussion a certain discipline, I shall concentrate upon the first chapter of Barth's commentary, which announces many of the themes which are subsequently developed.

2. Barth, *The Epistle to the Romans*, trans. Edwyn C. Hopkins (London: Oxford University Press, 1933), p. 10. In the present chapter, references to Barth's commentary will generally be given parenthetically within the text.

3. References in square brackets are to the German text: Karl Barth, *Der Römerbrief* (Munich: Kaiser Verlag, 1926).

4. On the Derridean notion of *différance*, see *Positions*, 7–11, cf. 24–29; *Margins of Philosophy*, 1–27.

5. Cf. 36: "The power of God stands neither at the side of nor above—supernatural!—these limited and limiting powers. . . . It can neither be substituted for them nor ranged with them, and, save with the greatest caution, it cannot even be compared with them." Barth's caution may reflect an awareness of the ironies and reversals delineated in Hegel's treatment of the master and the bondsman (*Phenomenology*, pp. 111–19; cf. Derrida, *Writing and Difference*, pp. 254–62).

6. *Margins of Philosophy*, p. 38; cf. *Writing and Difference*, pp. 6, 253; Gregory L. Ulmer, *Applied Grammatology: Post(e)-Pedagogy from Jacques Derrida to Joseph Beuys* (Baltimore: Johns Hopkins University Press, 1985), pp. 38, 51.

7. P. 28, emphasis added.

8. Søren Kierkegaard, *Concluding Unscientific Postscript*, trans. David F. Swenson and Walter Lowrie (Princeton: Princeton University Press, 1941), p. 219. Barth stands firm on this principle even with regard to Christ: "Here is the necessary qualification. The vision of the New Day remains an indirect vision" (97).

9. P. 10, emphasis added.

10. P. 53, emphasis added.

11. P. 40, emphasis added.

12. P. 40; see Moltmann, *The Crucified God*, trans. R. A. Wilson and John Bowden (New York: Harper & Row, 1974), pp. 252–53.

13. Metz, *Faith in History*, pp. 56–58, 128–30.

14. As Barth puts it at one point, what the hidden things contradict is "the obvious experience of the senses" (39). This is one line of thought contributing to Barth's mistrust of experience. Cf. 51: "They have wished to experience the known god of this world: well! they have experienced him." The prototype of unfaith is Pharaoh, whose experience of being "broken to pieces on God" was oppositional indeed (43).

15. P. 43, emphasis added; cf. p. 48.

16. Cf. 36, quoted earlier: "The power of God stands neither at the side of nor above—supernatural!—these limited and limiting powers."

17. Cf. *Positions*, 12.

18. "Whether in the order of spoken or written discourse, no element can function as a sign without referring to another element which itself is not simply present. This interweaving results in each 'element'—phoneme or grapheme—being constituted on the basis of the trace within it of the other elements of the chain or system. . . . Nothing, neither among the elements nor within the system, is anywhere ever simply present or absent" (Derrida, *Positions*, p. 26). As Derrida is frequently accused of making a "presence" of absence, it is important to note that he averts to this reading of deconstruction and gives specific reasons for rejecting it: see *Margins of Philosophy*, pp. 65–67; Spivak in *On Grammatology*, xv–xvi; Staten, *Wittgenstein and Derrida*, p. 53.

19. P. 33, cf. p. 36. The point invites comparison with the pattern of "something and—nothing, nothing and—something" observed earlier.

20. P. 48; this provides a way of understanding the powerful, extended description of the "mist," pp. 49–51.

21. *Romans*, p. 46. Adorno speaks of "a hope that animal creation might survive the wrong that man has done it, if not man himself, and give rise to a better species, one that finally makes a success of life. Zoological gardens stem from the same hope" (*Minima Moralia*, p. 115).

22. The exception which proves the rule is, of course, Sartre. There the reality of God or the infinite is denied; nevertheless the human being is defined by the (vain) desire to be that reality.

23. Kant, *Critique of Pure Reason*, trans. Norman Kemp Smith (London: Macmillan, 1929), p. 47.

24. See, for example, Derrida, *Positions*, p. 52.

25. Interestingly, a contrary objection is also possible. It may be argued that the finite/infinite difference as portrayed by our figure is not strong enough; that we have done what Barth forbids, placing God "fundamentally on one line with ourselves and with things." I think, however, that our representation of type 3 does as much as such any flat, two-dimensional figure can do, designating a hiatus between finite and infinite and thereby stipulating a prohibition, a "Nein!" Perhaps one could represent the finite/infinite difference by analogy with the difference *between* two dimensions and three (in the manner of Edwin Abbott's intriguing book, *Flatland: A Romance of Many Dimensions* (New York: Barnes & Noble, 1963). But even then, observers could imagine the infinite as one dimensions among others, or the sum of all dimensions, thus reasserting a continuity of finite and infinite.

3. Truth and Contextualization

1. Jacques Derrida, *Positions*, p. 5.

2. Freud's metapsychology is often portrayed as a misguided effort to submit psychology to the laws of Helmholtzian physics. See, for example, Hans Kung, *Freud and the Problem of God*, trans. Edward Quinn (New Haven: Yale University Press, 1979).

3. I borrow this suggestive term from Henry E. Allison, *Kant's Transcendental Idealism: An Interpretation and Defense* (New Haven: Yale University Press, 1983), pp. 10–13. Allison characterizes an epistemic condition as a condition "that is necessary for the representation of an object or an objective state of affairs," clearly distinguishing epistemic from logical, psychological, and ontological conditions.

4. Regarding the argument presented here and its relation to theology, cf. the important, untranslated work of Pierre Thévenaz, *L'Homme et sa raison. Vol. I: Raison et conscience de soi, Vol. II: Raison et histoire*, (Neuchatel: Editions de la Baconnière, 1956).

5. Husserl, *Logical Investigations*, trans. J. N. Findlay (London: Routledge & Kegan Paul, 1970), I:342; emphasis added.

6. Staten, *Wittgenstein and Derrida*, p. 34; quoting Husserl, *Formal and Transcendental Logic*, trans. Dorion Cairns (The Hague: Martinus Nijhoff, 1969), p. 233, emphasis Husserl's.

7. Husserl, *Logical Investigations*, I:254.

8. Husserl, *The Crisis of European Sciences and Transcendental Phenomenology*, trans. David Carr (Evanston: Northwestern University Press, 1970), p. 189.

9. Ibid., p. 159.

10. *Logical Investigations*, II, 584.

11. Derrida, *Positions*, p. 41; *Margins*, p. 17.

12. Ricoeur, *Husserl: An Analysis of His Phenomenology*, trans. Edward G. Ballard and Lester E. Embree (Evanston: Northwestern University Press, 1967), p. 204; cf. "the two intentive processes (*visées*)" (6). Following the sentence quoted, Ricoeur observes, "In short, in the first works, consciousness is at once speech (*la parole*) and perception"; the word (*la parole*) is associated with intention, perception with fulfillment, and the relation is that of the merely empty to that which completes it, the full. The premium is placed upon intuitive fulfillment. But in Ricoeur's own constructive work, *Fallible Man*, perception comes first, under the heading of finite perspective. Empty intention is introduced subsequently, in connection with language: i.e., the "ability to express sense," which "is a continual transcendence, at least in intention, of the perspectival aspect of the perceived here and now." Ricoeur, *Fallible Man*, trans. Charles A. Kelbley (New York: Fordham University Press, 1986), p. 27. Here primacy would seem to have shifted to the side of ("infinite") intention. Thus Ricoeur's own appropriation of phenomenology may reflect, expressly or inadvertently, the ambiguity which Derrida has since sought to explore.

13. Derrida, *Speech and Phenomena*, trans. David B. Allison (Evanston: Northwestern University Press, 1973), p. 90.

14. Ibid., p. 89.

15. Ibid., pp. 91–92.

16. Husserl, *Logical Investigations*, I:285–86; quoted by Derrida, *Speech and Phenomena*, p. 97.

17. *Speech and Phenomena*, p. 98; emphases Derrida's.

18. A turning point in the *Crisis* is the inquiry into "Descartes as the primal founder not only of the modern idea of objectivistic rationalism but also of the transcendental motif which explodes it." The section concludes with the observation that "Precisely those ideas which were supposed to ground this rationalism as *aeterna veritas* bear within themselves a *deeply hidden sense*, which, once brought to the surface, completely uproots it" (*Crisis*, pp. 73–74, emphasis Husserl's). The lines could almost have been written by Derrida. On Husserl as precursor of deconstruction, see Caputo, *Radical Hermeneutics*, pp. 36–59.

19. Staten, *Wittgenstein and Derrida*, p. 47; my exposition is indebted to Staten's treatment of this aspect of the Husserl-Derrida encounter.

20. Ricoeur, *Conflict of Interpretations*, p. 382.

21. Ibid., p. 396.

22. Ibid., p. 397.

23. Ibid.

24. Ibid., p. 398.

25. Ibid., p. 396.

26. Cf. the tension or contradiction between themes of holism and humanism traced in Lowe, "Introduction" to Ricoeur, *Fallible Man*, vii–xxxii. David E. Klemm's able commentary recognizes the three-part framework in Ricoeur, and indeed makes of it a major theme; see Klemm, *The Hermeneutical Theory of Paul Ricoeur: A Constructive Analysis* (Lewisburg: Bucknell University Press, 1983), pp. 13–14, 157.

27. For further reflection on the Ricoeurian hermeneutic, see Lowe, "Hans Frei and Phenomenological Hermeneutics," *Modern Theology* 8:2 (April 1992), pp. 133–44.

28. "Philosophy as Rigorous Science" in Peter McCormick and Frederick Elliston, eds., *Husserl: Shorter Works* (Notre Dame: University of Notre Dame Press, 1981), p. 193.

29. Husserl, "The Vienna Lecture: Philosophy and the Crisis of European Hu-

manity" in Husserl, *Crisis of European Sciences*, p. 275. Cf. p. 72: "to every primal establishment [*Urstiftung*] essentially belongs a final establishment [*Endstiftung*] assigned as a task to the historical process."

30. See Derrida, *Disseminations*, pp. 61–171. For the passages quoted, see Ferdinand de Saussure, *Course in General Linguistics*, Charles Bally and Albert Sechehaye with Albert Riedlinger, eds., trans. Wade Baskin (New York: McGraw-Hill, 1966), pp. 25, 31; cf. Derrida, *Positions*, p. 25.

31. Ricoeur, *Freud and Philosophy*, p. 65.

32. Cf. the subsections in Book III entitled "Psychoanalysis Is Not an Observational Science" (pp. 358–75) and "Psychoanalysis Is Not Phenomenology" (pp. 390–418).

33. Many have contended that it is possible and necessary to translate Freudian psychology entirely into the language of sense; see, for example, Jean-Paul Sartre, *Being and Nothingness: An Essay on Phenomenologicl Ontology*, trans. Hazel E. Barnes (New York: Philosophical Library, 1956), pp. 557–75; and Roy Schafer, *A New Language for Psychoanalysis* (New Haven: Yale University Press, 1976), *passim*. Ricoeur does little to indicate what would be lost by such translation. For an extended analysis of Ricoeur's "Analytic: Reading of Freud," see Lowe, *Mystery and the Unconscious: A Study in the Thought of Paul Ricoeur* (Metuchen, N.J.: Scarecrow Press, 1977).

34. Don Ihde, *Hermeneutic Phenomenology: The Philosophy of Paul Ricoeur* (Evanston: Northwestern University Press, 1971), pp. 155, 159; quoting Ricoeur, *Freud and Philosophy*, p. 464.

35. Ricoeur, *Lectures on Ideology and Utopia*, George H. Taylor, ed. (New York: Columbia University Press, 1986), p. 311. The lectures "were first delivered . . . in the fall of 1975" (p. ix).

36. George Taylor, Editor's Introduction to Ricoeur, *Lectures*, p. xxv; quoting Ricoeur, "Explanation and Understanding: On Some Remarkable Connections Among the Theory of the Text, Theory of Action and Theory of History" in *The Philosophy of Paul Ricoeur: An Anthology of His Work*, Charles E. Reagan and David Stewart, eds. (Boston: Beacon Press, 1978), p. 165, and Ricoeur, *The Rule of Metaphor*, trans. Robert Czerny (Toronto: University of Toronto Press, 1977), p. 313.

37. See David Pellauer, "The Significance of the Text in Paul Ricoeur's Hermeneutical Theory" in Charles E. Reagan, ed., *Studies in the Philosophy of Paul Ricoeur* (Athens: Ohio University Press, 1979), pp. 106–108.

38. *Lectures*, p. 8.

39. Ibid., p. 10.

40. Cf. Ricoeur, *Fallible Man*: "Man is not intermediate because he is between angel and animal; he is intermediate within himself, within his *selves*" (p. 3).

41. On conceptions of dialectic, see Derrida, "From Restricted to General Economy: A Hegelianism without Reserve" in Derrida, *Writing and Difference*, pp. 251–77.

42. See Hans Frei, "The 'Literal Reading' of Biblical Narrative in the Christian Tradition: Does It Stretch or Will It Break?" in McConnell, ed., *The Bible and the Narrative Tradition*, pp. 36–77.

43. My treatment of this topic is indebted to Gregory L. Ulmer's essay, "Sounding the Unconscious" in John P. Leavey, Jr., *Glassary* (Lincoln: University of Nebraska Press, 1986), pp. 23–129.

44. These classic cases are found in Freud, *Standard Edition*, pp. 12:1–82, 17:1–122.

45. Derrida, "*Fors*: The Anglish Words of Nicolas Abraham and Maria Torok," trans. Barbara Johnson in *The Georgia Review* 31:1, p. 106; the translation is reprinted as the foreword to Nicholas Abraham and Maria Torok, *The Wolf Man's*

Magic Word: A Cryptonymy, trans. Nicholas Rand (Minneapolis: University of Minnesota Press, 1986), where the passage appears with minor modifications on p. xl.

46. Here Derrida draws upon the thought of Jacques Lacan; see Ulmer, "Sounding the Unconsicous," pp. 51–57.

47. Ulmer, "Sounding the Unconsicous," p. 102.

48. Derrida, *Glas*, trans. John P. Leavey, Jr., and Richard Rand (Lincoln: University of Nebraska Press, 1986), 210; quoted in Ulmer, "Sounding the Unconscious," p. 93.

49. Ricoeur, *Conflict of Interpretations*, p. 119; I have modified the translation.

50. From "Limited Inc, a b c . . . ," trans. Samuel Weber, *Glyph*, 2 (Baltimore: Johns Hopkins University Press, 1977), p. 232.

51. "The Vienna Lecture," Quentin Lauer's translation in Husserl, *Phenomenology and the Crisis of Philosophy* (New York: Harper & Row, 1965), p. 189.

52. Ulmer, "Sounding the Unconscious," pp. 97, 103.

53. "The play of differences supposes, in effect, syntheses and referrals . . . ," Derrida, *Positions*, p. 26; cf. Ulmer's advocacy of a grammatology "beyond deconstruction," in *Applied Grammatology*, pp. 3–5 and *passim*.

54. Winfield, *Overcoming Foundations*, p. 1.

55. Husserl, *Crisis*, p. 299.

56. Christopher Norris, *The Contest of Faculties: Philosophy and Theory after Deconstruction* (London: Methuen, 1985), p. 206.

57. Derrida, *Writing and Difference*, p. 292; emphasis Derrida's.

58. The term "postmodern" has been invoked in a great variety of settings, sometimes simplistically, sometimes with subtlety. My use of the term at this point is sheerly for purposes of exposition, to designate a specific proposal regarding the nature of language.

59. Derrida, *Writing and Difference*, p. 293.

60. Derrida, *Edmund Husserl's "Origin of Geometry": An Introduction*, trans. John P. Leavey, Jr. (Stony Brook, N.Y.: Nicolas Hays, 1978), p. 102.

61. Staten, *Wittgenstein and Derrida*, p. 48.

62. In "White Mythology: Metaphor in the Text of Philosophy" Derrida shows not only that philosophy is irreducibly dependent upon a network of metaphors (a good "postmodernist" point), but also that the very notion of metaphor, especially when adopted as a fundamental explanatory device, is itself shot through with philosophic precommitments (*Margins of Philosophy*, pp. 207–71).

63. Caputo, *Radical Hermeneutics*, p. 97.

64. *Positions*, pp. 7, 9; cf. 29.

65. "The phenomenon of the *equiprimordiality* of constitutive items has often been disregarded in ontology, because of a methodologically unrestrained tendency to derive everything and anything from some simple 'primal ground.' " Heidegger, *Being and Time*, p. 170.

66. "The economy of the fetish is more powerful than that of the truth—decidable—of the thing itself or than a deciding discourse of castration (*pro aut contra*). The fetish is not opposable.

"It oscillates like the clapper of a truth that rings awry [*cloche*]" (*Glas*, p. 227).

67. Derrida, "Signature Event Context" in *Margins of Philosophy*, p. 327.

68. Derrida, *Speech and Phenomena*, p. 104.

69. Ulmer, "Sounding the Unconsicous," p. 27.

70. Derrida, *Limited Inc*, pp. 111–60. See particularly pp. 115–22, 136–41.

71. Ibid., pp. 136, 129.

72. Derrida, *Speech and Phenomena*, p. 102.

73. Ulmer, "Sounding the Unconscious," p. 111. Regarding Fate or Destiny, see Ulmer on *Moirae* and the *moire* effect, in *Applied Grammatology*, 44–48. Regarding

names, see Derrida, *Signeponge/Signsponge*, trans. Richard Rand (New York: Columbia University Press, 1984), on Francis Ponge; similarly, *Glas* on Genet and Hegel.

74. Cf. Robert S. Gall, "Of/From Theology and Deconstruction," *Journal of the American Academy of Religion* 58:3 (Fall 1990), pp. 413–37. I find much to agree with in Gall's insightful essay, though I would distinguish more than he does between Derrida and the various proponents of a deconstructive a/theology.

75. Cf. Hans, *Question of Value*, pp. 123–24 and *passim*; Caputo, *Radical Hermeneutics*, p. 6 and passim.

4. The Kantian Opening

1. For an excellent treatment of "Kant as Philosopher of Theodicy," see the dissertation by that title by Richard L. Velkley. The interpretation set forth in the present pages had been completed when Velkley's account became available to me.

2. Translated from Kant, *Anthropology*, VII 269 (136) by Susan Meld Shell in *Rights of Reason* p. 29. I am indebted to Shell for highlighting this passage and pointing to the theodicy issue in the Kantian philosophy. Regarding the significance of the anthropology lectures, see Frederick P. van de Pitte, *Kant as Philosophical Anthropologist* (The Hague: Martinus Nijhoff, 1971).

3. Adorno, *Minima Moralia*, p. 122.

4. *Kant's Cosmogony, as in His Essay on the Retardation of the Rotation of the Earth and His Natural History and Theory of the Heavens*, trans. W. Hastie (New York: Johnson Reprint Corporation, 1900), p. 151; Alexander Pope, *An Essay on Man*, 1:87–90; see Pope, *Selected Poetry*, ed. Martin Price (New York: New American Library, 1970), p. 126.

5. Kant, *Critique of Practical Reason*, trans. Lewis White Beck (Indianapolis: Bobbs-Merrill, 1956), p. 166. The significance of this turn of argument has been underlined, apparently independently, by Susan Meld Shell (*Rights of Reason*, p. 20) and by the French philosopher Jean-Luc Nancy (*L'impératif catégorique* [Paris: Flammarion, 1983], p. 86).

6. Blaise Pascal, *Pensées and The Provincial Letters* (New York: Modern Library, 1941), p. 75.

7. Leroy E. Loemker, *Struggle for Synthesis: The Seventeenth Century Background of Leibnitz's Synthesis of Order and Freedom* (Cambridge: Harvard University Press, 1972), p. 73.

8. *Dictionary of the History of Ideas: Studies of Selected Pivotal Ideas*, Philip P. Wiener, ed. (New York: Charles Scribner's Sons, 1968), I:325.

9. Arthur O. Lovejoy, *The Great Chain of Being: A Study of the History of an Idea* (New York: Harper & Brothers, 1936), p. 184.

10. In fairness to Pope, it should be noted that Order may be dynamic: see David Fairer, "Pope, Blake, Heraclitus and oppositional thinking" in *Pope: New Contexts*, ed. David Fairer (New York: Harvester Wheatsheaf, 1990), pp. 169–88.

11. "Gust" is an archaic term for taste or pleasure, according to the unabridged *Oxford English Dictionary*.

12. Lovejoy, *Great Chain*, p. 179.

13. Plato, *Timaeus* 29–30 in *The Dialogues of Plato*, trans. B. Jowett (New York: Random House, 1892, 1920) II:14; quoted in Lovejoy, *Great Chain*, p. 47.

14. Lovejoy, *Great Chain*, p. 49.

15. Ibid., p. 52.

16. "Where Spinoza had (ostensibly) asserted that the realization of the principle of plenitude, being necessary, cannot properly be called either good or bad, Leibnitz declared that, while necessary, it is also supremely good; he thereby gave

to that principle (without qualification) the status of a doctrine about value as well as (with a qualification) that of a doctrine about the constitution of reality," ibid., p. 180.

17. See Kant, *Kant's Cosmogony*. In the present section and the next, references to this work will generally be given parenthetically in the text.

18. G. J. Whitrow, "Kant's Contribution to Cosmology and Cosmogony: A New Assessment" in *Kant's Cosmogony*, pp. xix–xx.

19. W. Hastie, quoted by Gerald J. Whitrow, *Kant's Cosmogony*, pp. xxxvi–xxxvii.

20. Kant, "Universal Natural History and Theory of the Heavens," *Kant's Cosmogony*, p. 23.

21. Emphasis added.

22. P. 139, emphasis added.

23. Cf. Hans, *Question of Value*, p. 55: "Nietzsche seeks to overcome the relativity of truth by establishing the limits through which it can be arrived at, and as such, 'God is dead' is as essential as being delivered from revenge or accepting the eternal return. Each of these conceptual formulations is designed to make man turn away from his revulsion against time as it seeks to invert the Kantian Ideas of limit. Each of them is designed to show how man generates nihilism through his revulsion against time. They are the conditions of our humanity rather than the negation of it, as any careful reading of Nietzsche would show."

24. "But the primitive matter itself, whose qualities and forces lie at the basis of all changes, is an *immediate* consequence of the Divine existence; and that same matter must therefore be at once so rich and so complete, that the development of its combinations may extend over a plane which . . . is infinite" (p. 140, emphasis added).

25. P. 139, emphasis Kant's.

26. Cf. Kant's closing reflections on the human soul (154–56).

27. Kant, *Critique of Pure Reason*, B:1–2 (English, pp. 41–42); emphases added.

28. Joe Harold Hicks, "Divine and Human Subjectivity in Kant" (Ann Arbor: University Microfilms, 1970), p. 1.

29. Ibid., p. 4.

30. Kant, *Critique of Pure Reason*, p. 65.

31. Merold Westphal, "In Defense of the Thing in Itself," *Kant-Studien* 59:1 (1968), pp. 118–19, 122–23.

32. John Sallis, *The Gathering of Reason* (Athens: Ohio University Press, 1980), p. 20.

33. It must be added that Kant himself abetted the misunderstanding; see Ermanno Bencivenga, *Kant's Copernican Revolution* (New York: Oxford University Press, 1987). Cf. Peter Dews's sage remark that "one of the major differences between poststructuralism and Critical Theory is summarized in Adorno's contention that 'even when we merely limit the subject, we put an end to its power.' " This is in effect to say that unlike Kant's or Adorno's, the poststructuralist critique of the subject is too often oppositional (Dews, "Adorno, Poststructuralism and the Critique of Identity," p. 19).

34. Sallis, *Gathering of Reason*, p. 20.

35. Ibid., p. 21.

36. Ibid., 22; emphases Sallis's. I have dropped Sallis's reference to a gathering "into presence" because the phrase suggests the nostalgia for presence which Derrida discerns in similar passages by Heidegger.

37. For an illuminating treatment of intellectual intuition and its relation to the thing in itself, see Westphal, "In Defense of the Thing in Itself," pp. 118–41.

38. Sallis, *Gathering of Reason*, p. 25.

39. See, for example, Cantor, *Creature and Creator.*
40. Kant, *Critique of Pure Reason*, pp. 45–48.

5. The Otherness of the Ethical

1. Barth, *Romans*, pp. 38–39.
2. Cf. Ricoeur, *Conflict of Interpretations*, 441: "Accusation and protection are, so to speak, 'the corrupt parts of religion. . . .' " It is not clear, however, that Ricoeur's own Heideggerian resolution treats the issue with sufficient radicality.
3. See in particular Jeremy D. B. Walker, *To Will One Thing: Reflections on Kierkegaard's "Purity of Heart"* (Montreal: McGill-Queen's University Press, 1972), pp. 7–14. The task is to rescue existentialism from its own repudiation of the ethical: "Bultmann and Ebeling, with little concern for the Old Testament, have replaced the traditional Lutheran concept of accusation by the *law* with the idea that today it is the *world* which convinces man of his limitations, lostness and destiny for death," Dietrich Ritschl, *Memory and Hope: An Inquiry Concerning the Presence of Christ* (New York: Macmillan, 1967), p. 133. In contrast, see Metz, *Faith in History*, pp. 127–28.
   Thanks to the work of Ronald M. Green, we have increasing evidence of Kierkegaard's conscious, historical debt to Kant. See Green, "The Leap of Faith: Kierkegaard's Debt to Kant" in *Philosophy and Theology* III:4 (Summer 1989), pp. 385–421, and *Kierkegaard and Kant: The Hidden Debt* (Albany: State University of New York Press, 1992).
4. Kant, *Critique of Practical Reason*, p. 19; in the present section and the section following, references to this work will generally be given parenthetically in the text.
5. P. 18, emphases added.
6. Thus one takes quite seriously Kant's statement that the task "is merely to show that there is a pure practical reason" (*Critique of Practical Reason*, p. 3). See Robert J. Benton, *Kant's Second Critique and the Problem of Transcendental Arguments* (The Hague: Martinus Nijhoff, 1977), pp. 29–35.
7. Benton, *Kant's Second Critique*, p. 30.
8. Ronald M. Green, *Religious Reason: The Rational and Moral Basis of Religious Belief* (New York: Oxford University Press, 1978), p. 4.
9. Ibid., p. 90.
10. Ibid., p. 91.
11. Thévenaz, *L'Homme et sa raison. Vol II: Raison et histoire*, p. 151, translation mine.
12. Hicks, "Divine and Human," p. 187.
13. Reinhold Niebuhr, *The Nature and Destiny of Man: A Christian Interpretation* (New York: Charles Scribner's Sons, 1941), I:93.
14. See, for example, the "Symposium on Heidegger and Nazism" edited and introduced by Arnold I. Davidson in *Critical Inquiry* 15:2 (Winter 1989), 407–408; Jacques Derrida, "Like the Sound of the Sea Deep within a Shell: Paul de Man's War" in *Critical Inquiry* 14:3 (Spring 1988), pp. 590–652; and the collection of essays and responses on de Man in *Critical Inquiry* 15:4 (Summer 1989), pp. 704–873. Cf. Tolstoy's classic "The Death of Ivan Ilych."
15. Paul Fussell, *Thank God for the Atom Bomb and Other Essays* (New York: Ballantine Books, 1988), pp. 1–28; the essay is followed by an exchange of views between Fussell and Michael Walzer.
16. Attributed to Kierkegaard in *The Viking Book of Aphorisms: A Personal Selec-

tion, ed. W. H. Auden and Louis Kronenberger (New York: Viking Press, 1962), p. 91.

17. Kant, *Critique of Judgment*, trans. J. H. Bernard (New York: Hafner Press, 1951), p. 301.

18. Nancy, *L'Impératif catégorique*. See Derrida's response to Nancy in *Les fins de l'homme: A partir du travail de Jacques Derrida* (Paris: Editions Galilée, 1981), pp. 183–84; cf. Derrida's positive reference to the categorical imperative in *Limited Inc*, p. 152. In the present section, references to Nancy will generally be given parenthetically in the text. English translations are my own.

19. P. 65; cf. 29, n. 32.

20. W. B. Macomber, *The Anatomy of Disillusion: Martin Heidegger's Notion of Truth* (Evanston: Northwestern University Press, 1967), p. 108; cf. Derrida, *Limited Inc*, p. 129.

21. P. 112.

22. See entry on "Deontological Ethics" by Robert G. Olson in *The Encyclopedia of Philosophy*, Paul Edwards, ed. (New York: Macmillan, 1967), II: 343.

23. *Critique of Practical Reason*, p. 112.

24. Arthur Schopenhauer, *The World as Will and Representation*, trans. E. F. J. Payne (New York: Dover, 1958), I: 524; quoted by Allen W. Wood in *Kant's Moral Religion* (Ithaca: Cornell University Press, 1970), p. 39.

25. Wood, *Moral Religion*, p. 64.

26. Kant, *Critique of Practical Reason*, p. 24.

27. For a survey of current rethinking of the impassibility of God, see Warren McWilliams, *The Passion of God: Divine Suffering in Contemporary Protestant Theology* (Macon, Ga.: Mercer University Press, 1985).

28. *Critique of Practical Reason*, 112–13.

29. Wood, *Kant's Moral Religion*, pp. 28–29.

30. Kant, *Lectures on Philosophical Theology*, trans. Allen W. Wood and Gertrude M. Clark (Ithaca: Cornell University Press, 1978), pp. 122–23.

31. "All children have cheeks and all mothers spittle to wipe them tenderly. These things either matter or they do not matter. It depends upon the universe, what it is," Saul Bellow, *Herzog* (New York: Viking Press, 1961), p. 33.

32. Cf. Jürgen Moltmann, *The Crucified God: The Cross of Christ as the Foundation and Criticism of Christian Theology*, trans. R. A. Wilson and John Bowden (New York: Harper & Row, 1974), p. 223.

33. Cf. Paul Goodman, *Drawing the Line* (New York: Random House, 1946).

34. E. E. Cummings, *Complete Poems 1913–1962* (New York: Harcourt Brace Jovanovich, 1961), p. 339.

35. Fyodor Dostoyevsky, *The Brothers Karamazov*, trans. Constance Garnett (New York: Modern Library, 1950), bk. 5, ch. 4.

36. See Roger J. Sullivan, *Immanuel Kant's Moral Theory* (Cambridge: Cambridge University Press, 1989), pp. 193–211.

37. Cf. Jürgen Moltmann, "The 'Crucified God': God and the Trinity Today" in *New Questions on God*, Johannes B. Metz, ed. (New York: Herder & Herder), 1972, p. 27.

38. Cf. Philip Rieff, *The Triumph of the Therapeutic: Uses of Faith after Freud* (New York: Harper Torchbooks, 1966), p. 21: "Our cultural revolution does not aim, like its predecessors, at victory for some rival commitment, but rather at a way of using all commitments, which amounts to loyalty toward none." How is theology to proceed in a culture which regards ultimate concern itself as a hang-up? Cf. "Tillich's Ultimate Concern Is No More," Jacques Ellul, *Hope in Time of Abandonment*, trans. C. Edward Hopkin (New York: Seabury Press, 1973), p. 124.

39. Cf. Theodor W. Adorno, *The Jargon of Authenticity*, trans. Knut Tarnowski and Frederick Will (Evanston: Northwestern University Press, 1973).
40. Kant, *Critique of Practical Reason*, p. 117; see also Wood, *Moral Religion*, p. 85. Taken with full seriousness, the point is profoundly anti-Hegelian.
41. See Wood, *Moral Religion*, 87: "no common measure or equivalence between the *value* of the two goods is possible."
42. Derrida, *Margins*, pp. 109–36.
43. "Will modern man recognize his joy in truth, his quest for truth, his fanaticism for truth . . . in this looking glass? Will he put up with being taken so seriously . . . ?" Barth, *Protestant Theology in the Nineteenth Century: Its Background and History* (Valley Forge: Judson Press, 1959), p. 412.
44. Derrida, *Margins*, p. 120. In the text, "truth" is italicized.
45. Contrast Barth's use of *Aufhebung* as *non*presence, "dissolution"—which is then coupled with a divine *Begrundung* (Barth, *Romans*, pp. 30, 35, 36, 38, 46, 51).
46. Derrida, *Margins of Philosophy*, p. 121.
47. Cf. Jacques Taminiaux, *Dialectic and Difference: Finitude in Modern Thought*, ed. James Decker and Robert Crease (Atlantic Highlands, N.J.: Humanities Press, 1985), esp. p. 75.
48. Cf. ibid., pp. 118–19.
49. Cf. Ritschl, *Memory and Hope*, p. 127: "Nature *must* be evil, otherwise the whole system would collapse. For a non-christological understanding of grace presents the following impasse: As soon as grace is separated from Christ, who was *man* in Jesus, it cannot *affect* nature; it can either be nature, as in natural theology, or else it must bypass nature, as in Augustine's thinking."
50. Derrida, *Margins*, p. 115.
51. Ibid., 123; cf. footnote 15, pp. 121–22.
52. Kant, *Critique of Practical Reason*, p. 112, emphases altered. See Wood, *Kant's Moral Religion*, p. 91; though my argument presses in a direction somewhat different from Wood's, I am indebted to his exposition.
53. Kant, *Critique of Judgment*, p. 284; Wood, *Kant's Moral Religion*, p. 91.
54. Wood, *Kant's Moral Religion*, p. 91.
55. The chant and the image of a march figure importantly in the final chapter of Milan Kundera's *The Unbearable Lightness of Being*, trans. Michael Henry Heim (New York: Harper & Row, 1984).
56. See Wood's useful summary, *Kant's Moral Religion*, p. 98.

6. The Ethics of Otherness

1. See Kathryn Tanner, *God and Creation in Christian Theology: Tyranny or Empowerment?* (Oxford: Blackwell, 1988).
2. Jacques Derrida, *Limited Inc*, pp. 116, 127.
3. Mark C. Taylor, *Erring: A Postmodern A/theology* (Chicago: University of Chicago Press, 1984). In the present section and the section following, references to this book will generally be given parenthetically in the text.
4. Taylor, *Erring*, p. 6, quoting from Nietzsche, *The Gay Science*, trans. W. Kaufmann (New York: Random House, 1974), p. 182.
5. Ibid., p. 23, with paraphrase of Pierre Klossowski, quoted from Gilles Deleuze and Felix Guattrai, *Anti-Oedipus: Capitalism and Schizophrenia* (New York: Viking Press, 1977), p. 77; and with quotation from Norman O. Brown, *Life Against Death: The Psychoanalytic Meaning of History* (New York: Random House, 1959), p. 161.
6. Ibid., quoting Derrida, *Of Grammatology*, p. 277.

7. Ibid., p. 62, quoting Hayden White, *Tropics of Discourse: Essays in Cultural Criticism* (Baltimore: Johns Hopkins University Press, 1978), p. 234.

8. Ibid., p. 167, quoting Nietzsche, *The Twilight of the Idols* in *The Portable Nietzsche*, trans. Walter Kaufmann (New York: Viking Press, 1954), p. 554.

9. Ibid., quoting W. K. C. Guthrie, *The Greeks and Their God* (Boston: Beacon Press, n.d.), 156.

10. Taylor, *Altarity*, p. xxii.

11. Ibid., p. 5.

12. Ibid., pp. xxii, xxiii, xxii.

13. See particularly pp. 16, 19, 23, 31.

14. Barth, *Romans*, p. viii. In the remainder of the present chapter, references to the commentary will generally to be given parenthetically in the text.

15. I use this term with some reluctance, as the phrase is closely linked with the Ricoeurian hermeneutic, which I have criticized. Nevertheless, if we understand ourselves to be appropriating Ricoeur to Barth more than Barth to Ricoeur, Ricoeur's call for a "post-Hegelian Kantianism" serves as a useful pointer.

16. Cf. Ritschl, *Memory and Hope*, pp. 102–40.

17. Metz, *Faith in History*, p. 171.

18. *Romans*, p. 425, emphasis added.

19. For a treatment of this issue particularly as regards the later Barth, see Tanner, *God and Creation in Christian Theology*.

20. P. 465, emphasis added.

21. P. 426, emphasis added.

22. Barth quotes Luther: " 'Should I be able to make the whole world happy for one day, nevertheless I must not do so—if it be not God's will.' " *Romans*, p. 454.

23. Adorno, *Minima Moralia*, p. 238.

24. Pp. 425–26; emphasis added.

25. *Minima Moralia*, p. 247.

26. Adorno, *Negative Dialectics*, p. 6.

27. *Minima Moralia*, p. 243. On the significance of this aspect of Adorno, see Dews, "Adorno, Poststructuralism and the Critique of Identity," p. 19.

28. Cf. Pierre Thévenaz, *L'Homme et sa raison, Vol. I: Raison et conscience de soi*, passim.

29. Cf. Simone Weil, "Reflections on the Right Use of School Studies with a View to the Love of God" in Weil, *Waiting for God*, pp. 105–16.

30. Geoffrey Galt Harpham, *The Ascetic Imperative in Culture and Criticism* (Chicago: University of Chicago Press, 1987).

31. See Philip Rieff, *Freud: The Mind of the Moralist* (Garden City, N.Y.: Doubleday, 1959).

32. See, for example, Douglas Kellner, *Jean Baudrillard: From Marxism to Postmodernism and Beyond* (Stanford: Stanford University Press, 1989), pp. 70–71, 199.

33. See Jürgen Moltmann, *The Crucified God*, pp. 25–28; Gall, "Of/From Theology and Deconstruction," pp. 426–27.

34. Dietrich Ritschl, *Memory and Hope*, p. 133.

SELECTED BIBLIOGRAPHY

Abraham, Nicolas and Torok, Maria. *The Wolf Man's Magic Word: A Cryptonomy*, trans. Nicholas Rand. Minneapolis: University of Minnesota Press, 1986.

Abrams, M. H. *Natural Supernaturalism: Tradition and Revolution in Romantic Literature*. New York: W. W. Norton, 1971.

Adorno, Theodor W. *Minima Moralia: Reflections from Damaged Life*, trans. E. F. N. Jephcott. London: NLB, 1974.

———. *Negative Dialectics*, trans. E. B. Ashton. New York: Seabury Press, 1973.

———. "Subject and Object." *The Essential Frankfurt School Reader*, ed. Andrew Arato and Eike Gebhardt. New York: Urizen Books, 1978, pp. 497–511.

———. *The Jargon of Authenticity*, trans. Knut Tarnowski and Frederick Will. Evanston: Northwestern University Press, 1973.

Adorno, Theodor et al., *The Positivist Dispute in German Sociology*, trans. Glyn Adey and David Frisby. New York: Harper & Row, 1976.

Agger, Ben. *Fast Capitalism: A Critical Theory of Significance*. Urbana: University of Illinois Press, 1989.

Allison, Henry E. *Kant's Theory of Freedom*. Cambridge: Cambridge University Press, 1990.

———. *Kant's Transcendental Idealism: An Interpretation and Defense*. New Haven: Yale University Press, 1983.

Amnesty International Report: 1989. New York: Amnesty International USA, 1989.

Aquila, Richard E. *Representational Mind: A Study of Kant's Theory of Knowledge*. Bloomington: Indiana University Press, 1983.

Arendt, Hannah. *The Life of the Mind*. San Diego: Harcourt Brace Jovanovich, 1971.

———. *The Origins of Totalitarianism*. Cleveland: World Publishing Co., 1951.

Aries, Philippe. *The Hour of Our Death*, trans. Helen Weaver. New York: Alfred A. Knopf, 1981.

Aron, Raymond. *The Century of Total War*. Boston: Beacon Press, 1954.

Aronson, Ronald. *The Dialectics of Disaster: A Preface to Hope*. London: Verso, 1983.

Auden, W. H. and Kronenberger, Louis. *The Viking Book of Aphorisms*. New York: Viking Press, 1962.

Barraclough, Geoffrey. *An Introduction to Contemporary History*. New York: Basic Books, 1964.

Barth, Karl. *Protestant Theology in the Nineteenth Century: Its Background and History*. Valley Forge: Judson Press, 1959.

———. *The Epistle to the Romans*, trans. Edwyn C. Hoskyns. London: Oxford University Press, 1933.

Beck, Lewis White. *Early German Philosophy: Kant and His Predecessors*. Cambridge: Harvard University Press, 1969.

Bellah, Robert N. et al., *Habits of the Heart: Individualism and Commitment in American Life*. Berkeley: University of California Press, 1985.

Bellow, Saul. *Herzog*. New York: Viking Press, 1961.

Bencivenga, Ermanno. *Kant's Copernican Revolution*. New York: Oxford University Press, 1987.

Benedikt, Michael. "Critical Reflection on Recent Kant Literature in English," trans. F. P. van de Pitte. *Contemporary German Philosophy* 2 (1983), ed. Darrel

E. Christensen et al. University Park: Pennsylvania State University Press, 1983, pp. 257–87.

Benton, Robert J. *Kant's Second Critique and the Problem of Transcendental Arguments.* The Hague: Martinus Nijhoff, 1977.

Berman, Marshall. *All That Is Solid Melts into Air: The Experience of Modernity.* New York: Simon & Schuster, 1982.

Berman, Russell A. *Modern Culture and Critical Theory: Art, Politics and the Legacy of the Frankfurt School.* Madison: University of Wisconsin Press, 1989.

Bernstein, Richard J. *Beyond Objectivism and Relativism: Science, Hermeneutics and Praxis.* Philadelphia: University of Pennsylvania Press, 1983.

Blanchot, Maurice. *The Writing of the Disaster,* trans. Ann Smock. Lincoln: University of Nebraska Press, 1986.

Blumenberg, Hans. *The Genesis of the Copernican World,* trans. Robert M. Wallace. Cambridge: MIT Press, 1987.

———. *The Legitimacy of the Modern Age,* trans. Robert W. Wallace. Cambridge: MIT Press, 1983.

Bonhoeffer, Dietrich. *Act and Being,* trans. Bernard Noble. New York: Harper & Row, 1961.

———. *No Rusty Swords: Letters, Lectures and Notes 1928–1936,* ed. Edwin H. Robertson, trans. Edwin H. Robertson and John Bowden. New York: Harper & Row, 1947.

Bronner, Stephen Eric and Kellner, Douglas MacKay, eds. *Critical Theory and Society: A Reader.* New York: Routledge, 1989.

Brown, James. *Subject and Object in Modern Theology.* London: SCM Press, 1955.

Brown, Norman O. *Life against Death: The Psychoanalytical Meaning of History.* New York: Random House, 1959.

Buber, Martin. *I and Thou,* trans. Walter Kaufmann. New York: Charles Scribner's Sons, 1970.

Bubner, Rüdiger. *Essays in Hermeneutics and Critical Theory,* trans. Eric Matthews. New York: Columbia University Press, 1988.

Buck-Morss, Susan. *The Origin of Negative Dialectics: Theodor W. Adorno, Walter Benjamin, and the Frankfurt Institute.* New York: Free Press, 1977.

Buckley, Michael J., S. J. *At the Origins of Modern Atheism.* New Haven: Yale University Press, 1987.

Camus, Albert. *The Myth of Sisyphus and Other Essays.* New York: Vintage Books, 1955.

Cantor, Paul A. *Creature and Creator: Myth-making and English Romanticism.* Cambridge: Cambridge University Press, 1984.

Caputo, John D. *Radical Hermeneutics: Repetition, Deconstruction, and the Hermeneutic Project.* Bloomington: Indiana University Press, 1987.

Carnois, Bernard. *The Coherence of Kant's Doctrine of Freedom,* trans. David Booth. Chicago: University of Chicago Press, 1987.

Carroll, David. *The Subject in Question: The Languages of Theory and the Strategies of Fiction.* Chicago: University of Chicago Press, 1982.

Cassirer, Ernst. *Kant's Life and Thought,* trans. James Haden. New Haven: Yale University Press, 1981.

Chapman, G. Clarke. *Facing the Nuclear Heresy: A Call to Reformation.* Elgin: Brethren Press, 1986.

Chopp, Rebecca S. *The Praxis of Suffering: An Interpretation of Liberation and Political Theologies.* Maryknoll: Orbis Books, 1986.

Cioran, E. M. *The Temptation to Exist,* trans. Richard Howard. Chicago: Quadrangle Books, 1968.

Copleston, Frederick, S. J. *A History of Philosophy: Vol. VI: Wolff to Kant.* Westminster: Newman Press, 1964.

Culler, Jonathan. *On Deconstruction: Theory and Criticism after Structuralism.* Ithaca: Cornell University Press, 1982.

Darwall, Stephen L. *Impartial Reason.* Ithaca: Cornell University Press, 1983.

Dasenbrock, Reed Way, ed. *Redrawing the Lines: Analytic Philosophy, Deconstruction, and Literary Theory.* Minneapolis: University of Minnesota Press, 1989.

DeConcini, Barbara. "Narrative Hunger." *The Daemonic Imagination: Biblical Text and Secular Story*, ed. Robert Detweiler and William G. Doty. Atlanta: Scholars Press, 1990.

————. *Narrative Remembering.* Lanham: University Press of America, 1990.

Derrida, Jacques. "Deconstruction in America: An Interview with Jacques Derrida," ed. James Creech, Peggy Kamuf and Jane Todd. *Critical Exchange* 17 (Winter 1985), pp. 1–33 (Dept. of English, Miami University, Oxford, Ohio).

————. *Dissemination*, trans. Barbara Johnson. Chicago: University of Chicago Press, 1981.

————. *Edmund Husserl's "Origin of Geometry": An Introduction*, trans. John P. Leavey, Jr. Stony Brook: Nicolas Hays, 1978.

————. "Fors," trans. Barbara Johnson. *The Georgia Review* 31:1 (Spring 1977), pp. 64–116.

————. *Glas*, trans. John P. Leavey, Jr., and Richard Rand. Lincoln: University of Nebraska Press, 1986.

————. Interview from *Le nouvel observateur.* David Wood and Robert Bernasconi, eds., *Derrida and Différance.* Evanston: Northwestern University Press, 1988, pp. 71–82.

————. *Limited Inc.* Evanston: Northwestern University Press, 1988.

————. *Margins of Philosophy*, trans. Alan Bass. Chicago: University of Chicago Press, 1982.

————. "No Apocalypse, Not Now (full speed ahead, seven missiles, seven missives)." *Diacritics* 20 (1984), pp. 20–31.

————. *Of Grammatology*, trans. Gayatri Chakravorty Spivak. Baltimore: Johns Hopkins University Press, 1974.

————. *Positions*, trans. Alan Bass. Chicago: University of Chicago Press, 1981.

————. "Racism's Last Word." trans. Peggy Kamuf. *"Race," Writing and Difference*, ed. Henry Louis Gates, Jr. Chicago: University of Chicago Press, 1985.

————. *Speech and Phenomena*, trans. David B. Allison. Evanston: Northwestern University Press, 1973.

————. *Spurs: Nietzsche's Styles*, trans. Barbara Harlow. Chicago: University of Chicago Press, 1979.

————. "The Principle of Reason: The University in the Eyes of Its Pupils." *Diacritics* 19 (1983), pp. 3–20.

————. *Writing and Difference*, trans. Alan Bass. Chicago: University of Chicago Press, 1978.

Descombes, Vincent. *Modern French Philosophy.* Cambridge: Cambridge University Press, 1980.

Desmond, William, ed. *Hegel and His Critics: Philosophy in the Aftermath of Hegel.* Albany: State University of New York Press, 1989.

Dews, Peter. "Adorno, Poststructuralism and the Critique of Identity." *The Problems of Modernity: Adorno and Benjamin*, ed. Andrew Benjamin. London: Routledge, 1989, pp. 1–22.

————. *Logics of Disintegration: Post-structuralist Thought and the Claims of Critical Theory.* London: Verso, 1987.

Dostoyevsky, Fyodor. *The Brothers Karamazov*, trans. Constance Garnett. New York: Modern Library, 1950.

Ducrot, Oswald et al. *Qu'est-ce que le structuralisme?* Paris: Editions du Seuil, 1968.

Dunning, Stephen N. *Kierkegaard's Dialectic of Inwardness: A Structural Analysis of the Theory of Stages*. Princeton: Princeton University Press, 1985.

Dupré, Louis. *A Dubious Heritage: Studies in the Philosophy of Religion after Kant*. New York: Paulist Press, 1977.

Edgley, Roy and Osborne, Richard, eds. *Radical Philosophy Reader*. London: Verso, 1985.

Eksteins, Modris. *Rites of Spring: The Great War and the Birth of the Modern Age*. New York: Doubleday, 1989.

Elliot, Gil. *Twentieth Century Book of the Dead*. London: Penguin Press, 1972.

Ellul, Jacques. *Hope in Time of Abandonment*, trans. C. Edward Hopkin. New York: Seabury Press, 1973.

———. *The Betrayal of the West*. New York: Seabury, 1978.

———. *The Subversion of Christianity*, trans. Geoffrey W. Bromiley. Grand Rapids: Eerdman's, 1986.

Eucken, Rudolf. *Main Currents of Modern Thought: A Study of the Spiritual and Intellectual Movements of the Present Day*, trans. Meyrick Booth. New York: Charles Scribner's Sons, 1912.

Evans, C. Stephen. *Kierkegaard's "Fragments" and "Postscript": The Religious Philosophy of Johannes Climacus*. Atlantic Highlands: Humanities Press, 1983.

Fairer, David, ed. *Pope: New Contexts*. New York: Harvester Wheatsheaf, 1990.

Farley, Edward. *Good and Evil: Interpreting a Human Condition*. Minneapolis: Fortress Press, 1990.

Findlay, J. N. "Kant and Anglo-Saxon Criticism." *Kant's Theory of Knowledge*, ed. Lewis White Beck. Dordrecht, Holland: D. Reidel, 1974, pp. 187–207.

———. *Kant and the Transcendental Object: A Hermeneutic Study*. Oxford: Clarendon Press, 1981.

Floyd, Wayne Whitson, Jr. "The Search for an Ethical Sacrament: From Bonhoeffer to Critical Theory." *Modern Theology* 7:2 (January 1991), pp. 175–93.

———. *Theology and the Dialectics of Otherness: On Reading Bonhoeffer and Adorno*. Lanham: University Press of America, 1988.

Frankena, William K. *Ethics*. Englewood Cliffs: Prentice-Hall, 1963.

Frei, Hans. *The Doctrine of Revelation in the Thought of Karl Barth, 1909 to 1922: The Nature of Barth's Break with Liberalism*. Ann Arbor: University Microfilms International, 1956.

———. *The Identity of Jesus Christ: The Hermeneutical Bases of Dogmatic Theology*. Philadelphia: Fortress Press, 1967.

———. "The 'Literal Reading' of Bibilical Narrative in the Christian Tradition: Does It Stretch or Will It Break?" *The Bible and the Narrative Tradition*, ed. Frank McConnell. Oxford: Oxford University Press, 1986, pp. 36–77.

Frisch, Max. *Sketchbook 1946–1949*, trans. Geoffrey Skelton. San Diego: Harcourt Brace Jovanovich, 1977.

Fussell, Paul. *The Great War and Modern Memory*. London: Oxford University Press, 1975.

Gall, Robert S. "Of/From Theology and Deconstruction." *Journal of the American Academy of Religion* 58:3 (Fall 1990), 413–37.

Gasché, Rodolphe. *The Tain of the Mirror: Derrida and the Philosophy of Reflection*. Cambridge: Harvard University Press, 1986.

Girard, René. *Things Hidden since the Foundation of the World*, trans. Stephen Bann and Michael Metteer. Stanford: Stanford University Press, 1987.

Goodlove, Terry F., Jr. "Recent Work on Kant on Religion." *Religious Studies Review* 12:3/4 (July/October 1986), pp. 229–33.

Goodman, Paul. *Drawing the Line*. New York: Random House, 1946.

Goodman, Paul, ed. *Seeds of Liberation*. New York: George Braziller, 1964.

Grass, Günther. *The Tin Drum*, trans. Ralph Manheim. New York: Pantheon Books, 1961.

Green, Ronald M. *Kierkegaard and Kant: The Hidden Debt*. Albany: State University of New York Press, 1992.

———. *Religious Reason: The Rational and Moral Basis of Religious Belief*. New York: Oxford University Press, 1978.

Gutierrez, Gustavo. *A Theology of Liberation: History, Politics and Salvation*, trans. and ed. Sister Caridad Inda and John Eagleson. Maryknoll: Orbis Books, 1973.

Habermas, Jürgen. *Knowledge and Human Interests*, trans. Jeremy J. Shapiro. Boston: Beacon Press, 1971.

Hall, Douglas John. *God and Human Suffering: An Exercise in the Theology of the Cross*. Minneapolis: Augsburg, 1986.

Handelman, Susan A. "Jacques Derrida and the Heretic Hermeneutic." *Displacement: Derrida and After*, ed. Mark Krupnik. Bloomington: Indiana University Press, 1983, pp. 98–129.

———. *The Slayers of Moses: The Emergence of Rabbinic Interpretation in Modern Literary Theory*. Albany: State University of New York Press, 1982.

Hans, James S. *The Question of Value: Thinking through Nietzsche, Heidegger and Freud*. Carbondale: Southern Illinois University Press, 1989.

Harland, Richard. *Superstructuralism: The Philosophy of Structuralism and Post-Structuralism*. London: Methuen, 1987.

Harpham, Geoffrey Galt. *The Ascetic Imperative in Culture and Criticism*. Chicago: University of Chicago Press, 1987.

Harrington, Michael. *Socialism: Past and Future*. New York: Arcade, 1989.

Hart, Kevin. *The Trespass of the Sign: Deconstruction, Theology and Philosophy*. Cambridge: Cambridge University Press, 1989.

Hart, Ray L. *Unfinished Man and the Imagination: Toward an Ontology and a Rhetoric of Revelation*. New York: Herder & Herder, 1968.

Hartman, Klaus. "On Taking the Transcendental Turn." *The Review of Metaphysics* 20:2 (December 1966), pp. 223–49.

———. "Recent Anglo-American Literature on Kant," trans. Terry Pinkard, ed. Darrel E. Christensen et al. *Contemporary German Philosophy* 2 (1983), pp. 288–315. University Park: Pennsylvania State University Press, 1983.

Hartnack, Justus. *Kant's Theory of Knowledge*, trans. M. Holmes Hartshorne. New York: Harcourt, Brace & World, 1967.

Hartt, Julian N. *A Christian Critique of American Culture: An Essay in Practical Theology*. New York: Harper & Row, 1967.

Harvey, David. *The Condition of Postmodernity: An Enquiry into the Origins of Cultural Change*. Oxford: Basil Blackwell, 1989.

Heer, Friedrich. *The Intellectual History of Europe*, trans. Jonathan Steinberg. Cleveland: World Publishing Co., 1966.

Heidegger, Martin. *Basic Writings from "Being and Time" (1927) to "The Task of Thinking" (1964)*, ed. David Farrell Krell. New York: Harper & Row, 1977.

———. *Being and Time*, trans. John Macquarrie and Edward Robinson. London: SCM Press, 1962.

———. *Holzwege*. Frankfurt a. M.: Klostermann, 1950.

Heimsoeth, Heinz. "Metaphysical Motives in the Development of Critical Idealism."

Kant: Disputed Questions, ed. Moltke S. Gram. Chicago: Quadrangle Books, 1967, pp. 158–99.

Held, David. *Introduction to Critical Theory: Horkheimer to Habermas*. Berkeley: University of California Press, 1980.

Hendry, George S., "The Transcendental Method in the Theology of Karl Barth," *Scottish Journal of Theology* 37 (1984), pp. 213–27.

Hicks, Joe Harold. "Divine and Human Subjectivity in Kant." Ann Arbor: University Microfilms, 1970.

Horkheimer, Max. *Critical Theory: Selected Essays*, trans. Matthew J. O'Connell et al. New York: Herder & Herder, 1972.

———. *Critique of Instrumental Reason*, trans. Matthew J. O'Connell et al. New York: Seabury Press, 1974.

———. *Eclipse of Reason*. New York: Seabury Press, 1947.

———. "The End of Reason." *The Essential Frankfurt School Reader*, ed. Andrew Arato and Eike Gebhardt. New York: Urizen Books, 1978, pp. 26–48.

Horkheimer, Max and Adorno, Theodor W. *Dialectic of Enlightenment*, trans. John Cumming. New York: Herder & Herder, 1972.

Howard, Dick. *From Marx to Kant*. Albany: State University of New York Press, 1985.

Howard, Robert. *Brave New Workplace*. New York: Viking, 1985.

Hunsinger, George, ed. and trans. *Karl Barth and Radical Politics*. Philadelphia: Westminster Press, 1976.

Husserl, Edmund. *The Crisis of European Sciences and Transcendental Phenomenology: An Introduction to Phenomenological Philosophy*, trans. David Carr. Evanston: Northwestern University Press, 1970.

Jacoby, Russell. *Social Amnesia: A Critique of Conformist Psychology from Adler to Laing*. Boston: Beacon Press, 1975.

Jameson, Frederic. *Late Marxism: Adorno, or, The Persistence of the Dialectic*. London: Verso, 1990.

Jay, Martin. *Adorno*. Cambridge: Harvard University Press, 1984.

———. *Marxism and Totality: The Adventures of a Concept from Lukács to Habermas*. Berkeley: University of California Press, 1984.

———. *The Dialectical Imagination: A History of the Frankfurt School and the Institute of Social Research 1923–1950*. Boston: Little, Brown & Company, 1973.

Joyce, James. *Ulysses*, ed. Hans Walter Gabler et al. New York: Random House, 1986.

Jüngel, Eberhard. *The Doctrine of the Trinity: God's Being Is in Becoming*. Grand Rapids: Eerdman's, 1976.

Kant, Immanuel. *Critique of Judgment*, trans. J. H. Bernard. New York: Hafner Press, 1951.

———. *Critique of Practical Reason*, trans. Lewis White Beck. Indianapolis: Bobbs-Merrill, 1956.

———. *Critique of Pure Reason*, trans. Norman Kemp Smith. London: Macmillan, 1929.

———. *Foundations of the Metaphysics of Morals*, trans. Lewis White Beck. Indianapolis: Bobbs-Merrill, 1959.

———. *Groundwork of the Metaphysic of Morals*, trans. H. J. Paton. New York: Harper & Row, 1948.

———. *Kant's Cosmogony, as in His Essay on the Retardation of the Rotation of the Earth and His Natural History and Theory of the Heavens*, trans. W. Hastie. New York: Johnson Reprint Corporation, 1900.

———. *Lectures on Philosophical Theology*, trans. Allen W. Wood and Gertrude M. Clark. Ithaca: Cornell University Press, 1978.

————. *On History*, trans. Lewis White Beck. Indianapolis: Bobbs-Merrill, 1963.

————. "On the Failure of All Attempted Philosophical Theodicies," trans. Michel Despland. Michel Despland, *Kant on History and Religion*. Montreal: McGill-Queen's University Press, 1973.

————. "On the Form and Principles of the Sensible and the Intelligible World (Inaugural Dissertation)." *Kant's Latin Writings: Translations, Commentaries and Notes*, trans. and ed. Lewis White Beck et al. New York: Peter Lang, 1986, pp. 135–92.

————. *Prolegomena to Any Future Metaphysics*, ed. Paul Carus. LaSalle: Open Court, 1955.

————. *Religion within the Limits of Reason Alone*, trans. Theodore M. Greene and Hoyt H. Hudson. New York: Harper & Row, 1934.

Kaplan, Abraham. "Freud and Modern Philosophy." *Freud and the Twentieth Century*, ed. Benjamin Nelson. New York: Meridian Books, 1957.

Keat, Russell. *The Politics of Social Theory: Habermas, Freud and the Critique of Positivism*. Chicago: University of Chicago Press, 1981.

Kellner, Douglas. *Jean Baudrillard: From Marxism to Postmodernism and Beyond*. Stanford: Stanford University Press, 1989.

Kierkegaard, Søren. *Concluding Unscientific Postscript*, trans. David F. Swenson and Walter Lowrie. Princeton: Princeton University Press, 1941.

————. *Purity of Heart Is to Will One Thing: Spiritual Preparation for the Office of Confession*, trans. Douglas V. Steere. New York: Harper & Brothers, 1938.

Klemm, David E. "General Introduction." *Hermeneutic Inquiry. Volume I: The Interpretation of Texts*, ed. David E. Klemm. Atlanta: Scholars Press, 1986.

————. *The Hermeneutical Theory of Paul Ricoeur: A Constructive Analysis*. Lewisburg: Bucknell University Press, 1983.

Kofman, Sarah. *Lectures de Derrida*. Paris: Editions Galilée, 1984.

Konwicki, Tadeusz. *A Dreambook for Our Time*, trans. David Welsh. Harmondsworth, Middlesex: Penguin Books, 1969.

————. *The Polish Complex*, trans. Richard Lourie. Harmondsworth, Middlesex: Penguin Books, 1982.

Kortian, Garbis. *Metacritique: The Philosophical Argument of Jürgen Habermas*, trans. John Raffan. Cambridge: Cambridge University Press, 1980.

Kosiík, Karel. *Dialectics of the Concrete: A Study on Problems of Man and World*. Dordrecht, Holland: D. Reidel, 1976.

Kovel, Joel. *The Age of Desire: Reflections of a Radical Psychoanalyst*. New York: Pantheon Books, 1981.

Kroner, Richard. *Kant's Weltanschauung*, trans. John E. Smith. Chicago: University of Chicago Press, 1956.

————. *Speculation and Revelation in Modern Philosophy*. Philadelphia: Westminster Press, 1961.

Kundera, Milan. *The Art of the Novel*, trans. Linda Asher. New York: Grove Press, 1986.

————. *The Book of Laughter and Forgetting*, trans. Michael Henry Heim. Harmondsworth, Middlesex: Penguin Books, 1980.

————. *The Unbearable Lightness of Being*, trans. Michael Henry Heim. New York: Harper & Row, 1984.

Lacoue-Labarthe, Philippe and Nancy, Jean-Luc, eds. *Les fins de l'homme: à partir du travail de Jacques Derrida*. Paris: Editions Galilée, 1981.

Lalande, André, ed. *Vocabulaire technique et critique de la philosophie*. Paris: Presses Universitaires de France, 1960.

Lamb, Matthew L. *Solidarity with Victims: Toward a Theology of Social Transformation*. New York: Crossroad, 1982.

Lasch, Christopher. *The Culture of Narcissism: American Life in an Age of Diminishing Expectations.* New York: W. W. Norton, 1978.

————. *The Minimal Self: Psychic Survival in Troubled Times.* New York: W. W. Norton, 1984.

Leitch, Vincent B. *Deconstructive Criticism: An Advanced Introduction.* New York: Columbia University Press, 1983.

Levin, David Michael. *The Opening of Vision: Nihilism and the Postmodern Situation.* New York: Routledge, 1988.

Levinas, Emmanuel. *Totality and Infinity: An Essay on Exteriority,* trans. Alphonso Lingis. Pittsburgh: Duquesne University Press, 1969.

Lifton, Robert Jay and Falk, Richard. *Indefensible Weapons: The Political and Psychological Case Against Nuclearism.* New York: Basic Books, 1982.

Lindbeck, George A. *The Nature of Doctrine: Religion and Theology in a Postliberal Age.* Philadelphia: Westminster Press, 1984.

Loemker, Leroy E. *Struggle for Synthesis: The Seventeenth Century Background of Leibnitz's Synthesis of Order and Freedom.* Cambridge: Harvard University Press, 1972.

Lovejoy, Arthur O. *The Great Chain of Being: A Study of the History of an Idea.* New York: Harper & Brothers, 1936.

Lowe, Donald M. *History of Bourgeois Perception.* Chicago: University of Chicago Press, 1982.

Lowe, Walter. "Dangerous Supplement/Dangerous Memory: Sketches for a History of the Postmodern." *Thought* 61:240 (March 1986), pp. 34–55.

————. *Evil and the Unconscious.* Chico: Scholars Press, 1983.

————. "Hans Frei and Phenomenological Hermeneutics." *Modern Theology* 8:2 (April 1992), pp. 133–44.

————. *Mystery and the Unconscious: A Study in the Thought of Paul Ricoeur.* Metuchen: Scarecrow Press, 1977.

————. "On Using Heidegger." *Soundings* 60:3 (Fall 1977), 264–84.

Lyden, John C. "Karl Barth's View on the Knowledge of God and Its Relation to the Philosophical Epistemology of Immanuel Kant." Dissertation, University of Chicago, 1989.

Lyotard, Jean-Francois. *The Differend: Phrases in Dispute,* trans. Georges Van Den Abbeele. Minneapolis: University of Minnesota Press, 1988.

Mackintosh, Hugh Ross. *Types of Modern Theology: Schleiermacher to Barth.* New York: Charles Scribner's Sons, n.d.

Macomber, W. B. *The Anatomy of Disillusion: Martin Heidegger's Notion of Truth.* Evanston: Northwestern University Press, 1967.

Malantschuk, Gregor. *Kierkegaard's Thought,* ed. and trans. Howard V. Hong and Edna H. Hong. Princeton: Princeton University Press, 1971.

Mallard, William. *The Reflection of Theology in Literature: A Case Study in Theology and Culture.* San Antonio: Trinity University Press, 1977.

Malraux, André. *Anti-Memoirs,* trans. Terence Kilmartin. New York: Holt, Rinehart & Winston, 1968.

————. *Lazarus,* trans. Terence Kilmartin. New York: Holt, Rinehart & Winston, 1977.

Mann, Thomas. *Pro and Contra Wagner,* trans. Allan Blunden. Chicago: University of Chicago Press, 1985.

Marcuse, Herbert. *One Dimensional Man: Studies in the Ideology of Advanced Industrial Society.* Boston: Beacon Press, 1964.

————. *Reason and Revolution: Hegel and the Rise of Social Theory.* Boston: Beacon Press, 1941.

Masuzawa, Tomoko. "Original Lost: An Image of Myth and Ritual in the Age of Mechanical Reproduction." *Journal of Religion* 69:3 (July 1989), pp. 307–25.

McCarthy, Vincent A. *Quest for a Philosophical Jesus: Christianity and Philosophy in Rousseau, Kant, Hegel and Schelling.* Macon: Mercer University Press, 1986.

McGowan, John. *Postmodernism and Its Critics.* Ithaca: Cornell University Press, 1991.

McNeill, William. *The Rise of the West: A History of the Human Community.* Chicago: University of Chicago Press, 1963.

McWilliams, Warren. *The Passion of God: Divine Suffering in Contemporary Protestant Theology.* Macon: Mercer University Press, 1985.

Megill, Allan. *Prophets of Extremity: Nietzsche, Heidegger, Foucault, Derrida.* Berkeley: University of California Press, 1985.

Mehl, Roger. *The Condition of the Christian Philosopher,* trans. Eva Kushner. Philadelphia: Fortress Press, 1963.

Meilaender, Gilbert. *The Taste for the Other: The Social and Ethical Thought of C. S. Lewis.* Grand Rapids: William B. Eerdmans, 1978.

Melman, Seymour. *The Permanent War Economy: American Capitalism in Decline.* New York: Simon & Schuster, 1974.

Melville, Stephen W. *Philosophy Beside Itself: On Deconstruction and Modernism.* Minneapolis: University of Minnesota Press, 1986.

Metz, Johann Baptist. *Faith in History and Society: Toward a Practical Fundamental Theology,* trans. David Smith. New York: Seabury Press, 1980.

———. *The Emerging Church: The Future of Christianity in a Postbourgeois World,* trans. Peter Mann. New York: Crossroad, 1987.

Miller, J. Hillis, "The Critic as Host." *Deconstruction and Criticism.* New York: Continuum, 1979, pp. 217–53.

Moltmann, Jürgen. *The Crucified God: The Cross of Christ as the Foundation and Criticism of Christian Theology.* New York: Harper & Row, 1974.

———. *The Trinity and the Kingdom: The Doctrine of God.* San Francisco: Harper & Row, 1981.

Nancy, Jean-Luc. *L'Impératif catégorique.* Paris: Flammarion, 1983.

———. *La Remarque spéculative (un bon mot de Hegel).* Paris: Galilée, 1973.

Niebuhr, Reinhold. *The Nature and Destiny of Man: A Christian Interpretation.* New York: Charles Scribner's Sons, 1941.

Nietzsche, Friedrich. *Basic Writings of Nietzsche,* ed. and trans. Walter Kaufmann. New York: Modern Library, 1968.

———. *The Portable Nietzsche,* ed. and trans. Walter Kaufmann. New York: Viking Press, 1954.

Norman, Richard and Sayers, Sean. *Hegel, Marx and Dialectic: A Debate.* Atlantic Highlands: Humanities Press International, 1980.

Norris, Christopher. *Deconstruction and the Interests of Theory.* Norman: University of Oklahoma Press, 1989.

———. *Deconstruction: Theory and Practice.* London: Methuen, 1982.

———. *Derrida.* Cambridge: Harvard University Press, 1987.

———. *The Contest of Faculties: Philosophy and Theory after Deconstruction.* London: Methuen, 1985.

———. *What's Wrong with Postmodernism: Critical Theory and the Ends of Philosophy.* Baltimore: Johns Hopkins University Press, 1990.

O'Leary, Joseph S. *Questioning Back: The Overcoming of Metaphysics in Christian Tradition.* Minneapolis: Winston Press, 1985.

O'Neil, John, ed. *On Critical Theory.* New York: Seabury Press, 1976.

Ollman, Bertell. *Alienation: Marx's Conception of Man in Capitalist Society.* Second edition. Cambridge: Cambridge University Press, 1971.

Pascal, Blaise. *Pensées and The Provincial Letters.* New York: Modern Library, 1941.

Plato, *The Dialogues of Plato,* trans. B. Jowett. New York: Random House, 1892.

Pöggeler, Otto. "Being as Appropriation." *Heidegger and Modern Philosophy,* ed. Michael Murray. New Haven: Yale University Press, 1978, pp. 116–37.

Pojman, Louis P. *The Logic of Subjectivity: Kierkegaard's Philosophy of Religion.* University: University of Alabama Press, 1984.

Pope, Alexander. *Selected Poetry,* ed. Martin Price. New York: New American Library, 1970.

Poster, Mark. *Critical Theory and Poststructuralism: In Search of a Context.* Ithaca: Cornell University Press, 1989.

Rajchman, John. *Truth and Eros: Foucault, Lacan, and the Question of Ethics.* New York: Routledge, 1991.

Reboul, Olivier. *Kant et le problème du mal.* Montréal: Presses de l'Université de Montréal, 1971.

Reiss, Timothy J. *The Discourse of Modernism.* Ithaca: Cornell University Press, 1982.

Ricoeur, Paul. *Fallible Man.* New York: Fordham University Press, 1986.

———. *Freud and Philosophy: An Essay on Interpretation,* trans. Denis Savage. New Haven: Yale University Press, 1970.

———. *History and Truth,* trans. Charles A. Kelbley. Evanston: Northwestern University Press, 1965.

———. *Husserl: An Analysis of His Phenomenology,* trans. Edward G. Ballard and Lester E. Embree. Evanston: Northwestern University Press, 1967.

———. *Lectures on Ideology and Utopia,* ed. George H. Taylor. New York: Columbia University Press, 1986.

———. *The Conflict of Interpretations,* ed. Don Ihde. Evanston: Northwestern University Press, 1974.

Rieff, Philip. *Freud: The Mind of the Moralist.* Garden City: Doubleday, 1959.

———. *The Triumph of the Therapeutic: Uses of Faith after Freud.* New York: Harper & Row, 1966.

Ritschl, Dietrich. *Memory and Hope: An Inquiry Concerning the Presence of Christ.* New York: Macmillan, 1967.

Robinson, James M., ed. *The Beginnings of Dialectical Theology: Volume I,* trans. Keith R. Crim and Louis De Grazia. Richmond: John Knox Press, 1968.

Rose, Gilian. *Dialectic of Nihilism: Post-Structuralism and Law.* Oxford: Basil Blackwell, 1984.

———.*The Melancholy Science:* An Introduction to the Thought of Theodor W. Adorno. New York: Columbia University Press, 1978.

Rosen, Michael. *Hegel's Dialectic and Its Criticism.* Cambridge: Cambridge University Press, 1982.

Rosen, Stanley. "Thinking about Nothing." *Heidegger and Modern Philosophy,* ed. Michael Murray. New Haven: Yale University Press, 1978, pp. 116–37.

———. *Nihilism: A Philosophical Essay.* New Haven: Yale University Press, 1969.

———. *G. W. F. Hegel: An Introduction to the Science of Wisdom.* New Haven: Yale University Press, 1974.

Rosenfield, Denis. *Du Mal: Essai pour introduire en philosophie le concept de mal.* Paris: Aubier, 1989.

Rosenfield, Isaac. *An Age of Enormity: Life and Writing in the Forties and Fifties,* ed. Theodore Solotaroff. Cleveland: World Publishing Company, 1962.

Rossi, Philip J. and Wreen, Michael, eds. *Kant's Philosophy of Religion Reconsidered.* Bloomington: Indiana University Press, 1991.

Ryan, Michael. *Marxism and Deconstruction: A Critical Articulation.* Baltimore: Johns Hopkins University Press, 1982.

Sallis, John, ed. *Deconstruction and Philosophy: The Texts of Jacques Derrida*. Chicago: University of Chicago Press, 1987.

————. *Spacings—of Reason and Imagination in Texts of Kant, Fichte and Hegel*. Chicago: University of Chicago Press, 1987.

————. *The Gathering of Reason*. Athens: Ohio University Press, 1980.

Sartre, Jean-Paul. *Being and Nothingness: An Essay on Phenomenological Ontology*, trans. Hazel E. Barnes. New York: Philosophical Library, 1956.

Sayer, Derek. *Capitalism and Modernity: An Excursus on Marx and Weber*. London: Routledge, 1991.

Schell, Jonathan. *The Fate of the Earth*. New York: Alfred A. Knopf, 1982.

Schiffers, Norbert. "Suffering in History." *New Questions on God*, ed. Johannes B. Metz. New York: Herder & Herder, 1972, pp. 38–47.

Schmidt, Alfred. *History and Structure: An Essay on Hegelian-Marxist and Structuralist Theories of History*, trans. Jeffrey Herf. Cambridge: MIT Press, 1981.

Schnädelbach, Herbert. *Philosophy in Germany 1831–1933*, trans. Eric Matthews. Cambridge: Cambridge University Press, 1984.

Schrader, George. *Existential Philosophers: Kierkegaard to Merleau-Ponty*. New York: McGraw-Hill, 1967.

————. "The Constitutive Role of Practical Reason in Kant's Moral Philosophy." *Reflections on Kant's Philosophy*, ed. W. H. Werkmeister. Gainesville: University Presses of Florida, 1975, pp. 65–90.

Schroyer, Trent. *The Critique of Domination: The Origins and Development of Critical Theory*. New York: George Braziller, 1973.

Schwartz, Barry. *The Battle for Human Nature: Science, Morality and Modern Life*. New York: W. W. Norton, 1986.

Scott, Charles E. *The Language of Difference*. Atlantic Highlands: Humanities Press International, 1987.

Scott-Taggart, M. J. "Recent Work on the Philosophy of Kant." *Kant Studies Today*, ed. Lewis W. Beck. LaSalle: Open Court, 1969, pp. 1–71.

Sennett, Richard. *The Fall of Public Man: On the Social Psychology of Capitalism*. New York: Vintage Books, 1974.

Shell, Susan Meld. *The Rights of Reason: A Study of Kant's Philosophy and Politics*. Toronto: University of Toronto Press, 1980.

Silverman, Hugh J. and Ihde, Don, eds. *Derrida and Deconstruction*. New York: Routledge, 1989.

————.*Hermeneutics and Deconstruction*. Albany: State University of New York Press, 1985.

————. *Writing the Politics of Difference*. New York: State University of New York Press, 1991.

Slaatte, Howard A. *The Paradox of Existentialist Theology: The Dialectics of a Faith-Subsumed Reason-in-Existence*. New York: Humanities Press, 1971.

Slater, Philip. *Earthwalk*. Garden City: Doubleday, 1974.

————. *The Pursuit of Loneliness: American Culture at the Breaking Point*. Boston: Beacon Press, 1970.

Sloterdijk, Peter. *Critique of Cynical Reason*, trans. Michael Eldred. Minneapolis: University of Minnesota Press, 1987.

Smith, Steven G. *The Argument to the Other: Reason Beyond Reason in the Thought of Karl Barth and Emmanuel Levinas*. Chico: Scholars Press, 1983.

Sokolowski, Robert. *The Formation of Husserl's Concept of Constitution*. The Hague: Martinus Nijhoff, 1964.

Solzhenitsyn, Alexander. *One Day in the Life of Ivan Denisovich*, trans. Ralph Parker. Harmondsworth, Middlesex: Penguin Books, 1963.

Spengler, Oswald. *The Decline of the West*, ed. Helmut Werner, trans. Charles Francis Atkinson. New York: Modern Library, 1962.

Staten, Harry. *Wittgenstein and Derrida*. Lincoln: University of Nebraska Press, 1984.

Stillman, Edmund and Pfaff, William. *The Politics of Hysteria: The Sources of Twentieth-Century Conflict*. New York: Harper & Row, 1964.

Sturrock, John, ed. *Structuralism and Since: From Lévi-Strauss to Derrida*. Oxford: Oxford University Press, 1979.

Sullivan, Roger J. *Immanuel Kant's Moral Theory*. Cambridge: Cambridge University Press, 1989.

Surin, Kenneth. *Theology and the Problem of Evil*. Oxford: Basil Blackwell, 1986.

Taminiaux, Jacques. *Dialectic and Difference: Finitude in Modern Thought*, ed. James Decker and Robert Crease. Atlantic Highlands: Humanities Press, 1985.

Tanner, Kathryn. *God and Creation in Christian Theology: Tyranny or Empowerment?* Oxford: Blackwell, 1988.

Tauxe, Henri-Charles. *La Notion de finitude dans la philosophie de Martin Heidegger*. Lausanne: Editions L'Age d'Homme, n.d.

Taylor, Mark C. *Altarity*. Chicago: University of Chicago Press, 1987.

———. *Erring: A Postmodern A/theology*. Chicago: University of Chicago Press, 1984.

———. *Tears*. Albany: State University of New York Press, 1990.

Theunissen, Michael. *Der Andere: Studien zur Sozialontologie der Gegenwart*. Berlin: Walter de Gruyter, 1981.

Thévenaz, Pierre. *L'homme et sa raison: Vol. 1, Raison et conscience de soi; Vol. II, Raison et histoire*. Neuchatel: Editions de la Baconnière, 1956.

Thompson, William Irwin. *At the Edge of History*. New York: Harper & Row, 1971.

Thornton, Martin. *The Rock and the River: The Encounter between Traditional Spirituality and Modern Thought*. London: Hodder & Stoughton, 1965.

Thulstrup, Niels. *Commentary on Kierkegaard's "Concluding Unscientific Postscript" with a New Introduction*, trans. Robert J. Widenmann. Princeton: Princeton University Press, 1984.

Tilley, Terrence W. *The Evils of Theodicy*. Washington: Georgetown University Press, 1991.

Tracy, David. *Blessed Rage for Order: The New Pluralism in Theology*. New York: Seabury Press, 1975.

Trilling, Lionel. *Sincerity and Authenticity*. Cambridge: Harvard University Press, 1971.

Tuchman, Barbara W. *The Proud Tower: A Portrait of the World before the War, 1890–1914*. New York: Macmillan, 1966.

Ulmer, Gregory L. *Applied Grammatology: Post(e)-Pedagogy from Jacques Derrida to Joseph Beuys*. Baltimore: Johns Hopkins University Press, 1985.

———. "Sounding the Unconscious." *Glassary*, ed. John P. Leavey, Jr. Lincoln: University of Nebraska Press, 1986, pp. 23–129.

Vail, L. M. *Heidegger and Ontological Difference*. University Park: Pennsylvania State University Press, 1972.

Van de Beek, A. *Why? On Suffering, Guilt and God*, trans. John Vriend. Grand Rapids: William B. Eermans, 1990.

van de Pitte, Frederick P. *Kant as Philosophical Anthropologist*. The Hague: Martinus Nijhoff, 1971.

Van der Linden, Harry. *Kantian Ethics and Socialism*. Indianapolis: Hackett, 1988.

Velkley, Richard L. *Freedom and the End of Reason: On the Moral Foundation of Kant's Critical Philosophy*. Chicago: University of Chicago Press, 1989.

————. "Kant as Philosopher of Theodicy." Ann Arbor: University Microfilms International, 1978.

Viallaneix, Nelly. *Écoute, Kierkegaard: Essai sur la communication de la Parole*, Vols. I, II. Paris: Editions du Cerf, 1979.

Walker, Jeremy D. B. *Kierkegaard: The Descent into God*. Kingston and Montreal: McGill-Queen's University Press, 1985.

————. *To Will One Thing: Reflections on Kierkegaard's "Purity of Heart."* Montreal: McGill-Queen's University Press, 1972.

Wallace, Mark. *The Second Naiveté: Barth, Ricoeur and the New Yale Theology*. Macon: Mercer University Press, 1990.

Wallwork, Ernest. *Psychoanalysis and Ethics*. New Haven: Yale University Press, 1991.

Warren, Scott. *The Emergence of Dialectical Theory: Philosophy and Political Inquiry*. Chicago: University of Chicago Press, 1984.

Weber, Alfred. *Farewell to European History, or, The Conquest of Nihilism*, trans. R. F. C. Hull. Westport: Greenwood Press, 1948.

Weil, Simone. *Waiting for God*, trans. Emma Craufurd. New York: Harper & Row, 1951.

Welch, Claude. *Protestant Thought in the Nineteenth Century: Volume I, 1799–1870*. New Haven: Yale University Press, 1972.

Wells, William Walter. *The Influence of Kierkegaard on the Theology of Karl Barth*. Ann Arbor: University Microfilms International, 1971.

Wentz, Richard Eugene. *The Contemplation of Otherness: The Critical Vision of Religion*. Macon: Mercer University Press, 1984.

Westphal, Merold. "In Defense of the Thing in Itself." *Kant-Studien* 59:1 (1968), pp. 118–41.

Wiener, Philip P., ed. *Dictionary of the History of Ideas: Studies of Selected Pivotal Ideas*. New York: Charles Scribner's Sons, 1968.

Wiesel, Elie. *Night*. New York: Bantam Books, 1982.

Williams, T. C. *The Unity of Kant's "Critique of Pure Reason": Experience, Language and Knowledge*. Lewiston: Edwin Mellen Press, 1987.

Windelband, Wilhelm. *A History of Philosophy. Volume II: Renaissance, Enlightenment, Modern*. New York: Harper & Brothers, 1901.

Winfield, Richard Dien. *Overcoming Foundations: Studies in Systematic Philosophy*. New York: Columbia University Press, 1989.

Winling, Raymond. *La théologie contemporaine (1945–1980)*. Paris: Le Centurion, 1983.

Winquist, Charles E. *Epiphanies of Darkness: Deconstruction in Theology*. Philadelphia: Fortress Press, 1986.

Wolff, Robert Paul. *The Autonomy of Reason: A Commentary on Kant's "Groundwork of the Metaphysics of Morals."* New York: Harper & Row, 1973.

Wood, Allen W. *Kant's Moral Religion*. Ithaca: Cornell University Press, 1970.

Wood, Allen W., ed. *Self and Nature in Kant's Philosophy*. Ithaca: Cornell University Press, 1984.

Wood, David and Bernasconi, Robert, eds. *Derrida and Différance*. Evanston: Northwestern University Press, 1988.

Wyschogrod, Edith. *Spirit in Ashes: Hegel, Heidegger and Man-Made Mass Death*. New Haven: Yale University Press, 1985.

Yovel, Yirmiyahu. *Kant and the Philosophy of History*. Princeton: Princeton University Press, 1980.

INDEX

Absence, 31, 39, 42, 44, 98, 144, 154; divine knowing and, 98; Nietzsche, 87; of object, 57

Adorno, Theodor W., x, 1, 2, 8, 10, 11, 15, 21, 22, 30–31, 76, 79, 116, 140, 142, 143, 144, 148, 153, 155

Agnosticism, 81; positive, 84

Ambiguity, 105–108, 118–19, 138; mixed discourse, 63

Anthropocentrism, 69, 97–98

Aquinas, St. Thomas, 112, 131, 137

Archē (*see also* Origin, primal): 25, 62, 135; Barth on primal origin, 136, 141; Bultmann, 60; dialectic and, 66–67; Husserl, 63, 70; idealist diamond, 122–29, 134; Kant, 123–26, 128–29; Nancy, 110–11; Pope, 89; Ricoeur 65; Taylor, 134–36

Aristotle, 112

Askesis, 102, 126

Atheism, 90, 144; protest, 39

Aufhebung, Barth on, 36, 38, 41, 141; Derrida, 121–22; Hegel, 121–22

Augustine, St., 24

Auschwitz, 147

Autonomy, and heteronomy, 109–10, 112; of the ethical, 104, 134, 136; of reason, 115

Barth, Karl, ix, xii, 12, 20, 33–47, 48, 86, 100, 102, 119, 120, 127, 136–43, 144, 154

Begrundung, 36, 141

Big picture, 84, 93, 117, 121, 125

Bonhoeffer, Dietrich, ix, 23, 32, 37, 152

Bracketing, phenomenological, 52, 54

Buber, Martin, 17, 102

Buck-Morss, Susan, 30–31

Bultmann, Rudolf, 59–62, 119

Capitalism, 6, 9, 20, 22, 149

Child, 23, 118–19, 135, 162

Christ, 10, 38, 41–43, 132, 144, 149, 163

Command, 102, 112

Compossibility, 84, 117, 119

Concealment, 23, 29, 32, 74, 138

Condition, 124–26

Consciousness, 3, 16, 140, 143; Hegel, 120–22; Husserl, 54–56, 69–70; unhappy, 133–35

Consistency, 22, 39, 62, 88, 93, 108, 112, 115–16

Contextualization, 19–22, 25, 48, 101, 136; Barth, 138–39, 143; Derrida, 73; Hegel,

121–22; idealist diamond, 27–28; imperative as, 109–11; Kant, 95, 101, 111, 123, 126; metaphysics, 21–22, 27, 81–82; Pope, 82, 121–22; tradition, 22

Copernican revolution, Kant's so-called, 94, 95, 97, 99, 160

Coram Deo, 13, 98, 101, 114–15, 121, 128–29, 141–42

Correlation, method of, xii-xiii

Cosmology, 87, 95, 99

Cramponnement, 4, 70

Creation, 37, 41, 43–44, 127, 137, 141–43

Critical thought, xi, 21, 32, 48, 52, 65, 71, 129–30, 134, 144; Barth, 137, 142; Kant, 92, 95, 101, 117, 128–29, 135

Critique, first, 46, 75, 94–98, 103, 105, 106, 107, 110, 114, 120, 124, 128; second, 46, 75–78, 87, 96, 103–17, 120, 128; third, 96, 109

Cross, the, 10

Dasein, 123

Deconstruction (*see also* Derrida): 12, 13–16, 47, 55, 58, 62, 66, 73, 150, 151

De Man, Paul, 71, 108, 161

Demythologization, 59

Derrida, Jacques, x-xi, 11, 12, 13–17, 19, 22, 23, 28–29, 31, 33–36, 42, 44, 45–47, 48–50, 52, 55–58, 62–63, 67–74, 76, 80, 101, 109, 111, 120–21, 123, 125, 127–28, 130, 132, 133, 144, 147, 153, 154, 158

Descartes, René, 18, 19, 23,

Dialectic, 15, 30–31, 47, 69, 110, 139, 145; Adorno, 15, 30–31; Barth, 43, 138–43; Derrida, 15; Hegelian, 112, 133; Ricoeur, 64–67, 69, 110; tradition and, 17; two Enlightenments and, 30

Differance, 15, 47, 70, 72–73, 129, 151

Difference, 9, 13, 31, 47, 72, 130–31, 141; Adorno, 15; analogy of, 44; Barth, 33–35, 43–47, 127; Derrida, 15, 47, 158; dissolution of, 5–9, 13, 22, 36, 119, 124, 144; Enlightenment and, 30; Hegel, 133; Heidegger, 15; idealism and, 124, 129–30; innocent, 44, 144; Kant, 12, 31, 46, 90, 93, 98, 104, 111, 114, 120; qualitative, 33–35, 38; theology and, 13, 16, 35, 44–47, 75, 80, 121, 127, 143

Dilthey, Wilhelm, 59–60, 65, 122

Distinction, 3, 14, 16–17, 29, 41, 43, 44–47, 89; infinite qualitative, 34, 38

WALTER LOWE is Professor of Systematic Theology at Emory University. The author of *Mystery and the Unconscious* and *Evil and the Unconscious*, he has received fellowships from the Fulbright Foundation, the Alexander von Humboldt Foundation, and the American Council of Learned Societies.